The Social Software
of Accounting and
Information Systems

The Social Software of Accounting and Information Systems

Norman B. Macintosh
School of Business
Queen's University, Kingston, Canada

JOHN WILEY & SONS
Chichester · New York · Brisbane · Toronto · Singapore

Copyright © 1985 by John Wiley & Sons Ltd.

Library of Congress Cataloging in Publication Data:

Macintosh, Norman B.
    The Social software of accounting and information systems.

    Includes index.
    1. Accounting.   2. Managerial accounting.
    3. Management information systems.   4. Organizational behavior.
I. Title.
HF5657.M228   1985   658.4'0388   84-10447

ISBN 0 471 90543 7

British Library Cataloguing in Publication Data:

Macintosh, Norman B.
    The Social software of accounting and information systems.
    1. Accounting—Social aspects 2. Management information systems—Social aspects
    I. Title
    302.3'5   HF5625

ISBN 0 471 90543 7

Phototypeset by Input Typesetting Ltd, London
Printed in Great Britain at The Pitman Press, Bath

To Joan, Bruce, and Cameron

'All information is imperfect. We have to treat it with humility.'

(*J. Bronowski*)

'It is a capital mistake to theorize before one has data.'

(*Sir Arthur Conan Doyle*)

'It would be fine if we could swallow the powder of profitable information made palatable by the jam of fiction.'

(*W. Somerset Maugham*)

'A Minister's main function is answering yes or no on the basis of imperfect information.'

(Attributed to *Lord Bowen*)

'And what've I achieved? Three women in my life and one of *them* turned out to be a chartered accountant over thirty.'

(*John Mortimer*)

'Accounting is not boring; only chartered accountants.'

(*Monty Python*)

'I only ask for information.'

(*Charles Dickens*)

Acknowledgements

In the years that this manuscript has been in preparation, the number of friends, colleagues, and acquaintances to whom I am indebted for helping me with ideas, encouragement, and criticism has grown so large that it is impossible to list them all. As a way of getting round this, albeit an unsatisfactory one, I will single out only those upon whom I have called most frequently for help and those whose ideas have directly enriched my own meager understanding of the topic. I am much indebted to the many others and hope they will pardon me for not singling them out.

I am particularly indebted to a small group of academics who were kind enough to join my faculty for seminars which I have run over the past ten years for accounting and information systems executives: Carl Hammer of Sperry Univac who built one of the first computers and who covers the topic of the new information technology in a breathtaking yet realistic way; Anthony Hopwood, the UK Chartered Accountants' Professor of Accounting and Financial Reporting, London Graduate School of Business Studies, Distinguished International Lecturer in Accounting for 1981, founder and editor of the *Accounting, Organizations and Society* journal which is brimming with new and exciting ideas in the field, who taught us that accounting and information systems is a major institution in its own right in organizations and society and that managing them, not providing information for users, is the critical aspect; Bo Hedberg at the Swedish Center for Working Life, Stockholm, who made us realize that one of the primary purposes of accounting and information systems, particularly the new computer technology, is to create better and more humanistic organizations and jobs; Jack McDonough, with whom I shared many inspiring discussions in the doctoral program at Harvard University about control systems and organizational behavior, Professor of Accounting and Information Systems and Director of the Information Studies Research Program at the Graduate School of Management, UCLA, who made us uncomfortably aware of the realities of how formal accounting and information systems are used in the 'objective-accountability' game by organizational participants to pursue self-interests and who also gave us a blueprint for staying involved in this game with integrity and self-respect; Sid Huff at the University of Western Ontario who studied decision support systems at MIT and who gave us new insights, using his remarkable teaching skills, about how organizations can roll the computer, data bases, special software and managers into one very powerful decision system for many problems which previously eluded systematic analysis; Henry Mintzberg of McGill University, the world-renowned expert on managerial work who brought inspiration and insight about the realities of managerial information processing into our sessions; and Gerry Dermer of the University of Toronto who brilliantly covered the human relations aspects of budgeting systems. Also I am indebted to Jay Galbraith of the Wharton School, University of Pennsylvania, who chaired a session at the Athens TIMS meetings where I first presented our technology model of accounting and information systems and whose insight that organizations structure themselves around their information processing needs provided one of over-arching conceptual apparatus for the seminars. Although Jay could not arrange his schedule to come to these meetings, his ideas certainly were present.

Bob Tricker merits special mention. Bob, the first holder of a chair in accounting and information systems in the UK, director of the Oxford Centre for Management Studies, Oxford University during its formative years, now Research Fellow and Director of the Corporate Policy Group, Nuffield College, Oxford University, pioneered the idea that accounting, information systems and computing went together into something greater than the sum of their parts, and who developed several key notions regarding the need for, and the way to go about developing, an information system resource strategy as the cornerstone of corporate strategy. Bob helped me organize and chair these seminars and his marvelous knack of integrating into a coherent whole the various strands of thought of the rest of the faculty enabled us to take our thinking to new levels.

I must also mention those hundreds of executives who attended these programs at Queen's University. Many of the ideas in this book served as fodder for them to chew on against the teeth of their years of practical experience. These executives willingly shared their experiences, both failures and successes, about systems they had designed and implemented in their organizations. Thanks to them, I am constantly aware of the organizational terrain where the realities of accounting and information systems are put on the line each day.

These seminars were the outcome of a three-week management training program conceived and designed at Queen's University by Bob Crandall of Queen's University, Mike Gibbins now at the University of British Columbia, Jim Nininger formally at Queen's and now president of the Conference Board of Canada, and myself. We also served on the faculty along with Jim Sorensen from the University of Denver, who neatly related accounting systems with concepts about self-esteem and role expectations, and Larry Griener, from the University of Southern California, who cleverly put accounting and control systems into the perspective of long-run organizational development. My understanding of the social software of accounting and information systems is richer for associating with these colleagues.

I am also indebted to a small band of academics who gave birth to 'behavioral accounting' as a unique body of knowledge—John Livingstone, Jim Sorensen, Ed Lawler, Tom Hofstedt, Bob Swieringa, and Gene Haas. I was fortunate enough to attend their first 'dog-and-pony show', as they called it, sponsored by the American Accounting Association with the purpose of stimulating an interest in behavioral accounting on the part of academic accountants.

This book also owes a great deal to my friend and colleague, Dick Daft, an organizational sociologist who studied at the University of Chicago and who now researches and teaches at Texas A&M University. It was Dick who urged me to look at Perrow's work, and who collaborated with me to enrich and test some of the theories in this book. As well as acting as my tutor in organizational behavior and theory, he has tried to teach me a little bit about research design, multivariate statistical analysis, and especially writing. Without Dick this book would never have been written. And my thanks are due to another friend and colleague, Yoshi Tsurumi, whom I met in the doctoral program at the Harvard Graduate School of Business. Yoshi holds the belief that good teachers also research and write and has, consequently, been a source of constant encouragement to me. He is also a source of embarrassment as he is a prolific writer of articles and books in English—yet Japanese is his native language.

Important assistance was provided by Mrs Dawn Kiell who typed and retyped endless drafts of the original manuscript, and by Mrs Connie Raymond and her staff in our Word Processing Unit who so efficiently and effectively churned out endless drafts almost as quickly as I could revise them and get them back to her. Joan Harcourt, who reviewed each chapter for structure, grammar, and syntax, made this book as readable as it is and also encouraged me to keep at it. Finally, I must thank Donald Akenson of the History Department, Queen's University, who has written nearly a dozen books in as many years and who was kind enough to pass on some key pointers on how to write a book—work in concentrated blocks of time, do not let your family or social life take time from writing, rewrite and rewrite and rewrite, and drink lots of strong coffee to keep awake because it's going to be boring. Surprisingly, I enjoyed the writing as well as the coffee.

Contents

Preface

Accounting and information systems managers, students, and academics alike are beginning to realize that the crucial problems involved in designing and administering accounting and information systems are no longer simply a matter of getting the technical aspects right. Rather, the critical part is connecting the system in a valuable way with organizational participants. I have labeled the knowledge on how to do this the 'social software' of accounting and information systems. It will come as a surprise to many to learn that a substantial body of research and concepts about the social software already exists. The purpose of this book is to bring some of this knowledge, hopefully most of the important parts, to the attention of students, managers, and academics in the areas of management accounting, computer-based management information systems, and management science.

It is necessary to warn the reader that this book does not try to integrate all the findings and theories of the social software into one general all-encompassing theory as is being attempted, say, in positive theories of financial accounting. Some of the frameworks set forth in this book, however, do go part way towards this goal. Yet the lack of a grand unifying theory should not be too worrisome. For one thing, very few, if any, sciences have achieved such a state. Physics, for example, with the passing of Newtonian determinist mechanical laws of a clockwork-like universe, still lacks a general theory to unify the new quantum theory of particles with the concepts of relativity that Einstein formulated about planetary systems and galaxies. The social software of accounting and information systems remains, like quantum physics, a set of notions and theories, each of which works quite well on its own but sometimes seems to be in conflict with other parts of the theoretical base. But a more pervasive difficulty in achieving a unifying theory lies with the fact that the various theories look at the phenomenon of accounting and information systems through a wide variety of conceptual lenses such as: human relations; social psychology; role relations; expert judgement; cognitive structures; personality traits; organizational sociology; organizational theory; and uncertainty. To develop a unifying theory for such a diverse set of ideas will, no doubt, remain illusive for some time.

My own contribution to this body of knowledge remains modest. Such research and theory-building as I have done has followed, in the main, only one of the many perspectives—the impact of uncertainty on the design and subsequent workings of accounting and information systems. The origins of this line of inquiry stem from a few years back when I was serving as a Visiting Fellow at the Oxford Centre for Management Studies. I was puzzling with the idea that if, as many organizational theorists claim, the structural uncertainties of environment, goals, and technologies strongly influence patterns of organizational arrangements, they also should affect accounting and information systems and, further, that they should influence them in systematic ways. In general terms this seems highly plausible. But the specifics of such relationships remained elusive.

Shortly thereafter I found a way into this puzzle. Borrowing from Perrow's technology theory of organizational design, and Driver and Mock's model of human information processing systems, I outlined a general model of the influence of technology on the characteristics and use of information systems. This model is outlined at length in Chapter 11. I then sketched out the technology-based model of management control systems described in Chapter 12. These models suggest a systematic link between work-unit technology and accounting and information systems.

There are, of course, many ways to approach the problems of accounting and information system design. Some promising work is presently being done by researchers who are combining concepts from agency theory with Bayesian probability theory. Other researchers are puzzling with the problems of systematic analysis of accounting and information systems using the methodology of cybernetics and general systems theory. Still others are hoping to solve some of these problems with artificial intelligence embedded in electronic computers. Each of these camps, naturally, has its own avid believers and researchers; and it is my hunch that each of them, sooner or later, will enrich our understanding of accounting and information systems. So I urge readers to at least be familiar with them, even though the process may be tedious. These developments, however, are not discussed here. They are simply outside the scope of this book.

I hope that this book may be of some use to three groups of persons. First, to graduate and undergraduate students of accounting and information systems, especially those intending to make a career in this area and who wish to complement the technical side of their training with a closer look at the behavioral processes that make up the fabric of organizational systems. Second, to practical executives who are on the firing line in the midst of a never-ending round of implementing new systems and dismantling old ones. Hopefully, they might benefit from this book by importing an idea or two from these pages into their work. Third, to academics in the field of accounting, computer-based MIS, and management science who sense they are overly concerned with the technical side of their courses and who wish to have a bit of fun by teaching their students something about the fascinating social software of accounting and information systems at a level that is not found today in most technically oriented textbooks.

ONE. Personal Aspects of Accounting and Information Systems

CHAPTER 1

Introduction

This book is about accounting and information systems. It is not, however, a conventional book in that it is not concerned with either generally accepted accounting principles or with the principles of sound computerized management information system design. Rather it is about the 'social software' of accounting and information systems, a topic that until recently has been all but neglected by accounting and information systems managers, academics, and students alike.

The social software of accounting and information systems as we conceive of it here, and as we shall study it in much of this book, deals with the organizational behavioral ramifications of these systems. It is concerned with how these systems influence and are influenced by personal attributes, group dynamics, and impersonal forces in the organizational context. It deals with the impact these systems have on organizations and the people in them. This subject-matter is important. In the final analysis it is the social software which spells the difference between the success and the failure of our management accounting and information systems.

It must be made clear, however, that the social software of accounting and information systems has nothing to do with either 'human resource accounting' or 'corporate social accounting'. Human resource accounting has been soundly covered by authors such as Brummet *et al.* (1969) and Flamholtz (1972). It deals mainly with the development of techniques for recording the wages and related costs of employees as a capital asset and subsequently writing the cost off over a number of years. The idea is that such information will act to bring the value of human resources more closely to the attention of management. Corporate social accounting also has been dealt with solidly by researchers such as Epstein *et al.* (1976). It is concerned with the techniques for reporting corporate performance on matters of social responsibility, such as equal opportunity employment, environmental policy, and employee health and welfare.

Management accounting systems, of course, have been around for a long time even though they are a relatively recent phenomenon compared with financial accounting for reporting to external parties (Kaplan, 1982). Cost accounting, the precursor of modern management accounting, emerged as a major management tool at the turn of this century as a result of external reporting needs for inventory and cost of goods-sold valuations. In the

3

following years new techniques emerged and old ones were refined. By 1970, management accounting had grown into a well-rounded body of valuable and generally accepted tools and techniques. Standard cost accumulation systems, variance analysis methodologies, joint and by-product costing systems, process costing systems, cost–volume–profit analysis, net residual income, transfer pricing techniques, and relevant cost determination became common aids to management in organizations. This technical knowledge is contained in any one of a number of sound textbooks.

By the 1980s a new set of powerful quantitative analytical tools had been grafted on to the traditional management accounting tree. Excellent books such as Kaplan's (1982) advanced management accounting text are witness to this development. They demonstrate clearly the value of techniques such as Bayesean statistics, linear and non-linear multiple regression analysis, linear and dynamic programming, probabilistic decision theory and matrix algebra to sharpen the edge of the traditional management accounting tools.

Management information systems (MIS), by comparison, is a more recent phenomenon arriving on the heels of the computer invasion of organizations in the 1960s. Once the big projects, such as payrolls, inventory, and financial accounting systems were mechanized, computer departments discovered a need to utilize their excess capacity and so began to look for new information systems to serve their organizations. Management accounting and reporting systems proved to be the major customers for this capacity. And following in the footsteps of management accounting, MIS techniques developed and matured into a well-rounded body of generally accepted principles of how to develop, design, and implement computer-based information systems.

As a result, the demarcation point between management accounting and computer-based MIS became blurred. Like the plumbing system for a house, the management accountants provided the cold and hot water while the MIS people provided the pipes and plumbing. The two fields have merged into what is now called 'accounting and information systems'. Witness to this is the recent explosion of 'Accounting Information Systems' books which combine accounting and computing (Moscove and Simkin, 1981; Robertson *et al.*, 1982). Consequently what we have to say should be as vital to computing and MIS managers and students as it is to their management accounting counterparts.

The technical considerations of our accounting and information systems in organizations, by and large, would appear to be sound. However, they have received most of the professional attention, with a resulting imbalance in our knowledge of the social software which prevents us from having a broader vision of these systems (Hopwood, 1974). It is not the 'debit–credit' or 'bit–byte' aspects that are so troublesome any more. It is the social engineering that goes awry. Evidence continues to surface to suggest that systems create effects within organizations we had not bargained for. They are not, it seems, always embraced warmly by organizational participants. In fact, many authors, such as Ackoff (1967), Mason and Mitroff (1973), and

Hopwood (1974) argue that they often go unused and are widely ignored. And if you talk with practitioners in the field you soon realize that the number of accounting and information systems failures remains unacceptably high.

Consider an example which I witnessed recently. In a nationwide advertising firm the new financial officer, a qualified professional accountant, became concerned with the lavish expense accounts submitted by account executives. As a result, he designed an elaborate budgetary control system which collected expenses by every conceivable category, right down to individual taxi rides. He introduced a new computer system including a network of on-line terminals, which had to be brought up to the firm's suite of offices by a giant crane that lifted it off the truck, raised it up to the fifteenth floor, and carefully swung it through a large window frame. All the employees were on hand to witness the delivery and give a resounding cheer as the computer was lowered into place. Shortly thereafter, the new computerized system went on-line.

The managers were initially enthusiastic about the system. Yet it seemed not to help them very much, and after several months it fell into disuse, even though the managers were not unhappy with it. Shortly thereafter the accountant left the firm, blaming the managers for the failure of the system. What had happened was that the accountant had failed to analyze the nature of advertising work and client handling. By focusing on expenses, which are recovered from clients in any case, instead of on gross billings, his system was not congruent with the key factors involved in advertising work.

Even worse, our accounting and information systems sometimes lead unwittingly to dysfunctional negative consequences. Consider the case of a company which discovered that their liability for future pension obligations was significantly greater than had been recorded in the accounts. The auditors, quite rightly, insisted on recording the difference as a liability. The company thus set up the liability and allocated the expense side to their plants on the basis of years of seniority of all employees. This charge threw one plant into a loss position and senior management consequently decided to close the plant. In fact, of course, the plant's cash flow had not changed in the slightest. Senior management had made the classical mistake of including such sunk costs in decision-making. Accountants are well aware of this trap; but upper management, who were not financial experts, made an honest but unwarranted decision based on the formal information in the management accounting reports.

These types of errors when multiplied many times can have far reaching consequences. Consider the example cited by Kaplan at an accounting educators' conference. This company recorded all its headquarters staff costs in one overhead pool, including expenses for such departments as special engineering, R&D, operations research, institutional advertising, as well as accounting and MIS services. Top management insisted that these costs be allocated to the various decentralized product units. The accounting department used the normal percentage of total sales volume as the allocation method. As a result, some divisions, particularly those involved with mature products for the low end of the market, now reported losses. Subsequently, top management, receiving the accounting reports from the division, decided to abandon the low end products even though they produced a good cash flow. The accounting system, due to sloppy expense allocation, gave the wrong message.

Yet the ramifications do not stop here. When this type of behavior is repeated by many firms in the national economy, as researchers such as Magaziner and Reich (1982) believe, the long-run aftermath is alarming. As more domestic firms abandon the lower end of their product lines, foreign firms eagerly jump in to fill the gap, just as the Japanese have done in so many markets including automobiles, sewing machines, and television sets. As a result these foreign firms quickly develop their channels of distribution, marketing networks, and advertising campaigns. Once this marketing base is soundly established they begin to compete against the domestic firms with sophisticated products in the new and developing market segments. The impact of careless or narrow thinking on the part of management accountants can have unintended but far-reaching consequences for society.

Of course not all accounting and information systems work this way. There are as many, and likely more, success stories than horror ones. Yet enough do go astray to make it unsettling for accounting and information systems executives. Why they go astray often remains a puzzle. The important question before us, then, is why does one system fail and another succeed? This question, of course, is not new. It has troubled management accountants for a long time: and now this puzzle is shared with management scientists and computer-based MIS executives.

In order to answer this question some accounting scholars, and more recently a handful of management science and MIS academics, have turned their attention away from the technical design aspects of accounting and information systems, to investigate the organizational behavioral ramifications. In fact, considerable research and theory-building has ensued over the past couple of decades and a body of knowledge about how these systems influence and are influenced by organizational behavioral aspects is beginning to emerge.

This book is about these developments. It includes a review of studies undertaken from the perspective of the human-relations school of industrial psychology, studies that have investigated the effects of participation patterns and different leadership styles on the way systems are used and on motivation, productivity, and satisfaction. This body of research and the issues which have emerged are the subject of Chapter 2. In Chapter 3 we investigate the research and theory-building which uses social psychology as the basis for studying accounting and information systems. Chapters 4 and 5 review the evolution and findings of studies using the Brunswik lens model to analyze the way in which experts such as auditors, loan officers, and investment analysts make judgements using accounting and related data. In Chapter 6 we turn our attention to the way in which individual differences in personality and cognitive styles influence the use of formal accounting and information systems. Although the cumulative results to date of studies of this kind have been inconclusive and inconsistent, the long-run potential for tailoring our systems to the unique characteristics of the individual manager remains tantalizing.

At this juncture we shift our attention away from personal aspects to investigate the impact of impersonal forces on the design and use of accounting and information systems. Chapter 7 reviews some pioneering studies from the disciplines of organizational sociology and economics. These studies provided the foundation for linking, as covered in Chapter 8, organizational theory to accounting and information system design. Chapter 9 outlines a couple of milestone studies which investigate the impact of the cutting edge of uncertainty on our traditional accounting and information systems and signal a need for totally new types of systems. Chapter 10 continues this theme to review a small but fascinating set of studies which argue that accounting and information systems are a major sociological institution in their own right and influence the shape of other important organizational structures and processes in significant ways. Chapter 11 outlines a new theory which combines personal and impersonal forces to develop a general model of information systems, and Chapter 12 extends this line of thinking to focus on managerial control systems. These frameworks are based on established theories of technology and organizational design.

Chapter 13 reviews the remarkable developments in information technology centering on the evolution of the computer. We then speculate about the impact of the new information technology on organizations, and what our future organizations might look like. This chapter then makes the case that there is an urgent need for organizations to develop a comprehensive information resource strategy as the cornerstone for its overall corporate strategy. In the final chapter we take a shot in the dark and predict that the new information system technology will have profound impacts on the forces of industrial democracy as well as on those major institutions—both capitalism and socialism—which constantly reproduce our daily material needs.

While most management accountants and their computer and MIS colleagues are quick to recognize that the social software is more important to the success of their systems than are the technical considerations, it seems clear that in some respects our accounting and information systems knowledge has been like the physical sciences of this century: merrily booming along but without an equivalent for the engineering. This book attempts to bring what is now a surprisingly large and solid body of knowledge about the social software of these systems to the attention of accounting and information systems executives, teachers, and students.

8

References

Ackoff, R. L., 'Management misinformation systems', *Management Science*, December 1967, pp. B147–B156.

Brummet, R. L., E. G. Flamholtz, and W. C. Pyle (eds), *Human Resource Accounting: Development and Implementation in Industry*, Foundation for Research on Human Behaviour, 1969.

Epstein, M., E. Flamholtz, and J. J. McDonough, 'Corporate social accounting in the United States of America: state of the art and future prospects', *Accounting, Organizations and Society*, Vol. 1, No. 1, 1976, pp. 23–42.

Flamholtz, E. G., 'Assessing the validity of a theory of human resource value: a field study', *Empirical Research in Accounting: Selected Studies*, 1972, pp 241–266.

Hopwood, A. G., *Accounting and Human Behavior*, Haymarket Publishing Co., London, 1974.

Kaplan, R. S., *Advanced Management Accounting*, Prentice-Hall, Inc., Englewood Cliffs, NJ, 1982.

Magaziner, I., and R. Reich, *Minding America's Business*, Harcourt, Brace Jovanovich, New York, 1982.

Mason, R. O., and I. I. Mitroff, 'A program for research on management information systems', *Management Science*, January 1973, pp. 475–487.

Moscove, S. A., and M. G. Simkin, *Accounting Information Systems: Concepts and Practice for Effective Decision Making*, John Wiley & Sons, Inc., New York, 1981.

Robertson, L. A., J. R. Davies, and C. W. Alderman, *Accounting Information Systems: A Cycle Approach*, Harper & Row, Inc., New York, 1982.

CHAPTER 2

Human Relations and Budgeting Systems

Recently the organizational behavioral ramifications of management accounting and information systems have come under the scrutiny of both practitioners and academics in this field. Some evidence is surfacing to suggest that accounting systems have been creating effects within organizations we had not bargained for. Our systems, it seems, are not always embraced warmly by organizational participants; and the magnitude of the unintended negative consequences is alarming.

As a result, considerable research and theory-building has ensued over the past couple of decades; and a small number of accounting and MIS academics have devoted a lot of their time, considerably more than most accounting and information systems managers realize, to researching this problem. Early on it became something of a convenience to refer to this whole endeavor as behavioral accounting. Most of the early studies of these systems postulated that if we could somehow get the human relations aspects right, then our accounting and information systems would work as they are supposed to.

THE HUMAN RELATIONS PERSPECTIVE

The idea to involve participants in the design of organizational arrangements that affect them had its origin in the famous Hawthorne study conducted nearly fifty years ago by Mayo (1945) and Roethlisberger and Dickson (1947). This study revealed that human factors could have a profound effect on the productivity of our technical–economic organizations. From these beginnings, the human relations school of organizational behavior emerged and soon gained wide appeal.

The basic tenet of the human relations school is the belief that participation has great potential for curing many of our organizational problems. Increased productivity follows the release of an individual's creative energies. The leader's role, then, is to create a climate that allows all members of an organization to participate fully in the decision process. In turn, participating individuals appreciate the responsibility entrusted to them; morale is high and motivation is increased. The direction of influence, of course, is by no means clear, as Miles (1966) pointed out. Does higher morale lead to more productivity? Or does greater productivity lead to higher morale? Or are the two inextricably interwined?

9

Moreover, participation implies a process that is democratic, employee-centered, in which sound human relations are given priority. Few managers would deny that such a working climate has greater value than an autocratic, production-centered system, dominated by the bureaucracy. For many years participation in decision-making was thought to be a panacea for effective organizational effort.

But this school of thought was later to come under closer scrutiny. So much so that for many years participative decision-making became the most contentious and significant debate in the study of organizational behavior. More resources and energy were devoted to this issue than to any other in the history of organizational behavior. More recently, thoughtful and candid critiques of this approach, by notable theorists such as Perrow (1972), have helped to present a more balanced view of the human relations movement.

The outcome of the debate, unfortunately, has never been resolved. The believers have never been able to demonstrate rigorously that participative management really has a positive effect on productivity. The skeptics, for their part, have not been able to prove the opposite conclusively. So the issue remains unresolved. One cannot help but harbor the suspicion that enthusiasm for participation as a means to optimum efficiency and effectiveness outran careful research.

In any event it should be no great surprise to learn that the issue of participation found its way into the accounting and information systems field. And conventional thinking on management accounting soon embraced the concept of participation as the best means for getting managers and employees to make more effective use of accounting and information systems. Problems with imposed budgets were debated more than fifty years ago when a study by the National Industrial Conference Board (1931) indicated dissatisfaction with them and advised preparation by departments, followed by editing and revision in the central office. It was nearly twenty years later that Argyris (1952) reactivated the controversy by undertaking a study for the Controllership Foundation on the effects of budgets on people. The participation concept has troubled accountants for a long while.

Negative consequences of budgets

Argyris' study showed that budgets were viewed differently by budget people, factory supervisors, and front-line foremen and workers. To the budget people, who perceived themselves as the 'answer-men' of the organization, the budget served the extremely important function of being 'the eyes and ears of the plant'. As they saw it, one part of their job involved a continuous uncovering of errors and weaknesses, as well as the examination and analysis of plant operations with an eye to increased efficiency. The next stage was to report the findings to top management so that pressure could be brought to bear on the lower echelons to increase productivity and achieve greater efficiency. They also believed that budgets present a challenging goal to front-line foremen and workers. For budget people, then, budgets were a powerful lever for motivating the workforce.

Factory supervisors held a somewhat different perspective, although all those interviewed considered that the budget department affected their world to a great extent. Top factory supervisors, in particular, invoked budgets frequently and strongly to maintain their authority. Front-line factory supervisors, by contrast, hardly ever used them. Nor did they mention budgets to production people for fear of crossing them, resentment, hostility, and aggression of the workers toward the company, with a consequent reduction in production.

The research team, although they did not interview any production workers, gained the impression that budgets were viewed with suspicion by the workforce. All factory supervisors pretty much agreed on the major problems with budgets: they were geared to results only, with no discussion of the process; they emphasized past instead of future performance; they were based on rigid standards; they were used to apply pressure for increasingly higher goals; they insulted a man's integrity rather than offering him motivation; and they included unrealistic goals that were almost impossible to meet.

These observations led to speculations about the underlying behavioral dynamics of budgeting. Workers, it was posited, form cohesive groups to counteract and combat the pressure management exerts through the arbitrary imposition of budgets. This, in consequence, leaves top management in a quandary. When they relax the pressure the groups do not disintegrate; on the contrary, unreal conditions are created and existing ones are exaggerated, so that the groups continue to 'do battle' with management. Yet if further pressure is then applied, the result is head-on 'do-or-die' battles.

As a way out of this dilemma, the study recommended that supervisors participate—in a truly genuine fashion—in making or changing the budgets that affect them. Another remedy proposed was to bring all the supervisors together in small face-to-face groups where they would confront each other and their mutual problems, reveal their own feelings, attitudes, and values towards budgets and then form new ones. The report also suggested training in human relations for controllers and accountants, as well as for accounting students. And, of course, like all good academics, Argyris recommended more research. These remedies—participation, T-groups, and human relations training—would be recognized today, of course, as the standard human relations response to problems of almost any sort.

Still, for the management accountant the study makes some telling points. The first is that since foremen and workers often form cohesive groups the budget person must realize that he is dealing with groups, not individuals. The management accountant, then, should be familiar with the basics of group dynamics. The second point is that any success the budget people have in uncovering errors and weaknesses (which they then report to upper management), has the fault that it implies failure on the part of the front-line supervisors and the workforce. After all, the latter are responsible for the errors. And since the culprits can be easily singled out, they are particularly vulnerable. In short, management accountants only achieve success when they point to the failure of others. It is this dilemma that creates conflict between the management accountant and the foremen and workers. Unfortunately, this conflict is a fact of life. Once recognized, however, the management accountant may be able to find a mutually satisfactory and workable resolution to this problem.

Participation and group dynamics

Argyris' study, together with the momentum achieved by the participative management school, had a lasting influence on research into behavioral accounting. But, as it happened, participation in budgeting turned out to be more complex than Argyris anticipated. A decade later, Becker and Green (1962) wrote a thoughtful, if controversial, theoretical article on the subject. They showed how participative budgeting was not merely a simple progression from participation, through budget and performance, and finally to comparison. Rather, they argued, while budgets act as controls to limit and inform people operating under budgets, these same people determine and limit each succeeding round of budgeting. And how they affect subsequent rounds depends upon first, the cohesiveness of the work group, and, second, on the group's acceptance of the stated goal. These two factors combine in four ways as shown in Table 2.1.

Table 2.1

Cohesiveness	Attitudes re. goal acceptance	Outcome
1. High	Positive	Maximum motivation and efficiency
2. Low	Positive	Efficient performance
3. Low	Negative	Production depressed
4. High	Negative	Most conducive to a production slow-down

The main lesson seems to be that if participation is encouraged, then the budgeting process inevitably becomes enmeshed in the group dynamics of the work force. A highly cohesive work force with a positive attitude toward the budget goal will yield maximum motivation and efficiency. But a similar highly cohesive work group with negative attitudes to the proposed goal will result in a production slow-down. Under participative budgeting, Becker and Green argue, the group process is a most important intervening determinant of final production. They also go on to show how goal aspiration levels, as suggested by Stedry (1960), complicate the process even further. Becker and Green concluded that participation can work either for or against you. It all depends upon the attitudes of the work group.

Budgets and leadership style

In another effort following up the Argyris study, DeCoster and Fertakis (1968), investigated the idea that supervisors use budgets as a way of expressing their own patterns of leadership. They used the two Ohio State leadership dimensions, initiating structure and consideration. (The first refers to leadership action which establishes ways of getting the work done, clearly delineates roles, establishes channels of communication, provides detailed job instructions, and displays a definite concern for the task. The second includes respect for the ideas and feelings of subordinates, friendship, mutual trust, and communication about the process of work relationships.) Thus, they proposed that budgetary procedures encouraging supervisory consideration should be more effective than those linked with initiating structure. This proposition stemmed from the prevailing human relations belief that considerate managers achieve better performance than do those who stress output and production. The reasoning assumed that a participative approach to budget goal formulations would result in concerted effort to reach the goal, but with little felt pressure. It was also assumed, however, that when under budget pressures, supervisors would switch to structuring behavior, take greater initiative in work assignment, emphasize the need for production, make most decisions themselves, and act like a directive boss. Therefore, when supervisors felt high budget pressure, consideration efforts would be neglected or ignored. In sum, it was anticipated that budget pressure would lead to greater initiating structure behavior on the part of supervisors and to a neglect of consideration efforts.

This, however, proved not to be the case. A survey of supervisors in eight manufacturing firms indicated that *both* initiating structure and consideration were positively correlated with budget pressure. Also, the degree of pressure from immediate superiors proved to be positively correlated with both initiating structure and consideration efforts by supervisors. What might be happening, the study speculated, is that when supervisors induce budget-related pressure, supervisors increase both initiating structure and consideration efforts in order to get higher effectiveness out of the work group. They become ideal leaders. Such behavior, if applied consistently, could be constructive to the organization.

The study, then, showed that pressure from above induces leadership behavior which mirrors the ideal leadership style, rather than the detrimental effects alleged by the Argyris study. Budgets, it seems, may not be, after all, a major source of human relations problems.

Budget participation and the 'game spirit'

The next milestone study of the association of human-relations variables and financial controls is Hofstede's (1967) investigation of budget-related behavior in six large manufacturing firms. Hofstede was puzzled by the

14

contradiction between findings in the US and his own observations in Holland. Whereas the former reported that an emphasis on budgets was associated with pressure, aggression, conflict, inefficiency, and staff-line clashes, in Holland, in many instances, not only were such conflicts and negative human relations not noticeable, but in addition, neither managers nor employees appeared to be concerned with budgets. In fact, they seemed to motivate no-one at all. Believing these two conditions to be extremes, he set out to discover the precise conditions that lead to successful and positive attitudes to budgets. The key, he believed, would be found in participation in budget level setting.

The research plan followed a model of the effect of participation in standard setting which was much richer than the traditional model (see Figure 2.1). Participation was thought to be the key ingredient in bringing aspiration levels in line with budget standards and ultimately lead to greater motivation and, thus, higher productivity. Participation should lead to standards which are neither impossible to achieve nor so easy as to be useless. As a result, balance and fairness are brought to the financial control system. The result is an enhancement of autonomy, affiliation, and achievement needs.

There are, however, other factors which naturally limit the positive motivation of participation. These include: personality, culture, leadership practices, machine speeds, work standards studies, and other interdependent departments. Authoritarian personalities, for example, may be quite willing to accept, even welcome, non-participative standard-setting; and machine

A. The traditional view of the effect of participation in standard-setting

B. Improved model of the effect of participation in standard-setting

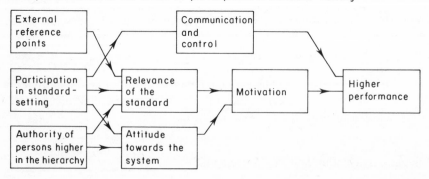

Figure 2.1 Two views of the effect of participation in standard-setting. (Source: Hofstede, 1967, p. 178. Reproduced by permission of Tavistock Publications Ltd and Koninklijke Van Gorcum & Company NV, Assen, The Netherlands)

speeds and capabilities often are the major determinant of standards. Attitudes towards the financial controls are also important, and these are shaped by people in positions of higher authority, as well as by participation.

The research sites, six plants in five large manufacturing firms, all held a reputation for being well managed and having good organizational practices. The questionnaire, administered to nearly 140 managers, supervisors, and staff officers, contained hundreds of questions about a wide range of factors including demographics, job attributes, departmental characteristics, market conditions, leadership style, attitudes, satisfaction, and morale, in addition to questions about the financial control systems. A number of major results emerged.

As anticipated, participation in the budget setting process proved to be positively associated with motivation to fulfill budget targets, but only for managers from the second level up—those who participated a great deal in setting the budget target. For first-level supervisors and employees, however, the situation was quite different. Although they did not participate in the budget process, they did participate to some extent in setting the technical production standards, thus indirectly influencing the budgets. This participation by first-level supervisors in setting technical standards did not lead to greater motivation to meet them. The results regarding participation, therefore, were mixed.

Generalizations of this sort, however, can be dangerous. In one plant, for example, budget standards were based on levels used in another company-owned plant, so the managers participated little in setting them. Yet these externally set standards were seen as valid and relevant. In another plant, first-line supervisors participated in budget setting because upper management believed that foremen should be considered part of the management team. As a result, they established separate cost centers so the foremen could have their own budgets. The company was highly cost-conscious and believed that all managers are responsible for performance. Budget performance also had a large influence in overall job appraisal. Budget participation and responsibility was a key element in this company's management philosophy and practices; and the foremen in this plant held positive attitudes to budget participation. In the other plants, by contrast, the foremen had mixed reactions.

Another important finding proved to be that the budgetee's supervisor plays a key role in the motivation to meet the budget. The communication between superior and subordinate proved most crucial, particularly the frequency of person-to-person contacts about budget results and efforts related to its achievement. Positive attitudes resulted from superiors using budget results in performance appraisal, and holding meetings to discuss budget performance. The budget-related behavior of higher authorities turned out to be an important factor.

Participation in budget target setting would appear to be a necessary, but not sufficient, condition for high budget motivation. Target levels must be correct. Superordinates must hold the proper attitudes. But the key ingredient, Hofstede came to believe, was the 'game spirit' which managers relied on to 'play the budget game'. Again and again, during his interviews and investigations, he was impressed with the different ways in which managers played the budget game. Some ignored the budget, others became overly concerned with it and carefully weighed every move in terms of its effect on meeting standards, while still others treated it in a positive but not pathological manner.

The way to establish this game spirit, Hopstede believed, was to create an atmosphere where the budget process is seen as a game with the budget an end for its own sake. People play games for the game itself. Players become highly involved and enjoy the challenge of competition. Play also involves certain rules which the players accept and conscientiously follow. It is this attitude that has the potential for creating team spirit.

Similarly, planning and control, essential factors for any organization, can be seen as a game by managers. The trick, then, is to get managers to approach the budget as if it were a game—in a positive and high-spirited way. A well-played budget game means involvement, co-operation, excitement, and a positive contribution. The key to this positive game spirit, Hofstede believed, was budget participation.

Hofstede, then, had solved his puzzle. Participation by itself is not enough to get managers to live with budgets and be motivated by them. Sufficient communication, correct target levels, judicious performance appraisal, and appropriate superordinate behavior are also necessary. But even then, only with a positive game spirit will healthy budget motivation emerge. Consequently, accountants and top management must strive to instill a game spirit into the budgeting process in their organizations.

Importantly, Hofstede also concluded that external circumstances, such as technology and markets, also explain the way organizational systems, including financial control systems, are designed and used. A good company will align its organizational and control systems to the demands of external circumstances; and, he came to believe, these external and impersonal causes are more fundamental than internal and personal ones.

LEADERSHIP BEHAVIOR AND FINANCIAL CONTROLS

The next major human-relations study with respect to the budgeting process investigated the effect of the way supervisors use budget performance information on cost-consciousness, job tension, interpersonal relations, and manipulation of accounting reports (Hopwood, 1973 and 1976). The study rested on the overriding proposition that the impact of an accounting system on job-related behavior depends more on the style in which it is used than on its technical design.

The study identified three styles of evaluation. Some managers use a 'budget-constrained' style whereby the subordinate's performance is evaluated primarily on the basis of meeting short-term targets. These managers over-emphasize budget performance information and use it in an overly zealous and unquestioning manner. They give subordinates negative feedback for budget overruns regardless of any mitigating circumstances. Accounting information is taken at face value and used rigidly for performance evaluation.

By contrast, other managers utilize a 'non-accounting' style. They are indifferent to budgetary performance information or are unaware of its intended purposes. Accounting information plays a relatively unimportant role in evaluating the performance of their subordinates.

Still other managers follow a 'profit-conscious style'. The budget is not an end in itself, but rather a means to an end. Performance is evaluated on the ability to increase the general effectiveness of departmental operations as dictated by long-term organizational and departmental goals and programs. Accounting and budget performance information is used as part of performance evaluation, but in a careful and flexible way.

In order to test these ideas, a survey was made of 167 cost centre department heads in one large manufacturing firm. The results are shown in Table 2.2. Surprisingly, nearly half of the department heads reported a non-accounting evaluation style. As expected, involvement with costs proved lowest for this style. Budget-constrained managers were more concerned with meeting

Table 2.2 Style of evaluation and relations with superiors, relations with peers, and rating of evaluative criteria

	Style of evaluation		
	(a) Non–accounting (N=73)	(b) Budget–constrained (N=33)	(c) Profit-conscious (N=43)
(1) *Relations with supervisor*			
(a) Trust	4.0	3.3	4.2
(b) Respect	4.3	3.7	4.6
(c) Reasonableness of expectations	3.9	3.3	4.1
(d) Satisfaction	4.4	3.3	4.6
(2) *Relations with peers*			
(a) Supportiveness	3.9	3.6	3.8
(b) Agreement	3.8	3.4	3.7
(c) Helpfulness	4.2	3.8	4.0
(d) Friendship	3.7	3.3	3.7
(3) *Rating of evaluative criteria*			
(a) Cost concern	4.1	4.3	4.8
(b) Effort	4.5	4.1	4.7
(c) Quality concern	4.5	4.5	4.7
(d) Meeting budget	3.9	4.4	4.5
(e) Attitude to work and firm	4.6	4.1	4.8
(f) Co-operation with colleagues	4.4	3.7	4.3

The above indices are based on a scale of 1 to 5.
Source: Data selected from tables in Hopwood (1973), pp. 77, 79 and 88.

budget targets, but exhibited defensive behavior. They reported widespread tension and job worry, and believed their superiors' evaluations of their performance to be improper and unjust. As a result, many of them responded with a host of negative and dysfunctional activities, including manipulation of accounting reports, avoidance of innovation, adoption of short-term expedients at the expense of higher long-run costs, and development of negative attitudes to accounting reports.

This last description is familiar to those who have studied enterprise managers throughout the USSR. The results, which have been documented widely, include massive underutilization of productive resources, avoidance of innovation, and preoccupation with short-run plan fulfillment at the expense of long-run improvements. The rigid plans and budgets from state central planning agencies are adhered to even in the face of blatantly obvious incongruities.

Budget-constrained cost center heads also reported a deterioration of relationships with their superiors. They felt superiors had little understanding of departmental problems. They believed the budget expectations of superiors to be unreasonable; and they reported significantly lower trust, respect and satisfaction with superiors than did the other two groups. A budget-constrained style is obviously detrimental to superordinate relationships.

The budget-constrained evaluation style also led to a deterioration of interpersonal relationships with peer managers. When superiors continually focused on budget variances beyond the control of the department heads, they adopted a parochial stance and moved to improve their performance, regardless of any detrimental effects on other departments. They also blamed other units for budget variances. Consequently, co-operation, so vital to interdependent activities, gave way to rivalry and conflict.

Profit-conscious superiors, by contrast, proved considerably less rigid in the use of accounting information. Although they too applied budget pressure, they focused on long-run and goal-congruent cost reductions; and while they were not easy to satisfy, they applied pressure fairly, and willingly accepted reasonable explanations of variances. As a result, department heads working under a profit-conscious evaluation style had better relations with both their superiors and their peer managers, higher concern for cost and quality, and better attitudes to work and the firm. They also felt that effort was rewarded. Although this style was viewed as very demanding, it was accepted and respected. The profit-conscious style, then, very nearly mirrored Hofstede's positive game spirit of budgeting.

The profit-conscious style of evaluation also included a significantly higher degree of budget participation than did the other two styles. This finding stimulated an investigation of the impact on job-related behavior of participation by department heads in the budgeting process. The results are noteworthy; participation appeared to have a widespread salutory effect on both the budget-constrained and the non-accounting department heads. It reduced job-related tension. It sharpened awareness of the financial aspects of performance. It improved relations both with superiors and peer managers. It increased the amount of discussions with superiors about the limitations and inadequacies of the accounting system. For the non-accounting group, it significantly boosted concern for budget attainment and cost control. In general, then, the results indicate that participation in the budgeting process has a substantial wholesome effect on department heads subjected to inappropriate use of accounting information. Importantly, though, it has little effect when accounting information is used appropriately, as is the case for the profit-conscious style, where it stimply is not necessary.

The general pattern to emerge from the above data, as summarized in Table 2.3, is both revealing and instructive. The non-accounting style is fine for superior and peer relations but, as expected, suffers in terms of concerns for, and meeting, budgets. A shift to an overconcern for meeting budgets improves attention to cost, but at the expense of attitudes, co-operation, and relations with superiors and peers. A more balanced use of accounting information, as embedded in the profit-conscious style, yields the best of all worlds—good relations with superiors and peers and high levels of concern for cost control and meeting budgets, co-operation with colleagues, and positive attitudes to work and company. Participation in the budgeting process moderates the negative effects of non-accounting and budget-constrained styles, but does not help much—indeed is not needed—under the profit-conscious style.

Table 2.3 Effects of different evaluation styles

	Style of evaluation		
	Budget-constrained	Profit-conscious	Non-accounting
Involvement with costs	High	High	Low
Job-related tension	High	Medium	Medium
Manipulation of the accounting reports	Extensive	Little	Little
Relations with the supervisor	Poor	Good	Good
Relations with colleagues	Poor	Good	Good

Source: Hopwood (1976), p. 113.

The study also investigated the relationship between performance evaluation style and leadership behavior. Cost center heads rated their superiors on two traditional leadership characteristics—initiating structure (clearly delineated roles, clear channels of communication, well-defined patterns of organization, detailed job instructions and a definite concern for the task) and consideration (rapport, trust, communication, and respect for the ideas and feelings of others). A comparison of evaluation and leadership styles shown in Table 2.4, revealed that leadership style did influence evaluation style. Budget-concerned superiors were high on initiating structure and low on consideration, the classic 'task-oriented' boss. By contrast, non-accounting superiors were low on initiating structure and high on consideration, the classic 'country club' style. Profit-conscious superiors, by contrast, proved to be high on both dimensions. Further, some superiors, mainly the profit-conscious ones, exhibited a flexible evaluation style, depending on the past budget performance of the cost centre head and the particular circumstances such as the size of the department, the nature of the work, and the degree of skilled labor in the department. Leadership style, then, proved to have a significant effect on the manner in which accounting information was used in performance evaluation.

Table 2.4 Evaluation style and leadership characteristics

	Style of evaluation		
Leadership characteristics	Budget-constrained	Profit-conscious	Non-accounting
Initiating structure	High	High	Low
Consideration	Low	High	High

Source: adapted from Hopwood (1973), p. 178.

The study also uncovered evidence to support the notion of a 'contagion' effect in evaluation styles. This occurs when a performance-evaluation style is transferred from a superior to a subordinate at the next lower level in the hierarchy. This proved to be very strong for the budget-constrained style. It also was present for the profit-conscious managers, but they seemed to be capable of resisting it, depending on their own managerial abilities and their assessment of the situational needs. They deflected it, not by reducing the importance attached to meeting the budget, but by increasing the importance attached to other performance criteria. Non-accounting managers were successful in diverting it when they thought it unsuitable.

Hopwood's study goes well beyond previous approaches by placing the issue of participation in the budgeting process in a wider setting, including the evaluation manner of superiors, leadership styles, and situational needs. The findings are intriguing and important. The budget-constrained perform-ance evaluation can lead to a host of negative consequences—manipulation of accounting data, short-term horizons, distrust, parochial attitudes, peer rivalry, and hostility. The non-accounting style avoids these consequences but at the expense of lower concerns for cost and budget performance. In both cases the problems are modified by participation in the budgeting process. By contrast, a leadership style concerned with both task and human relations gives rise to a profit-conscious use of accounting information which does not require participation and which avoids the problems encountered by either of the other styles.

In reviewing his findings, Hopwood calls for an expansion of the role of accounting and information systems managers. They should not merely prepare and present information to managers. Rather, they need to get involved in educating and preparing managers in the use of accounting information. A first step would be to make sure managers are informed of the assumptions and guesses that are necessary to produce accounting information. Then line managers will, in turn, recognize the inadequacies and limitations of the information and so avoid the unhappy results of attaching undue importance to it. Accountants should also emphasize the value of information for learning and improvement and de-emphasize the practice of using accounting information for 'responsibility, accountability, past achievement and piling up a track record'. In short, accounting and information systems designers need to take an increased responsibility for the way in which line managers use accounting systems.

The important message for management accounting and information systems executives seems to be that human relations play an important role in how accounting information is used in organizations. By itself, it does not result in either negative or positive effects. Rather it is the way it is used that is critical. Use is not a straightforward matter, nor is it an inevitable consequence of mere availability.

The study also has something to say about the issue of participation in the budgeting process. Participation seems not to be a panacea. Rather, it is a complex social process that is related closely to other phenomena, including situational needs and evaluation styles. A strong concern for budget performance in evaluation styles can be moderated by a managerial style which attempts to create a friendly supportive climate conducive to trust and respect. Without this, however, accounting information can be stressful and threatening. In the final analysis, accounting information is a vehicle that assists managers to run their departments. Accounting and information system designs can play an important role by helping managers understand the best style for its appropriate use in the performance evaluation process.

Environmental stress and budget behavior

In a related study, Otley (1978) took a close look at the generally accepted premise that evaluations of managerial performance based primarily on budget performance lead to a variety of negative outcomes, including distrust and feelings of being treated unfairly and, consequently, practices featuring short-run action and organizational slack-ridden budgets. The research site consisted of one organization with several large production units each of which was treated as a profit centre. This particular company was selected since it had a well-developed and soundly designed accounting system, one which was highly suitable for the application of budgetary control. Several important findings emerged, not the least of which was refutation of the generally accepted premise stated above.

The data uncovered more insights into the effect of the different evaluation styles identified by Hopwood and discussed earlier in this chapter. For one thing, managers working under a budget-constrained style easily adapted to the budget system by employing a variety of covert practices. They manipulated spending, adopted 'income-smoothing' accounting customs, bargained hard for pessimistic budget levels and even resorted to 'creative' bookkeeping techniques. Not surprisingly, then, their actual results consistently matched budget targets; and, contrary to Hopwood's findings, the budget-oriented evaluation style did not lead to high levels of job- and budget-related tension.

Unit managers under a profit-centered evaluation style tended to be less accurate. These managers tended to be optimistic in target setting, or they merely submitted unrealistic but acceptable budgets to a docile upper management. Moreover, when actual results fell short of targets, upper management reacted in a flexible manner. Profitable units produced accurate budgets whereas unprofitable ones tended to produce unrealistic ones which were not used later in evaluating performance. Trust in superiors was higher for the profit-conscious group but, contrary to expectations, job-related tension also was higher. Interestingly, when unit managers had either less or more than average influence on budgeted levels, both job-related and budget-related tension increased and perceived fairness of evaluation dropped. Even so, managers at all levels and under various budget evaluation styles reacted flexibly and intelligently to the budget system.

The study also indicated that the effects of participatory budget setting may not be as salutory as was previously thought, thus supporting Cherrington and Cherrington's (1973) findings during a laboratory experiment that managers operating under conditions where budget targets were either imposed or revised upward immediately after being set by the managers, outperformed those whose budgets were accepted on submittal.

Contrary to previous findings, evaluation styles did not seem to affect job-related and budget-associated tension. Nor did differences in style explain differences in performance. What seems to have happened, Otley speculates, is that senior managers adopted an evaluation style which suited the prevailing circumstances and was, therefore, appropriate for each independent operating unit. These circumstances are dependent upon factors such as the toughness of the competitive environment, the general economic conditions, the size of the operating unit (and thus the relative magnitude of the investment in the unit), the relative experience of its manager, and the degree of profitability of the unit. Senior managers seemed able to match their evaluation style to each set of circumstances; for example, they exercised closer control through a budget-constrained style, on relatively inexperienced unit managers and on the larger units. New managers were given a chance but monitored closely and replaced quickly at the first sign of incompetence. The managers generally felt that a certain degree of emphasis on meeting budget levels is helpful for technical efficiency and interpersonal relations.

This proved to be an important finding. Prevailing circumstances may have more influence on the use of accounting information than does the individual's own personality and philosophy of management.

These results point toward the need to develop a more contingent theory of budgeting control based on differences in organizational types, the environmental circumstances in which they operate, and the norms and values current both within the organization itself and within the society in which it is set (Otley, 1978, p. 146).

CONCLUSION

The idea of involving participants in the setting of targets for financial control systems as a remedy for reported negative consequences of financial controls proved to be naive. Clearly participation is not a panacea for effective budgeting systems. Nevertheless, we have learned a great deal from such studies. For example, one previously overlooked aspect is that financial people are dealing with groups and, as the groups may be protective or negative towards the company, participative target setting can have either a positive or a negative effect on motivation.

What seems to be even more important, however, is the way in which superiors use the budgets. Some use it in an overly zealous and unquestioning way to pressure subordinates continually to meet short-run budget targets. Others attribute little validity to budgetary performance, thus losing the potential positive aspects of financial controls. Still others use it in a flexible and intelligent way, treating it as a means to move their organizational units towards long-term goals. Subordinates tend to imitate their supervisors in the way they, in turn, use financial controls. The manner in which line managers use the budget proved more important than participation. Management accountants, then, should pay close attention to this aspect of budgeting, even to the extent of counselling line managers about the behavioral ramifications of budgeting systems.

The amount of environmental stress also seems to have an important impact on the way budgets are used and the amount of job-related tension. Under laboratory conditions, some line managers reacted by increasing both initiating structure and consideration efforts in their use of budgets and got constructive results. In a real-life tough competitive situation, upper line managers appeared to match their evaluative style of budget use to each set of circumstances for the various component parts of their organization.

Another critical aspect to emerge is the idea that the spirit with which managers play the budget game is important. When it is played in a high-spirited, competitive, and sportsmanlike way, it can result in involvement, co-operation, and excitement and so make a positive contribution towards the healthy functioning of the organization. The creation by financial people of a game spirit for budgeting appears to be more important than mere participation in target setting.

Finally, these studies also pointed to the important fact that the financial people are so placed that their own success is dependent on spotting and reporting the failure of others. The natural conflicts that follow is a point

24

worth underscoring. Thus, even though the participative budgeting concept proved to be a myth, we have learned a great deal about the way financial controls work in our organizations. Even more important, it gave birth to the field of behavioral accounting and information systems.

References

Argyris, C., *The Impact of Budgets on People*, Controllership Foundation, Inc., Cornell University, Ithaca, NY, 1952.

Becker, S., and D. Green, 'Budgeting and employee behavior', *The Journal of Business*, October 1962, pp. 392–402.

Cherrington, D. J., and J. O. Cherrington, 'Appropriate reinforcement contingencies in the budgeting process', *Journal of Accounting Research: Empirical Research in Accounting: Selected Studies*, 1973, pp. 225–253.

De Coster, D. T., and J. P. Fertakis, 'Budget induced pressure and its relationship to supervisory behaviour', *The Journal of Accounting Research*, Autumn 1968, pp. 237–246.

Hofstede, G. H., *The Game of Budget Control*, Koninklijke Van Gorcum & Comp. N.V., Assen, The Netherlands, 1968.

Hopwood, A. G., *An Accounting System and Managerial Behavior*, Saxon House, Hampshire, UK, 1973.

Hopwood, A. G., *Accounting and Human Behavior*, Prentice-Hall, Inc., Englewood Cliffs, NJ, 1976.

Mayo, I., *The Social Problems of an Industrial Civilization*, Harvard University Press, Cambridge, Mass., 1945.

Miles, R. E., 'Human relations or human resources', *Harvard Business Review*, July–August 1966, pp. 148–155.

National Industrial Conference Board, *Budgetary Control in Manufacturing Industries*, New York, 1931.

Otley, D. T., 'Budget use and managerial performance', *Journal of Accounting Research*, Spring 1978, pp. 122–149.

Perrow, C., *Complex Organizations: A Critical Essay*, Scott, Foresman and Company, 1972.

Roethlisberger, F. J., and W. J. Dickson, *Management and the Worker*, Harvard University Press, Cambridge, Mass., 1947.

Stedry, G. H., *Budget Control and Cost Behavior*, Prentice-Hall, Inc., Englewood Cliffs, NJ, 1960.

CHAPTER 3

The Social Psychology of Accounting and Information Systems

The field of behavioral accounting, spurred on by the unexpected findings of the studies of the human relations school on budgeting, widened its scope to include the social-psychological aspects of accounting and information systems. A major impetus for this was the dawning realization that the human relations perspective was at odds with the traditional management accounting one.

On the one hand, the traditional management accounting literature had emphasized the merits of accounting and information systems such as budgets. According to this view, they reflect organizational plans and goals, and budget targets provide the motivation to participants to strive towards these goals. Further, financial controls contain the critical means by which managers can exercise surveillance over the objectives, functions, methods, and costs of their responsibility centers. Financial controls also force managers to look ahead, anticipate changes, assess the feasibility of plans, and consider how the various functions of the organization fit together. They also serve as a means of co-ordinating activities throughout the organization by creating interdependencies amongst the various units. Finally, financial controls give upper management a common means for measuring, evaluating, and guiding progress. From the perspective of management accounting, then, budgets play a very positive role in organization.

On the other hand, from the human relations viewpoint, individuals often tend to regard accounting and information systems with apprehension. Employees, especially in the lower echelons, perceive financial controls as coercive mechanisms whose purpose is relentlessly and unilaterally to increase production goals. Frequently they are seen as an unfair means of evaluating performance. In consequence, employees develop resentment, hostility, and even fear and aggression towards financial control systems. In some cases this results in psychological breakdown. Finally, financial controls force managers to stress the interest of their individual responsibility centers, thus creating interdepartmental rivalries, hostilities, and energy-consuming competition, all of which is detrimental to overall organizational purpose. From the human relations vantage point, then, accounting and information systems play a negative role in organizations.

This chapter investigates the obvious discrepancy between these two views. It does this by reviewing the research and theory dealing with the social-

26

psychological aspects of these systems. These studies deal with a variety of social-psychological phenomena including interpersonal relations, role conflict and ambiguity, path goal leadership ideas, and organizational slack practices. They go a long way to explaining the discrepancy between the two conflicting views; and they yield a rich set of insights for accounting and information systems managers into the workings of these systems.

INTERPERSONAL BEHAVIOR, ROLES, AND BUDGET-RELATED BEHAVIORS

In one of the milestone social psychological studies of managerial accounting, Swieringa and Moncur (1974), investigated the association of a host of variables with managers' budget-related behavior using the powerful, neat and creative research model shown in Figure 3.1. The logic of the research model is as follows. Budgets lead to budget-related behavior. A manager may be motivated by a budget to develop a well-laid plan or expand the product line. He might also be motivated to go over plans with superiors, discuss spending levels with accounting officers, and pressure other departments for prompt delivery of raw materials and discuss cost variances with subordinates. Budget-oriented behavior, then, is the variety of actions and interactions of managers that is precipitated by a budgetary control system. The central idea is that the use of budgeting elicits budget-oriented behavior from a manager.

Arrow 1 in Figure 3.1 indicates that the local manager's budget-oriented behavior can be influenced by the demands and expectations of other managers, including superiors, peers, and accounting and budget officers, about how to compile budgets or about the consequences of not meeting budget targets. The expectations of others are in turn influenced by feedback,

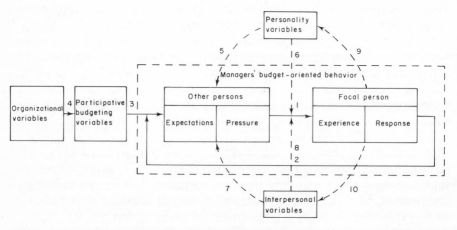

Figure 3.1 Factors influencing budget-oriented behavior. (Source: Swieringa and Moncur (1974), p. 26. Reproduced by permission of the National Association of Accountants, New York.)

as shown in Arrow 2, about the extent to which the manager does or does not conform to the behavior and expectations of others. The other managers get feedback about how the manager responds to the communications and pressures from others, and so these expectations are either reinforced or altered.

Turning to Arrow 3, the model proposes that the style of participative budgeting influences the content of the expectations held by others for the budget-related behavior of the focal managers. Participative budgeting refers to the extent to which managers are allowed to participate in establishing budget targets to be used for evaluating and measuring their performance. In some organizations, top management unilaterally set operating budget targets and then issue them to the operating managers. In other organizations, operating managers have a say, usually a limited amount, in setting budget levels. In still other organizations, top management and operating managers share this responsibility. The type of participation (Arrow 3) effects the pattern of interaction between operating and top management. In the case of shared responsibility all managers, including the budgeting officers, are involved extensively in developing plans and translating them into budget targets.

The type of participation, in turn, is shaped by organizational variables as shown in Arrow 4. These variables may be size, the number of management levels, the products and services produced, and the financial base of the organization, combined into a unique operating environment which can systematically influence the way the organization shapes its budgeting participation patterns. It is of more than passing interest to note that the model proposes that the pattern of budget participation for any organization is dictated largely by its impersonal operating environment as opposed to the personal beliefs and assumptions of the top managers. Finally, to complete the model, personality and interpersonal variables are expected to influence the budget-oriented behavior of both other and focal managers, as indicated by Arrows 5 to 10.

The study collected data from 137 budgeted managers in four firms manufacturing electronic products in the San Francisco Bay area. Eight personality traits were also measured, including cautiousness, original thinking, tolerance and trust, vigorousness, self-assurance and assertiveness, perseverance and responsibility, emotional stability, and sociability. The interpersonal variables included leadership style, attitude about 'Machiavellian' behavior, and whether or not individuals perceive themselves to be masters of their own destinies as opposed to victims of chance, fate, or luck. This personal trait is known as internal versus external locus of control. Personality, of course, had been seen for a long time to be an important moderating factor in any participation process (Vroom, 1964).

The large number of predictor- and budget-oriented variables included in the study makes the results difficult to summarize. Nevertheless, some of the general findings are of interest. The personality and attitudinal variables seemed to influence how the managers used budgets, although not to the extent anticipated. Some of the strongest relationships suggested by the data are as follows:

(1) The most important predictors of how managers achieve their budgets, how influential they are in the budgeting process, and how positive their attitudes are about budgeting proved to be emotional stability, self-assurance, and assertiveness, and then internal versus external locus of control attitude.

(2) Managers who engage more in nefarious activities to cope with budget overruns tend to be intellectually curious but less stable emotionally; while those who engage less in such practices tend to be less intellectually curious but more self-assured and assertive.

(3) Managers who take a passive role in their relationships with others tend to spend more time on activities involved in explaining budget variances.

(4) Managers who think that rewards depend on their own behavior spend more time discussing budget issues with their superiors than do those who believe that rewards result from luck, chance, and the control of persons of power.

(5) Managers who are relatively emotionally stable and intellectually curious tend to believe that their methods of achieving their budgets will be accepted by superiors.

(6) Managers who are more stable emotionally, less assertive, and more accepting of a following role, and have high internal feelings of control, spend more time with financial people in preparing budgets and have more influence in the budget setting behavior.

(7) Managers who are self-assured and assertive in their relationships with others spend more time discussing budget matters with others.

(8) Managers who are more assertive and less emotionally stable spend more time with financial staff personnel and with other peer managers discussing budget matters.

(9) Managers who are more trusting of others, more gregarious and social, but less stable emotionally spend more time preparing and working with budgets.

Many of these relationships, however, were not particularly strong. In fact, the personality and attitudinal variables, which were thoroughly measured, proved to be much less important than expected. This led the researchers to conclude that the effects of these types of variables are more limited than is generally thought to be the case. Surprisingly, the organizational variables proved to be more important than personality and attitude in explaining budget-related behavior. This was an unexpected but important finding. Nevertheless, personality variables do influence the actions and interactions of budgeted managers. While this in itself is not unexpected, the study demonstrates the potential utility for accounting and information system designers of systematically measuring personality traits, predicting how the managers will react to and use financial controls, and tailoring systems to anticipate and overcome potential problems and misuse.

Locus of control and budget participation

The influence of personality as a moderating factor in the budgetary participation process was looked at later by Brownell (1981) in a controlled laboratory experiment. The personality variable selected was 'locus of control', the degree to which individuals accept personal responsibility for what happens to them. Those of us with an external locus tend to perceive events, both good and bad, as unrelated to our own behavior and thus beyond our control. Those of us with an internal locus do the opposite.

The subjects in the experiment, undergraduate accounting students and management personnel, participated in a controlled business game where each assumed the role of one of four senior managers in a firm manufacturing and marketing a perishable product. They were required to submit a budget recommendation to top management for the level of sales for the next period. They then received a contrived recommended budget sales level for the other three managers. Finally, they received notification of the final budget level as determined by top management. This final budget was a weighted average of the estimates made by all four 'managers' in the experiment. Each was informed of the level set by top management and received a statement of the percentage by which all of the four recommended budget levels deviated from the final decision. For the 'high' participation group, the recommendation was given a weight of 90 percent, while for the 'low' participation group, it was given a weight of only 5 percent. The amount of influence an individual had on the final jointly set budget was deemed to be the budget participation factor. Each 'manager' also received the level of advertising expenditure which would produce an actual sales volume equal to the final budget. This information could be used to avoid either a costly stockout or an excess inventory of perishable products which could not be sold.

The general results are shown in Figure 3.2. When personality type and influence in budget target setting were congruent, as in cells 1 and 4, performance on the business game proved to be high. By contrast, when these factors were incongruent, as in cells 2 and 3, performance was lower. These results support the idea that personality and participation patterns interact in an important way.

Several other interesting findings emerged. For example, influence in budget target setting through participation resulted in better performance *only* for individuals who saw events as being a consequence of their own actions. External locus of control individuals, it seems, perform best when budget levels are assigned to them by top management. Learning rates also proved better for those subjects in their preferred participation mode (cells 1 and 4).

		Locus of control	
		Internal	External
Influence in *budget target-* *setting*	High (participative)	High performance and fast learning 1	Low performance and slow learning 2
	Low (non-partic-ipative)	3 Low performance and slow learning	4 High performance and fast learning

Figure 3.2 Locus of central influence in budget target-setting and performance and learning. (Source: adapted from Brownell, 1981.)

These results suggest that people who find themselves working under conditions which suit their personality learn faster, and consequently perform better, than when under unsuitable conditions. These results are consistent with previous psychological experiments which found that individuals who believe they have personal control over their environment preferred and performed better under conditions of self-control; while those with an external locus of control preferred and did better under conditions which were controlled by the experimenters.

Interestingly, internals outperformed externals and performance was generally superior for those, except for extreme externals, in the high participative group. The important implication is that high participation is generally the preferred condition except in extreme cases. No explanation is offered for the fact that internals do better than externals. Perhaps internals believing they have control over events become more involved in the game, whereas externals, attributing outcomes as beyond their control, are more inclined merely to go through the motions. In any event, the experiment provides evidence that accounting and information system designers should be careful to create the right chemistry between personality traits, participative budgeting patterns, and the roles imposed upon the manager. These findings were supported by studies by other researchers such as Milani (1975) and Collins (1978).

AN EXPECTANCY THEORY OF BUDGETS

Ideas stemming from expectancy theory were used by other researchers to understand the intricate workings of financial controls. Ronen and Livingston (1975), for example, proposed that ideas incorporated in path–goal theories of leadership could be used to integrate and accommodate some of the fragmentary and contradictory findings from previous behavioral accounting studies and went on to develop a new and insightful set of ideas about the workings of financial controls.

Expectancy theory holds that motivation is a combination of factors which are external (or extrinsic) and internal (intrinsic) to the individual as well as the satisfaction and personal utilities (called valences) the individual experiences from being involved in goal-directed activities and from completing tasks. The strength of external motivators depends on the expectations and beliefs one holds about whether effort will result in accomplishment and, importantly, whether effort and accomplishment will be recognized and rewarded. The strength of internal motivation to work stems from internal satisfactions experienced by involvement in goal-directed activities and the pleasures experienced from successful performance of a goal-directed task.

Superiors can influence these motivations, the theory holds, in several ways. They can express approval of accomplishment and reward an individual's contribution to the overall organizational purpose. They can influence the amount of control subordinates have over task-directed efforts and goal setting. And they can make the path to the goal easier to travel by creating an environment of trust and friendship, providing support in times of stress, reducing frustrating barriers, and permitting subordinates to get involved in a variety of interesting tasks.

Budgets, then, Ronen and Livingston argue, represent an excellent vehicle through which a superior can communicate with subordinates, reflecting his expectations about what constitutes successful goal performance. They imply that external rewards will be forthcoming for budget accomplishment. They help clarify the potential level of external attractiveness to the organization of work–goal accomplishment. They influence, through the perceived difficulty of reaching the budget target, the expectations of subordinates that effort will lead to budget achievement. They bias, by the manner in which the superior delivers the contingent rewards for budget accomplishment, the expectations of subordinates of future rewards associated with task accomplishment. And they provide structure to ambiguous tasks. Thus, the way a superior utilizes the budgeting process holds great potential for influencing the motivation of subordinates.

These ideas are used to re-examine a number of the traditional generally accepted management accounting assumptions about financial controls as summarized in Table 3.1. The first assumption holds that budgets should be set at reasonably attainable levels. Research has found, however, that the subordinate's aspiration level (the goal one explicitly undertakes to reach where maximum effort will be exerted just to meet the aspired-to goal) is more important than the budget target level, and that aspiration levels are influenced by the level at which standards, imposed or otherwise, are set. Previous research indicated that performance significantly different from the aspiration level led to an adjustment of the aspiration level in the direction of the actual performance level (Stedry, 1960). This suggests that budget standards should be changed periodically so that they are met some of the time, but are slightly higher than attainable levels the rest of the time. This way, aspiration levels continually creep upward. Budget levels slightly higher than aspiration levels will, if occasionally reached, push aspiration levels higher; and intrinsic motivation will be high because of the satisfaction that comes from meeting, or nearly meeting, the set goal. Finally, extrinsic motivation will be enhanced when the subordinate's effort is recognized and rewarded.

Table 3.1   Traditional versus expectancy theory management accounting assumptions

Traditional generally accepted management accounting assumptions	Expectancy theory management accounting assumptions
1. When budget levels are reasonably attainable the motivation of budgeted managers is at or near maximum	1. Budgets should be set close to, but above, aspiration levels to maximize intrinsic and extrinsic satisfactions and, thus, motivations
2. When budgeted managers participate in developing their budgets they will be highly motivated to achieve them	2. Participation by budgeted managers will only enhance external valences if group cohesiveness is high and group norms are supportive to the organization; otherwise motivation will not be increased and may even decline
3. Upper management should practice 'management by exception' and focus only on unfavorable budget variances	3. Upper management should reinforce extrinsic valences by giving attention to, and rewarding, positive budget variances and they should help remove obstacles along the budget path before they become negative budget variances
4. Budgets should include only items that are within the control of the budgeted manager	4. Budgets which include both ambiguous and partly controllable items enhance extrinsic, and perhaps intrinsic, valences associated with motivation for work activities associated with such items
5. Budgets and budget-related behavior by superiors should not include dimensions of performance that cannot be measured in monetary terms	5. Introduce non-monetary criteria into the formal control systems, link their accomplishment to extrinsic rewards, clarify them, and make their accomplishment intrinsically valent to the subordinate

Adapted from Ronen and Livingston (1975).

The traditional view also holds that when budgeted managers have a say in the setting of budget target levels they will internalize the standards embodied in the budgets and will be highly motivated to achieve them. Path–goal theory suggests that this will hold only if group cohesiveness is high and group norms are supportive of the organization. The reason for this is that individuals maintain their acceptance of budget targets in a positive cohesive group when they achieve budget targets. The group cohesiveness is an extrinsic valence associated with accomplishment of goals; but if the work group is not cohesive, no additional valence is introduced. In the case of a cohesive but negative group, extrinsic valence may actually be decreased. When participation is unwanted but forced on managers, as in the case when they fear censure will be forthcoming for not meeting budget targets, intrinsic valences associated with goal-directed behavior will likely decline.

The next traditional assumption—that budget-related behavior by superiors should be limited to management by exception, thus focusing on only negative variances—is clearly at odds with path–goal ideas. Non-reinforcement of favorable budget results, the expectancy model suggests, will tend to decrease the expectancy that budget accomplishment will lead to intrinsic rewards. Consequently, the motivation to meet budget targets will not be enhanced and may even be reduced. Upper management can also play a positive role during the budget period by helping to remove obstacles, such as getting other departments to meet their previously agreed upon commitments before problems arise rather than waiting until they surface in budget reports.

The next widely held assumption is that budgets should include only items that are within the control of the budgeted manager because these are likely to be associated with expectations that task-directed behavior will accomplish budget targets. To some extent this idea conforms to path–goal concepts. Further, only tasks that are seen as controllable lead to higher intrinsic personal satisfaction; but, in reality, the line between controllable and uncontrollable is usually hard to draw. Since many activities, being either ambiguous or only partly controllable, are excluded from budgets, the motivation to achieve budget levels operates on only those activities that are seen to be instrumental to attaining over-all organizational goals, with other beneficial activities tending to be neglected. But when partly controllable items are included in the budget, assuming the appropriate reinforcement contingencies are in place, the budgeted managers will be motivated to exert effort towards them.

A concrete example may make this clearer. In one of my research sites the plant manager of a tin-can plant operated under a profit budget which included, in addition to product costs and expenses, sales and revenue accounts. The plant manager had considerable control over product quality and prompt delivery, both key competitive factors; but he had no line responsibility over the sales force which, due to economies of scale in covering the various geographic territories, served several plants. By including sales responsibility in the budget, extrinsic valences, backed up with appropriate reinforcement contingencies in the form of a substantial bonus for meeting budgeted profit levels, motivated the plant manager to exert effort to meet sales levels as well as to control costs. Had sales been excluded from the budget, extrinsic valences associated with satisfying customers would be absent.

Finally, it is generally held that budgets and budget-related behavior by superiors should not include dimensions of performance that cannot be measured in monetary terms. Financial controls, due to the nature of accounting structures, are usually restricted to reporting only financial performance. They motivate managers to emphasize things that are measured and neglect those that are not. In terms of the expectancy model, non-monetary objectives that are formally introduced into the control system will motivate the subordinate to spend effort to accomplish them. This can be done by linking extrinsic rewards to their accomplishment; by clarifying these tasks so that the expectancy that goal-directed behavior will accomplish them is enhanced; and by making their accomplishment intrinsically valent to subordinates.

Ronen and Livingston, then, use expectancy leadership concepts to derive a much richer understanding of budget motivation than was previously available. The prescriptions which emerge from their analysis modify, in important ways, our classical management accounting assumptions. These ideas help to accommodate some of the fragmentary and contradictory findings from previous studies relating human relations variables and financial controls.

A path–goal theory of financial controls

Along similar lines, Macintosh (1983) used some of the path–goal leadership findings of House (1971) to reconcile several of the contradictions between the traditional management accounting and the human relations perspectives of financial controls outlined at the beginning of this chapter.

House unexpectedly found a positive relationship between formal bureaucratic initiating structure (clear-cut roles, formal communication channels, and detailed job instructions) and the job satisfaction of higher-level managers. He speculated that this was due to the ability of these activities to clarify equivocal path–goal relationships and thus reduce the manager's role ambiguity, and that this in turn would lead to increased efforts to achieve task goals. House also unexpectedly found that consideration efforts (trust, respect, and rapport) by superiors had little effect either on job satisfaction or that resulting from the initiating structure–satisfaction relationship. The reason for this, he surmised, is that the work path for higher-level managers is already challenging, varied, and intrinsically satisfying—so consideration efforts are not necessary.

Routine, lower-level jobs, by contrast, frequently lack intrinsic satisfaction. They contain self-evident paths and clear-cut goals. Any attempt to introduce more structure is therefore bound to engender hostility and suspicion. Since the job of low-level employees is already unambiguous, they view any additional structuring as more external control imposed solely to keep them working at unsatisfying activities. In fact, House found that, for these jobs, leader-initiating structure was negatively associated with satisfaction and did little in the way of clarifying path–goal relationships. The successful leader of employees in routine jobs, he concluded, gives priority to consideration and support, thereby maximizing the social satisfaction of the job.

These dual aspects of House's path–goal theory show promise for finding a solution to the presently opposed views on the functions of budgets. After all, budgeting involves both motivation and leadership behavior; and financial controls are used at all levels in organizations.

To understand this we must think of financial controls in general, and budgets in particular, as part of an organization's initiating structure. That is to say, a budget serves to delineate the budgeted manager's relationship between himself and his superior. It provides an important channel of subordinate–superior communication; and it helps to define the pattern of organizational authority and responsibility. In this way, a budget becomes an important part of the total initiating structure package. It emphasizes the rationalistic needs of the organization.

Now the path–goal theory suggests that for the high-level managers, budgets help clarify their often ambiguously defined jobs. Upper management jobs are rife with uncertainty, conflict, and ambiguity. Managers can act by treating the budget as a surrogate for ambiguous path–goal responsibilities. By referring to the budgets they can assess decisions in terms of their effect on budget versus actual outcomes. This serves to reduce sharply role ambiguity; and, if this is the case, it follows that managers will feel positive about budgets as they provide structure to an ambiguous task. For them, then, working towards budget accomplishment provides motivation and satisfaction.

The theory also predicts that for the high-level manager, consideration factors, such as participation in the budgeting process, will have little, if any, moderating effect on his attitude to the budget. Given these factors, and assuming the budget to be a reasonably accurate surrogate of achievable goals, it should motivate high-level managers to work towards the over-all organizational goals, even in the absence of consideration efforts.

At lower levels in the organization, however, the path–goal theory suggests that budgets work the other way around. Here, financial controls, such as budgets and cost standards, may tend to be perceived as redundant parts of the unnecessary and overloaded initiating structure. The well-defined path, often void of intrinsic satisfaction, is at least familiar; and if upper management view the financial controls as important to the operational control system they will, conversely, be thought of negatively by the lower-level employees. In other words, financial controls will not be as welcome at lower levels and may even correlate negatively with employee satisfaction. Under these conditions, consideration efforts such as active employee participation in the budgeting process may mitigate against these negative attitudes.

Macintosh surveyed 333 managers in 22 large industrial and commercial firms as a partial test of these ideas. The results revealed that an overwhelming majority of the managers in the sample held highly favorable attitudes towards budgets. A closer analysis of demographic factors indicated that when the budgeting process was seen as very important, attitudes to the budget were significantly higher than average. Conversely, when the budget process was considered to be only moderately important, budget attitudes were significantly less than average. This situation is similar to Hopwood's (1973) non-accounting style where the budget plays an unimportant part in the evaluation of performance.

Budget attitudes were also more favorable than average when perceived freedom to carry out responsibilities was more than needed. When freedom was felt not to be enough, they fell sharply. An explanation for this is that when the manager has more freedom than needed, the budget is one of the few official guidelines in an otherwise virtually unrestricted situation. By contrast, when job freedom is not enough the budget might be perceived as a further restricting device.

Budget attitudes also were more favorable for managers in their first year with the firm, and for those in widely diversified firms. Under both these conditions environmental uncertainty is probably higher than normal, in which case the budget would serve to reduce the uncertainty. It would serve also to provide concrete task-related feedback which achievement-oriented managers would appreciate. Attitudes were also significantly higher when the budget was seen as very important, and significantly lower when seen as only moderately important. Presumably, budgets only serve to reduce role ambiguity if they are an important part of the formal initiating structure of the firm and if they have the necessary top management support.

Other indirect support for the idea that budgets are positively accepted under conditions of high role ambiguity, such as in the higher and even middle-level managerial jobs in large organizations, comes from achievement motivation theory. McClelland (1961) argued that high achievers, such as managers, seek situations in which they get concrete feedback on how well they are doing. Such people like moderately difficult but achievable goals. They respond favorably to information about their work and they want to know the score. Affiliation and consideration factors loom less large for these managers than does feedback on achievement. Budgets, when accurately set, represent one of the most important sets of feedback information for managers. It follows, then, that budgets should be received positively by these managers.

Another important idea that emerges from the path–goal concepts is that at lower levels financial controls do not help reduce ambiguity since it is already low. Consequently, in routine jobs, as Argyris (1952) found, budgets are prone to be viewed negatively. Low-level supervisors believed the quickest way to cause trouble was to mention the budget to his employees, who saw it as a straightforward strategem to apply pressure on them to increase their productivity. Budgets, taboo with employees on the line, were not invoked by the supervisors. Gerold (1952) reported similar findings. According to the factory foremen in his study, budgets breed fear and aggression in the employees towards the company, and dwelling on them has led to decreased productivity.

The path–goal framework suggests, however, that the natural tendency towards negative budget attitudes at lower levels may be lessened through participation in the budget process. In support of this idea, Hofstede (1967) found that participation in the setting of financial standards was much less general for first-line supervisors than for other levels of management. He argued that participation in budget setting could be fruitfully lowered to first-level supervisors. Argyris (1952) also suggested genuine participation in the budget process as a remedy to negative budget attitudes at lower levels; and others found that participation in budgeting resulted in an improvement in the relations of cost center heads with supervisors, and that without the

moderating effects of considerate attitudes to subordinates and the maintenance of a supportive organizational climate, the structural concern with the
accounting information was seen as threatening and served as a trigger for
defensive dysfunctional behavior (Hopwood, 1973).

Macintosh, then, used some of the path–goal ideas as a framework which
subsumed both the traditional management accounting and human relations
perspectives of financial controls. Conventional knowledge about management accounting tends to emphasize the merits of budgeting and focus on
their positive roles in organizations. At the same time, the human relations
view of financial controls has tended to emphasize their negative effects. The
budget attitude survey described above indicates that budgets tend to be
positively received in the organizations included in the sample. Evidence
from other studies suggests they are not always so well received. Aspects of
the path–goal leadership framework, however, appear to provide a reasonable basis for a refined view of financial controls which accommodates both
points of view.

PARTICIPATIVE BUDGETING AND ORGANIZATIONAL SLACK

Investigation into participative budgeting, however, was to take a curious
twist. Evidence based on careful research began to appear which suggested
that, rather than helping productivity, participative budgeting actually
promotes inefficiency, because it leads to the creation of organizational slack.

Schiff and Lewin (1970) conducted one of the milestone studies on this
dysfunctional aspect of participative budgeting. Their study included an
extensive analysis of the budget and control process in different divisions of
three very large firms. It focused on divisional managers' behavior in connection with the budgetary control system imposed upon them by their corporate
headquarters. Their findings are illuminating.

Schiff and Lewin argue that, in the first place, the budgeting process is a
highly participative effort on the part of all managerial levels. So we need
not advocate that organizations adopt participative budgeting; it is already a
reality. The reason for this is straightforward. Since budget performance is
used by corporate headquarters to judge divisional performance, divisional
managers actively bargain for the final budget target levels. Contrary to the
generally accepted view, then, the budgetary process, at least in our large
divisional organizations, is already highly participative.

It is during the budget formulation process, Schiff and Lewin continue,
that divisional managers deliberately build slack into their budgets. Since
budgets are the main criteria for the measurement of performance, the
divisional manager's interest is best served by obtaining a slack budget—one
that is acceptable to headquarters officials and, more important, practically
speaking, attainable as well. The result is bargained budgets which in most
cases have 20–25 percent built-in slack. The data and statistical analysis in
the study provide solid evidence to support this conclusion.

Further, Schiff and Lewin observe, the opportunities for incorporating slack are numerous, especially for managers with an intimate knowledge of the budgetary control and accounting systems. These managers employ simple budget-making decision rules that result in sales volume targets that are highly likely to be attained, and use initial price estimates which are lower than expected ranges and which find their way into the final budget at lower than their expected average. As a result, the level of budgeted sales frequently falls well below the division's estimated attainment.

On the cost side, divisional managers also introduce slack estimates. They use cost standards that exclude the effect of *known* planned improvements. These improvements are introduced subsequently only if needed to assure budget attainment. Managers use discretionary cost budgets in a similar manner. Discretionary spending, such as marketing expenses, training, special promotion and the like, appear on budgets. Yet the actual spending is contingent on budget progress. For example, the advertising dollars actually spent are based upon the amount of budgeted spending remaining, rather than on an objective estimate of the effect of advertising on income. Likewise, divisional managers frequently budget for increased personnel levels and then delay hirings as another simple method of creating slack.

These practices make it relatively easy for managers to build slack into their budgets; also, divisional accounting officers actually assist divisional managers in these practices. Such complicity is widespread. Participation, it seems, includes divisional accounting personnel.

The research also found evidence that top management are aware of this padding and sandbagging. They even cater to it by imposing increased profit requirements during difficult years and accepting budgets without change in favorable years. So the process of creating slack is, it seems, legitimized and universally employed by managers at all levels to further their personal goals and desires. Schiff and Lewin conclude, not surprisingly, that the traditional participative budgeting process, contrary to general belief, does not result in the optimal use of resources.

Pressure and organizational slack

Onsi (1973) also took a look at the phenomenon of budgeting and organization slack. His study paid particular attention to the motivation underlying this custom. It involved 39 middle managers of five large national and international companies. Over 30 of these managers stated that they bargained for slack, not only in discretionary cost items, but also in manufacturing costs, in estimated sales volume, and in sales price. The prime reason given was the pressure of top management for both budget attainment and steady growth. This pressure was an over-riding concern for these managers. A second, although less important, reason they gave was the need to hedge against uncertainty.

The study also found that the practice of building-in slack was not limited to good times. Managers used slack to protect themselves during bad business conditions. Further, slack budgeting practices seemed to be influenced by the firm's growth patterns. Firms with steady growth had more slack practices than those in a widely fluctuating market. This research, then, adds a great deal of legitimacy to the notion that budget participation plays a key role in the creation of organizational slack.

These two research studies provide a dramatic warning that the use of participative budgeting advocated by the human relations school of financial controls must not be taken at face value. The realities are not nearly as one-sided nor as simple as this perspective suggests.

CONCLUSION

The emerging human relations view of management accounting and information systems proved to be at odds with the traditional management accounting one. Studies based on a social psychological approach to understanding these systems proved helpful in reconciling this discrepancy. We learned, for example, that personal attributes, such as emotional stability and locus of control, had a lot to say about reactions to, and use of, these systems, as did the role expectations of other managers. We also saw that many of the generally accepted management accounting principles, such as the idea that budgets should include only items that are within the budgeted manager's control, do not square with the realities of organizational life nor with research findings. We came to realize that some of our traditional management accounting principles should be modified in light of findings from expectancy theories of leadership; and we discovered that concepts from path–goal leadership theory could help us see financial controls in a richer and more realistic way. At higher organizational levels, budgets help reduce role ambiguity and are received with enthusiasm, while at low levels they can be seen as a redundant part of the already oppressive initiating structure and must be accompanied by large doses of consideration. The social psychological approach provided the basis for accommodating both the traditional and the human relations perspectives of management accounting and information systems.

We also learned a great deal more about the issue of participative approaches to budget setting. Some of the research suggests that participative budgeting has the potential for producing higher motivation and satisfaction on the part of the budgeted managers. Other research indicates that participative budgeting leads to budgets which are below what is truly attainable. This is disturbing. It seems that participative budgeting facilitates the deliberate creation of slack on the part of those very managers who are so motivated and satisfied.

The management accountant, therefore, faces an uncomfortable dilemma—participation sometimes leads to high motivation to achieve the budget; yet at the same time it also reduces budget accuracy and facilitates organizational slack. We cannot, it seems, have it both ways. Maybe there are established ways to finesse the trade-off; but as yet they have not been widely researched and understood.

This dilemma leaves management accountants in an unprotected position. There seems to be a real possibility that the creation of slack is caused—not totally, of course, but in no small measure—by the widespread practice of participative budgeting in our large organizations. It is small comfort to learn that similar practices have been reported by Berliner (1957) and others as the major problem of low productivity in the Russian industrial enterprise system.

Nor does it help to know that over 20 years ago Parkinson propounded his famous law that people will stretch a given piece of work as far as time and the possibility of making themselves more important by adding underlings will allow. Organizations, according to Parkinson's law, can only grow, and grow exponentially inefficient. Participative budgeting, it seems, may be aiding, rather than preventing, this phenomenon.

All of this points to a need for new theories. It is likely that any new theories will have to deal with variables such as group attitudes, game spirit, managerial leadership styles, and participation, as if they were distributed randomly throughout organizations. They will have to be more general; and new theories will have to deal with such factors as environmental influences, character of resources, departmental interdependencies, types of structure, level in the hierarchy, role ambiguity, and technology. A number of personal factors also enter the equation, since they clearly moderate the effects of participation on important outcomes such as performance, satisfaction, learning and slack.

It seems likely that, as Brownell (1982) concludes, impersonal factors dictate the specific requirements for participation, while personal factors influence its effects. We now turn our attention away from the social–psychological aspects of financial controls to focus on the rapidly developing body of knowledge about how individual experts process and use accounting information to make decisions.

References

Argyris, C., *The Impact of Budgets on People*, Controllership Foundation, Inc., Cornell University, Ithaca, NY, 1952.

Berliner, J. S., *Factory and Manager in the USSR*, Harvard University Press, Cambridge, Mass., 1957.

Brownell, P., 'Participation in budgeting, locus of control and organizational effectiveness', *The Accounting Review*, October 1981, pp. 844–860.

Brownell, P., 'Participation in the budgeting process: when it works and when it doesn't', *Journal of Accounting Literature*, Vol. 1, No. 2, 1982, pp. 124–153.

Collins, F., 'The interaction of budget characteristics and personality variables with budgetary response attitudes', *The Accounting Review*, April 1978, pp. 324–335.

Gerold, W. B., 'The impact of budgets on people', *Controller*, March 1952, pp. 116–118.

Hofstede, G. H., *The Game of Budget Control*, Koninklijke Van Gorcum & Comp. N.V., Assen, The Netherlands, 1968.

Hopwood, A. G., *An Accounting System and Managerial Behavior*, Saxon House, Hampshire, UK, 1973.

House, R. J., 'A path–goal theory of leader effectiveness', *Administrative Science Quarterly*, September 1971, pp. 321–328.

Macintosh, N. B., 'Budget attitudes: a survey and speculation', *Cost and Management*, January–February 1983, pp. 19–24.

McClelland, C. C., *The Achieving Society*, Van Nostrand-Reinhold, Princeton, NJ, 1961.

Milani, K., 'The relationship of participation in budget setting to industrial supervisor performance and attitudes: a field study', *The Accounting Review*, April 1975, pp. 274–284.

Onsi, M., 'Factor analysis of behavioral variables', *The Accounting Review*, July 1973, pp. 636–648.

Ronen, J., and J. L. Livingston, 'An expectancy theory approach to the motivational impacts of budgets', *The Accounting Review*, October 1975, pp. 671–685.

Schiff, M., and A. Y. Lewin, 'The impact of people on budgets', *The Accounting Review*, Vol. 45, No. 2, 1970, pp. 259–268.

Stedry, G. H., *Budget Control and Cost Behavior*, Prentice-Hall, Inc., Englewood Cliffs, NJ, 1960.

Swieringa, R., and R. Moncur, *Some Effects of Participative Budgeting on Managerial Behavior*, National Association of Accountants, New York, 1974.

Vroom, V. H., *Work and Motivation*, John Wiley & Sons, New York, 1964.

CHAPTER 4

Information Processing During the Expert Judgement Process

Although accountants and information systems designers spend much of their working lives developing and maintaining information systems for professional experts and managers, relatively little attention is given to analyzing how these experts in turn process and utilize such information in making judgements and decisions. Yet there is considerably more available knowledge than most designers would suspect; and some familiarity with it could prove the difference between the success and failure of any information system.

THE EXPERT JUDGEMENT COGNITIVE PROCESS

A few examples of the way sundry experts process and use information will demonstrate the nature of this phenomenon. An investment analyst, assessing the potential value of a common stock, will consider the following: data on the company's products, diversification plans, the stock of equipment and machinery, managerial talent, and the health of the industry. He will also scrutinize such financial information as ratios of the company's profitability, liquidity, stability, and growth. He will then somehow assimilate all this information and make a judgement about the potential capital appreciation of the stock. Over the course of a year he will probably undertake more than fifty similar analyses.

A physician, checking a patient's health, also processes a great deal of information. Known symptoms are discussed with the patient, and checks for unnoticed symptoms by examination of temperature, heart rate, lungs, eyes, ears, throat, reflexes, and so forth, are made. The case history is reviewed and the results of various lab. tests studied. Finally, a diagnosis is made. This process is repeated, on average, over a hundred times a week.

An admissions officer for a graduate program in management processes a large amount of data in reviewing an application from a young woman currently working in the forecasting department of an international bank. He will begin with a review of her undergraduate transcript. He will note carefully the grades obtained in mathematics, statistics, and a money and banking economics course and also review the results of her graduate management admissions tests, paying particular attention to her quantitative score. He will make a mental note of her work experience. Then, after reviewing letters of recommendation and the results of an interview with a faculty member, he will make a decision whether or not to recommend the applicant for admission to the program. During the course of a year he will make over 3000 similar judgements.

A partner of a professional accounting firm will review the audit of a large manufacturing company before signing the auditor's certificate attesting to the accuracy of the company's wealth and income as shown on the directors' financial statements. He will study the permanent file containing historical data, such as articles of incorporation and stock option agreements. He will review the specific audit procedures undertaken to meet the evidence requirement. He will check audit working papers, scrutinize the detailed schedules showing the activity in each balance sheet and profit and loss account during the year, and note the test procedures undertaken. He will trace all adjusting and reclassification entries to the final trial balance and check summaries of the latter against the financial statements. He will discuss any controversial items with both the chief financial officer of the company and the audit supervisor. When all matters are cleared to his satisfaction he will sign the audit report. He may certify over 200 sets of statements in a year.

In each of these examples the subject-matter of the judgement is distinct and the education and experience of each expert is different. Yet all the judgement processes follow similar patterns. None of the objects being judged—the value of a stock, the physical health of an individual, the ability of an applicant to complete an MBA, and the wealth and income of a company—can be assessed as whole cloth, so to speak; rather they must be 'seen' through accumulated pieces of information. Each expert is a highly trained, competent professional specialist who judiciously collects the data, carefully weighs their information content, and makes an informed judgement.

This procedure raises several important questions for designers of accounting and information systems. What type of information do these experts use as they formulate decisions? What data are ignored or discarded? Do they assess each piece of information singly, or do they merge two or more into a configuration which is richer than the individual pieces? Is the accuracy of their judgement affected by more, or less, information? Likewise, does the amount of information increase or decrease confidence in their judgements? How closely does the information being used correspond to the reality of the situation under consideration? How accurately do their judgements match the reality of the object being analyzed? Unquestionably, answers to these questions could prove of great value to accounting and information systems designers.

As it turns out, most research into the information processing capabilities of experts has been carried out by psychologists. This is not surprising; after all, thought processes are central to the study of psychology.

As in all areas of scientific inquiry, however, each piece of knowledge gained sprouts more puzzles—which in turn require more research. The research on expert judgement-making has not escaped this cycle. A major development, however, consists in a model of the expert judgement process known as the 'Brunswik lens'. This has been used extensively for studying the way experts utilize accounting systems.

This chapter reviews the development of our existing knowledge of information processing by experts. The next chapter reviews studies which focused on the judgement process utilized by investment analysts and professional auditors, and offers some guidelines for accounting and information systems designers.

THE EXPERT JUDGEMENT PHENOMENON

The 'expert judgement phenomenon' has been of interest to psychologists for some time. More recently this process has also attracted the attention of behavioral accounting researchers. A review of the development of our understanding of this process will help the reader to appreciate the possibilities inherent in such knowledge for accounting and information systems research. After all, the process of how professionals in all fields use information systems to make judgements is germane to the social engineering of accounting and information systems.

First, consider the way the clinical psychologist makes judgements about the mental health of a patient. Initially he pieces together the case history. Next he conducts a series of interviews pursuing those topics which seem important to the patient at the time. Then he might administer a few psychological tests wherein the patient responds to various stimuli (such as ink blots in a Rorschach test). The responses may reveal key aspects of the patient's thought processes. Finally, he assimilates all this information, identifies key symptoms, matches them to various structural dynamic theories of personality, and decides if the patient is suffering from some particular mental disease.

The process appears to be highly organic. It is not unlike that surrounding the formation of slugs, where an amebocyte cell swims around in isolation from other amebocytes until acrasin is released by special amebocytes causing them to form up in stellate ranks, touch, fuse, and construct a solid slug. The new body raises a magnificent stalk with a fruiting horn on top from which the next generation of isolated amebocytes are spewn (Thomas, 1975). In a similar manner, clinical psychologists develop theories about their patients. Sundry pieces of information about patients float around separately as case histories and diagnoses are thus recorded. Eventually, through exchanges of such information at conferences and in publications they, like the isolated amebocytes, form up in a new theory of personality. The whole marvelous arrangement goes on in an evolutionary fashion.

Yet until recently this process was little understood. Even though most psychologists spent much of their time diagnosing patients in the manner described above, not a great deal was known about the diagnostic process or its accuracy. Since accuracy of diagnosis was a matter of concern, studies followed, the results of which could be generalized to any kind of exercise involving expert judgement. Consequently, they eventually became of interest to accounting and information systems researchers.

Expert judgement accuracy

For the past thirty years a host of scientific studies investigating the accuracy of expert clinical judgements have appeared. The overall results have been both discouraging and alarming. In study after study, using a variety of subjects (such as clinical psychologists, radiologists, medical practitioners, and investment analysts) the judgements made by professional experts proved to be inaccurate. One such study vividly demonstrates the disparity in judgement among the experts.

A sample of 1000 schoolchildren was examined for tonsillitis by a group of doctors who found about 600 children required tonsil removal (Bawkin, 1945). The remaining 400 were examined by a second group of physicians who found nearly 180 also needed a tonsillectomy. The remaining 200 children were examined by yet another group of doctors who selected a further 120 for surgery. Of the original 1000, only 65 remained with tonsils. (Fortunately, as one observer commented, the program was called off before tonsils became extinct.) The expert judgement of the doctors differed radically on what would seem to be a relatively simple diagnostic situation.

Exhaustive research into judgements by clinical psychologists revealed a similar lack of accuracy (Meehl, 1954; Goldberg, 1965). Alarmingly, in many experiments, clinical psychologists did not perform any better than graduate students; in some situations experts did not even outperform laymen and sometimes they even did worse (Oskamp, 1965). Remarkably, years of training and experience did not appear to affect judgement accuracy (Goldberg, 1965); and the subjectiveness of preconditioned biases and agreement among experts easily supplanted objective observation and factual information.

Information processing and expert judgement

Puzzled by these findings, researchers shifted their efforts from studying the accuracy of judgement to investigating the way in which experts process information. The purpose of the shift was to identify different processing patterns which, in turn, might explain differences in the rate of accuracy. If such patterns could be uncovered, it was argued, experts' judgement could be improved by training in information processing. The results did not settle this issue. They did, however, prove highly relevant to accounting and information systems designers.

One study, for example, exposed untrained subjects to drawings of human figures (Chapman, 1967). Each drawing contained statements about the characteristics of the patients who allegedly drew the figures. The statements were selected deliberately so that there would be no relationship between them and the drawings. The results were alarming. The subjects were more influenced by their preconceived biases than by the information content of the drawings and the statements. Subjects concluded, for example, that uncertain suspicious people drew humans with big eyes; and individuals worried about their manliness drew muscular figures. The subjects also saw the same relationships between the drawings and personality that clinical psychologists are known generally to report in their treatment of patients, even though these relationships did not exist in the experimental materials. The subjects 'learned' to see what they already 'knew'. The experiment placed into bold relief the pervasive power of preconditioned biases and common beliefs. These factors, literally, can overwhelm new information content.

Further studies uncovered other unexpected aspects of the use of information. For example, Ryback (1967) found that the accuracy of expert judgement was unrelated to the quantity of information available and processed. More information, however, tended to increase the confidence of experts in the accuracy of their initial judgement. In one experiment, for example, eight clinical psychologists were given a four-part case history of a patient (Oskamp, 1965). For each part they answered the same set of twenty-five questions about the patient and each time the confidence level was recorded. The subjects estimated after the first part that 33 percent of their answers were correct, while the actual rate was 26 percent. By the end of the fourth part, however, they were grossly overconfident, estimating 53 percent of their answers to be correct, against an actual correct source of 28 percent. It would appear that more information not only does not improve judgement accuracy, it makes experts overconfident in the extreme.

Interestingly, then, more information serves only to fossilize judgements. Although we might expect new information to cast doubt on the original judgement, the opposite phenomenon occurs. Once an expert judgement is formed, subsequent information supporting it is accepted readily and serves to increase the judge's confidence in the correctness of the original judgement. By contrast, non-supporting information is either discarded, discounted, or even distorted to fit the judgement. Once commitment to a judgement takes place, any disconfirming or contradictory information has no effect. Accountants have long argued that the timing of information is important. They have not known, however, that, after a point, new information will have no impact.

Other studies regarding the accuracy and consistency of expert judgement followed. Mixed results emerged regarding consensus among experts on the same task. Some studies found an extremely high degree of consensus while others indicated very little (Goldberg and Werts, 1966). Unfortunately, there have been no studies which examine the nature of the various experimental tasks. It was assumed that experts would tend to exhibit more agreement on straightforward tasks than for more complex ones. It was found, however, that judges were consistent over time. They seem to develop a patterned method of judgement which allows them to reproduce similar judgements when faced with similar tasks.

Thus, the studies into use of information and the accuracy and consistency of expert judgement are revealing. Consistency across a sample of experts is generally low, although individual judges are consistent over time. Judgements are unduly vulnerable to preconceived biases, generally held beliefs, and the influence of fellow experts. Judgement is highly inconsistent when the same object is under consideration, but different sources of information are used. Neither experience, nor training, nor the amount of information available would appear to be related to the accuracy of judgement. Yet, as information increases, reliance on the accuracy of the judgement soars to the point of overconfidence.

Perhaps these findings are not so unexpected. After all, in expert judgemental situations two polar opinions usually emerge. A striking example comes from astrophysics. One well-supported view argues for the 'big bang' idea of the universe. It states that in the beginning a huge mass of tightly packed matter exploded as a result of internal pressure. Thus, all galaxies will continue to move out into infinite space and time, until gravity eventually impedes their outward motion and pulls them back together to form another huge mass, whence the cycle is repeated. The competing idea is the 'steady-state' notion. It asserts that the universe is stable because the tension in the fabric of free (i.e. non-gravity) space produces hydrogen to replace that consumed by stars as they give off the energy vital to life. Similarly, accounting has witnessed several long-standing debates, including full versus direct costing, flow-through versus deferred tax, and historical cost versus current value accounting. Professional experts, it seems, prefer one side or the other of the critical issues facing their profession. We should, then, be neither surprised nor alarmed when rigorous studies reveal substantial differences in judgements, as most expert judgement tasks are both complex and not yet well understood. Different views are thus bound to emerge.

CLINICAL VERSUS STATISTICAL JUDGEMENT

These disturbing studies nevertheless cast a dark shadow of doubt on the entire area of expert judgement. It was only natural, then, for psychology to embark on a lengthy debate centering on the relative merits of judgements by expert clinicians as compared to those based on statistical prediction.

A clever analogy known as 'Meehl's box', was developed to highlight the debate (Meehl, 1954). The box, illustrated in Figure 4.1, is opaque and has a series of colored lights on the front with rows of buttons on the back. A complex arrangement of gears, wires, and pulleys which cannot be seen from outside the box connects the buttons to the lights. Different combinations of buttons pressed simultaneously result in different combinations of lights

48

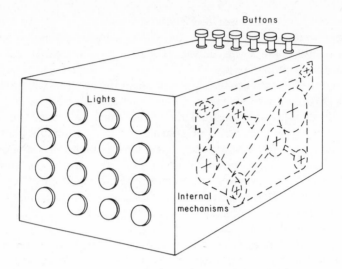

Figure 4.1 Mehl's box: an analogy of clinical judgement. (Source: Wiggins, *Personality and Predictions*, © 1973 Addison-Wesley, Reading, Massachusetts, Page 154, Figure 4.3. Reprinted with permission.)

flashing. The buttons represent the stimuli received by a patient, with the lights being the response; and the arrangement of gears, wires, and pulleys connecting the buttons to the lights represents the patient's cognitive mechanisms and processes linking stimulus and response.

First, the box is presented to a statistician who is asked for an explanation of the relationship of buttons and lights. He begins by making a number of observations of the associations between different combinations of buttons and lights. He identifies a number of different classes of relationships. Then he records, in a frequency table, the historical odds concerning relations observed between classes of button-presses and classes of light display. Armed with this table of odds, the statistician is ready to make educated guesses about the most likely combination of lights to go on, given any particular combination of buttons pressed. He then classifies combinations of buttons pressed as belonging to a specific category which he knows is related to a class of light displays. The process is similar to that undertaken by a statistician in predicting the mental health of a patient on the basis of statistical analysis of those psychological tests for which frequency tables are available.

Next, the box is presented to a skilled mechanic who has considerable experience in dismantling and repairing similar boxes. He also observes the relationship in these boxes between button-pressing and light display; but, rather than developing frequency tables, he adopts a trouble-shooting approach. He makes a small number of carefully chosen button-presses. Then, based upon his experience with similar boxes, he constructs theories about the internal arrangements of gears, wires, and pulleys. The clinical psychologist, to complete the analogy, operates in a like manner. He has a great deal of experience in dismantling mental processes and putting them back together again. He is privy to a store of dynamic theories of personality which explain structural relationships between stimuli and responses. He is able to diagnose mental health by building on theories concerning the internal mechanisms of the patient's mind. Use and development of theories of personality distinguish his approach from that of the statistician.

THE BRUNSWIK LENS MODEL

The analogy of Meehl's box illustrates the point that expert clinical judgement is a dynamic process involving the interaction of pieces of information with judgement and intuition. Obviously, some expert judges made good judgements, while others consistently made poor judgements; and many make mediocre ones. Consequently, it was realized that better clinicians are capable of outperforming statisticians. This insight shifted the field of study to a search for the traits inherent to good clinical psychologists.

The better experts, however, do well compared with statistical estimates because statistical prediction is based on the law of averages. It follows that statistical predictions will be consistently average. The better experts, obviously, will nearly always thus outperform the statistician; and, of course, the statistician will consistently outperform the poorer experts. The possibility of surpassing statistical predictions, it was concluded, is due to the ability of the clinician to understand, utilize, and derive theories of personality.

A search for theoretical models of the clinical method followed. The idea was that a theoretical reconstruction of the human judgement process held great potential for improving expert clinical judgement. By coincidence, a highly suitable model of this sort had already been developed by Egon Brunswik, the well-known psychologist. The model, which became known as the 'Brunswik lens', combined aspects of both clinical judgement and statistical prediction (Brunswik, 1952 and 1956).

Brunswik pictured the cognitive process (that is, the mental act of knowing) as including both awareness and judgement, not as the motivating force, but as a reaction to an environmental object or event which the individual focuses upon. Perception, from this view, is the process of paying attention to certain of these focal variables in the environment. It works much like a lens which absorb rays from one place, refocuses them, and then projects them elsewhere. Brunswik's original depiction of this lens is reproduced in Figure 4.2. The initial focal variables are related by information cues to terminal focal variables, such as an individual's judgement. The cues mediate between the initial and terminal focal variables, acting much as a filter in a lens. Judgements, therefore, must be based upon indirect and impoverished stimuli.

For example, every morning when the mailman approaches our house, the dog becomes agitated, barks viciously, and claws the door. As the mailman

50

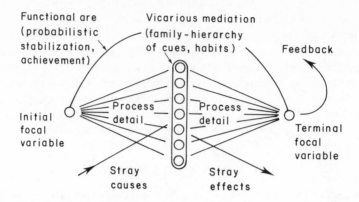

Figure 4.2 The Brunswik lens model. (Source: Brunswik, 1952, p. 20. Reproduced by permission of the University of Chicago Press. © 1952 by the University of Chicago.)

stuffs the mail through the slot the dog's agitation mounts. In a frenzy he seizes the nearest piece of mail (mercifully often a bill) and tears it apart with his teeth. Now the dog never actually sees the object of his fury. The distal variable, the mailman, is filtered through cues of sound and smell. The cues enable the dog to judge the intruder to be the mailman. In a similar fashion I hear the dog running amuck and, making an educated guess, judge that the mail has arrived.

From here, in what proved to be an important step, Brunswik generalized the model to groups of variables. Both environmental events and objects, as well as the responses, he argued, can be regarded as classes—not merely individual occurrences. It follows that the patterned connections between classes of initial and terminal focal variables are identifiable. Then the associations between the three classes of the judgement process can be made by taking random samples from each. Linear multiple regression analysis then can be applied to describe these relationships in quantitative terms. The point to underscore is that, from the vantage-point of classes of events, cues, and responses, the judgement process can be modelled mathematically. This connection has proved invaluable to subsequent researchers. Brunswik described his idea as follows:

The total pattern involved, when viewed as a composite picture of numerous cases of individual mediation from initial to terminal focus, bears resemblance to a bundle of rays scattering from a light-source and brought back to convergence in a distant second point by a convex lens. While correlation between the focal variables is assumed to be relatively high although in general not perfect, those of each focus with the single elements or chains of mediation may be low. A semi-circular arrow is appended in the figure to the terminal focus to indicate that lens patterns do not stand in isolation but are apt to reflect back upon the organism in a future state in what is now sometimes called a 'feedback' loop, such as when arriving at the food is followed by satiation and reinforcement of the preceding behaviour.

Considering the relative chaos in the regions intervening between focal variables, focal connections may also be called 'interrupted'. Although they do not require action-at-distance, they are relations-at-distance.

Recent psychology has shown that variables located in certain 'areas', 'layers', or 'regions' of the environment or of the organism seem more often to be focal than those in others. Any organism has to cope with an environment full of uncertainties. Forced to react quickly or within reasonable limits of time, it must respond before contact with the relevant remote conditions in the environment, such as foodstuffs or traps, friends or enemies, can be established.

The probability character of intra-environmental relationships, becomes of concern in two regional contexts: on the reception or stimulus side as the equivocality of relationships between distal physical or social objects and proximal sensory stimuli or cues, and on the effection or reaction side as the equivocality of relations proximal outgoing behavioural responses, or means, and their more remote distal results and effects. In one or the other of these ways behavioural responses are, of necessity based upon 'insufficient evidence'.

Another way of stating this state of affairs is by pointing toward the fact that the relationship between the mediated event and its mediators is one of probable partial causes and partial effects. In line with the inherent probability character of object–cue and of means–end relationships, gross organismic coming-to-terms with the environment can thus never become foolproof, especially so far as the more vital remote distal variables are concerned. It is in this sense that, as William James has phrased it, perception is 'of probable things'. Perceptual and behavioural functioning is spoiled much in the manner in which rays are apt to interfere with perfect focusing. Imperfections of achievement may in part be ascribable to the 'lens' itself, that is, to the organism as an imperfect machine. More essentially, however, they arise by virtue of the intrinsic undependability of the intra-environmental object-cue and means-end relationships that must be utilized by the organism; these are comparable uncontrolled lateral light-sources. (Brunswik, 1956, pp. 19–23.)

In sum, the lens model was developed as a way of understanding situations where objects and events can be perceived only indirectly and where judgements must be made on the basis of a set of cues. The pattern of association between classes of objects, cues, and judgements can be captured mathematically. Consequently, the relationships between judgemental ability and the specific pieces of information utilized can be brought into bold relief. The common way of portraying the lens and the mathematical relationships is shown in Figure 4.3.

The Brunswik lens was initially developed to be applied to a wide variety of expert judgement situations, including jurists, radiologists, psychologists, and managers. Not surprisingly, it also attracted a great deal of interest from accounting and information system researchers to study judgements involved in stock evaluation, loan assessment, audit programs, and materiality disclosure practices. Before turning, in the next chapter, to the results of these studies, however, a related and relevant issue—the linear versus configural thinking controversy—of the expert judgement process should be introduced.

Linear versus configural judgements

Experts from all walks of life describe the judgement process as configural. Yet careful research indicates, to the contrary, a predominance of linear thinking in the way experts process information. The Brunswik lens model provided a much-needed mechanism for detailed analysis of this puzzle. Before reviewing these efforts, however, linear and configural thinking must be defined.

Linear thinking involves sequential processing of information where the

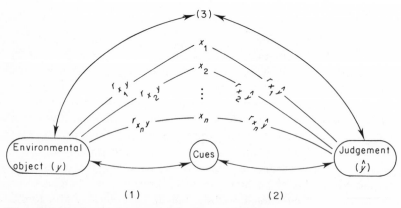

Figure 4.3 The basic elements of the Brunswik lens.
(1) Probabilistic relationship between object and cues ($y = b_1x_1 + b_2x_2 + \ldots b_nx_n$)
(2) Probabilistic relationship between cues and judgement ($\hat{y} = b_1x_1 + b_2x_2 + \ldots b_nx_n$)
(3) Probabilistic relationship between judgement and object ($r_{y.\hat{y}}$)

expert moves from one piece of information to the next in a logical sequence. It is not unlike the serial steps involved in constructing an apartment or a spaceship where each step is linked to the preceding step, and will be linked in turn to the subsequent step until the job is complete. In linear thinking, each piece of information used is handled in a reliable and sequential manner. The specific importance of each piece of information can be isolated easily by the simple linear, additive, multiple-regression model. Under this approach it is assumed, perhaps naively, that the way individuals respond to a judgement task can be described in the form:

$$Y = b_1X_1 + b_2X_2 + \ldots b_nX_n$$

where Y is the vector of judgemental responses, the Xs are the values of information cues presented to the judge and the bs or regression weights are the values of each cue indicating their relative importance in the judgement process. The key assumptions are that a linear relationship exists between cues and responses and that the values of the cues are additive.[1]

Configural thinking is quite different. Here the judgement is formed not by simply summing the value of each information cue. Rather, the value of a cue is dependent upon some relationship to the value of at least one other cue.[2] Configural (or interactive as it is sometimes called) thinking has been described vividly in the context of stock evaluation as follows:

> Take the case of the security analyst: where two companies have the same trend of earnings, the emphasis placed on growth rates will be weighed quite differently depending on their respective industries and their financial strength. In addition, the assessment will be tempered by the dividend trend, the current payout ratio, profit margins, returns on capital, and the host of analytical criteria we looked at previously. The evaluation will also vary with changes in the state of the economy, in the level of interest rates, and in the companies' competitive environment. Thus, a successful investor must be adept at configural processing, integrating many diverse factors, since changes in any may require a revision of the total assessment. Not unlike juggling, each factor weighed is another ball in the air, increasing the difficulty of the process. (Drenan, 1977, pp. 87–88.)

Verbal descriptions such as this from experts in all fields support the idea that experts process information configurally.

Several studies have employed the lens model to investigate the relative use of linear versus configural thinking during clinical judgement. The following experiment is typical. The task, supposedly a highly configural one, consisted of the differential diagnosis of benign versus malignant gastric ulcers from visible signs of an X-ray (Hoffman et al., 1968). Six experienced radiologists and three radiology residents diagnosed ninety-six hypothetical combinations of the seven major signs which can be seen in X-rays of gastric ulcer patients. The seven signs were all either present or absent in the X-ray and one cue occurred only in the presence of another. The doctors believed that a diagnosis could be made only by using the seven signs in a configural fashion. They judged each case on a seven-point scale ranging from 'definitely benign' through 'uncertain' to 'definitely malignant'. Each judge made a repeat diagnosis of the ninety-six cases.

The results revealed that individual judgement was highly consistent in the repeat diagnosis, but that consensus among doctors was distressingly low. (Evidently, experienced physicians disagree in their diagnoses to the same extent as clinical psychologists.) The data were analyzed by means of a statistical test (ANOVA) to determine the extent of both linear and configural thinking and the pattern of cue utilization. On average, 90 percent of the variation for any one combination of cues was 3 percent. The separate cues accounted for ten to forty times as much variation as the largest interaction. These results indicate that the doctors used a linear rather than a configural information-processing style.

This is puzzling. Two competing explanations have been suggested. One is human judges actually follow a process that is remarkably linear while believing that it is more complicated. According to this view, experts actually handle information and make judgements in a rather simple, straightforward way; but it is rationalized as a much more complex process (Goldberg, 1968).

The competing explanation is that experts do process information in a configural manner, but that the linear regression model is powerful enough to screen this out. This is analogous to the way a straight line gives an excellent approximation of many curved lines. An example is a sailboat navigating to its next mark. What appears to be a straight route is, in fact, an arc. Similarly, both the linear regression and ANOVA models are powerful enough to obscure anything but the most obvious kinds of configural cognitive patterns (Rorer, 1967).

To summarize, even though most experts describe their judgemental processes as configural, the simple linear model, in fact, adequately describes what actually transpires (Hammond and Summers, 1965). Studies failed to show any but very small amounts of configural thinking. We will return to this issue later when the lens accounting studies are reviewed.

CONCLUSION

Several issues relevant to accounting and information systems designers emerged from psychological lens studies. First, experts tend to be surprisingly unreliable. Second, individual experts tend to be consistent in their judgements over time. Third, the degree of consensus among experts about the same object or event tends to be low. Fourth, more information, after a point, does not improve expert judgement; rather it serves only to make the experts extremely over-confident in the accuracy of their initial judgements.

Finally, while they describe their use of information as configural, the evidence suggests that it is linear thinking that dominates the expert judgement process. An awareness of these findings should result in the development of more appropriate accounting and information systems.

It is against this background of the development of the lens model and its related issues that we move, in the next chapter, to a review of the accounting and information systems studies which employed the Brunswik lens. As might be expected, many of the issues and findings of the psychological studies reviewed above reappear in the accounting studies.

Notes

1. Linear in the sense that if vertical lines are drawn from each of the X, Y points to the least-squared line, and if the distance between these lines is squared and summed, the resulting amount will be less than a comparable sum of squares from any other possible straight line. Additive in the sense that the simple addition of the least-squares explained by each cue (X) of variation in the responses (Y) will sum to the total explanatory power of the equation.
2. Configural thinking can be captured readily by finding mathematical expressions which approximate configural cue usage. One way of doing this is by examining the interaction effects of independent variables in analysis of variance (ANOVA). Another common way is to express the interactive use of two cues, X_1 and X_2, using multiple regression analysis which includes the product term $X_1 \cdot X_2$. In a similar manner, more than two cues can be used in a product to test for more complex interactions. The new product term is then introduced into the multiple regression analysis to compete with each separate cue in explaining variance in the dependent variable.

References

Bawkin, H., 'Pseudodoxia pediatricia', *New England Journal of Medicine*, Vol. 232, 1945, pp. 691–697.
Brunswik, E., *The Conceptual Framework of Psychology*, University of Chicago Press, Chicago, 1952.
Brunswik, E., *Perception and the Representative Design of Experiments*, University of California Press, Berkely, 1956.
Chapman, J. L., 'Illusory correlation in observational report', *Journal of Verbal Learning and Verbal Behaviour*, Vol. 6, 1967, pp. 151–155.
Drenan, D., *Contrarian Investment Strategy: The Psychology of Stock Market Success*, Random House, Inc., New York, 1977.
Goldberg, L. R., 'Diagnosticians versus diagnostic signs: the diagnosis of psychosis versus neurosis from the MMPI', *Psychological Monographs*, Vol. 79, No. 9, 1965.
Goldberg, L. R., 'Simple models or simple processes? Some research on clinical judgements', *American Psychologist*, Vol. 23, 1968, pp. 483–496.
Goldberg, L. R., and C. E. Werts, 'The reliability of Americans' judgements: a multitrait–multimethod approach', *Journal of Consulting Psychology*, Vol. 30, 1966, pp. 196–206.
Hammond, K. R., and D. A. Summers, 'Cognitive dependency on linear and non-linear cues', *Psychological Review*, Vol. 72, 1965, pp. 215–224.
Hoffman, P. O., P. Slovic, and L. G. Ròrer, 'An analysis of variance model for the

assessment of configural cue utilization in clinical judgement', *Psychological Bulletin*, Vol. 69, 1968, pp. 338–349.

Meehl, P. E., *Clinical Versus Statistical Prediction: A Theoretical Analysis and a Review of the Evidence*, University of Minnesota Press, Minneapolis, 1954.

Oskamp, S., 'Overconfidence in case study judgements', *Journal of Consulting Psychology*, Vol. 29, 1965, pp. 261–265.

Ròrer, L. G., 'Conditions facilitating discovery of moderators', Paper presented at the Meeting of the American Psychological Association, Washington, DC, September 1967.

Ryback, D., 'Confidence and accuracy as a function of experience in judgement-making in the absence of systematic feedback', *Perceptual and Motor Skills*, Vol. 24, 1967, pp. 331–334.

Thomas, L., *Lives of a Cell*, The Viking Press, New York, 1975.

Wiggins, J. J., *Personality and Prediction: Principles of Personality Assessment*, Addison-Wesley Publishing Company, Reading, Mass., 1973.

CHAPTER 5

Lens Model Accounting Studies

The previous chapter provides some clues for accounting and information systems designers about how experts such as managers, investment analysts, and even auditors process information as they go about making important decisions. Following these leads, several researchers employed the lens model as the research paradigm to undertake controlled experiments involving auditors and investment analysts. This chapter reviews these studies. While not conclusive, they have added a valuable dimension to our understanding of a critical dimension of the design problem.

LENS MODEL AUDIT STUDIES

The process followed by professional accountants in conducting audits of the financial affairs of organizations clearly requires a great deal of expert judgement. Auditing is defined as the analytical process of gathering sufficient evidence, on a test basis, to enable a competent professional to express an opinion as to whether a given set of financial statements meet established standards of financial reporting (Arens and Loebbecke, 1976). More specifically, auditing involves a highly judgemental process which includes developing an intimate knowledge of the firm (its products, manufacturing methods, marketing, and its environment), reviewing and evaluating the accounting and internal control systems, gathering evidence on the integrity of these systems, collecting evidence related to the amounts and quantities represented in the financial statements, and formulating a judgement on the basis of the available evidence. The auditor's statement reflects the nature of the process involved, '. . . we have examined . . . made in accordance with . . . included such tests as we considered necessary in the circumstances . . . in our opinion . . . present fairly . . . in conformity with . . . applied on a basis consistent with'. The net result is the auditor's evaluation of the fairness of the financial statements presented by the enterprise.

All of this suggests a rather complex, subjective process involving a great deal of expertise. In adopting the lens model approach to investigate this important dimension of organizational life, we will focus mainly on findings and implications rather than on issues of experimental design. The studies did, however, involve interesting and innovative design aspects and the interested reader is encouraged to read the original sources.

One such study involved eighteen partners of CPA firms and fifteen securities analysts (Boatsman and Robertson, 1974). These experts judged, on the basis of eight cues, thirty hypothetical cases dealing with materiality disclosure. Subjects sorted the cases into one of three categories: (1) no separate disclosure; (2) footnote, or (3) separate line item and a footnote. The study design is outlined in Figure 5.1. The results of a best-fit multiple discriminant analysis model for each of the three disclosure models is shown in Table 5.1. The 'percentage of the item to current year net income' emerged as the most dominant cue. This is consistent with conventional guidelines. Since materiality is relative, it is necessary to have a reference point for establishing whether or not an error is material. Net income normally is regarded as the most critical piece of information, and so it is the most important basis for deciding what is material (Arens and Loebbecke, 1976). The 'percentage of item to total revenue or expense' and the 'reversed 2-year earnings trends' also emerged as important. Other items appeared to have little influence on the judgement process.

Table 5.1 Beta weights of the discriminate analysis multiple-regression model for the three types of disclosure* (Boatsman and Robertson, 1974)

	Disclosure judgment		
Characteristic of item	Not Required	Footnote	Line Item
1. Gain or loss on sale of non-current asset	5.54	3.66	4.59
2. An accounting change	8.03	8.87	8.46
3. Reversed the two-year earnings trend	−15.43	−16.60	−16.29
4. Percentage of current year net income	28.17	30.33	31.99
5. Percentage effect on net working capital	6.14	5.73	5.97
6. Percentage of total revenue or expense	−10.13	− 9.96	− 9.86
7. Absolute dollar size	0.15	0.17	0.18
8. Percentage of the two-year growth rate in net income	1.06	0.85	0.88
9. Riskiness (on a five-point scale)	−28.95	−30.69	−35.18

*All items significant at the 0.01 level.

The study also indicated that the subjects were substantially in agreement regarding which cases should receive some form of higher-order disclosure. Such consensus among experts is unusual for lens model studies. This may be accounted for by the pervasiveness of generally accepted auditing principles. In any event, the results revealed that materiality judgement across professional auditors was consistent.

In an innovative maneuver the researchers developed a multiple-regression model of the materiality judgement process. The model was used to predict the judgement for each expert. When placed against random assignments of the cases to the three disclosure categories, the model outperformed random assignments by a significant margin. The implication is that such a model (which is a mathematical consensus of subjects' materiality standards) could

OBJECTS

CUES

JUDGES

– 18 Partners of CPA firms and 15 security analysts

JUDGEMENT

– Materiality treatment judged as:

(1) No separate disclosure required

(2) Footnote disclosure, or

(3) Separate line item and a footnote

– 30 Hypothetical firms

– Nine situational variables

(1) A gain or loss on the sale of noncurrent assets (yes or no)

(2) An accounting change (yes or no)

(3) Reversed the 2 year earnings trend (yes or no)

(4) Percentage of the item to current year net income

(5) Percentage of the item to net working capital

(6) Percentage of item to total revenue or expense

(7) Absolute size of item

(8) Two year growth rate in net income

(9) Riskiness of the firm

Figure 5.1 Study of auditor's materiality judgements (Boatsman and Robertson, 1974)

be used to supplement, or even supplant, professicnal accountants for materiality disclosure decisions. (The issue of the 'statistician' versus the 'clinical expert' should be recalled.) While the statistical model has the merit of consistency, the possibility that the professional accountant may make better judgements remains. Undoubtedly this possibility supports the practice of retaining professional accountants for materiality decisions.

The researchers also performed a test to determine whether differences existed between the judgements of the professional accountants and the security analysts. This was done because CPA's have been publicly charged in media (such as the *New York Times*) with using standards in making materiality judgements which are more liberal than desired by security analysts. The insinuation is, of course, that auditing firms do not wish to be 'fired' by important clients over a materiality judgement. This charge has to do with the obvious contradiction encountered by professional auditors in their work. On the one hand they undergo extensive professional training in how to make objective judgements about financial reporting. On the other hand they are paid handsome fees by the very clients whose financial statements are being 'objectively' judged. Skeptics assume that auditors' judgements are politicized by fee considerations. Protagonists argue that professional training and ethics mitigate against such practices. The researchers' exhaustive tests indicated no important differences between auditors and the security analysts in terms of materiality disclosure judgements. The study therefore provided some ammunition for countering charges of 'politicized' judgements by auditing firms, although the experimental situation was hypothetical and the politicized factor was not included in the test.

Another study using the lens model investigated auditing internal control judgements in a payroll setting (Ashton, 1974). The study is outlined in Figure 5.2. Six indicators of payroll internal control were selected as cues:

(1) Are timekeeping and payment tasks separated from payroll preparation?
(2) Are tasks of payroll preparation and payment separated from bank reconciliations?
(3) Are payroll names checked periodically against active employee files of the personnel department?
(4) Are formal procedures established for changing names on payroll, pay rates, and deductions?
(5) Is the payroll audited periodically by internal auditors?
(6) Was the internal control over payroll found to be satisfactory during the previous audit?

The subjects, sixty-three professional auditors, rated thirty-two randomly selected combinations of these cues on a six-point scale ranging from 'extremely weak' through 'adequate to strong'. The cues were presented in a pre-answered 'yes' or 'no' form, where 'no' indicated a weakness in internal control and 'yes' represented a strength.

JUDGES

– 63 Independent
auditors

JUDGEMENT

– Internal control judged on a scale
ranging from extremely weak to
adequate or strong

CUES

32 Combinations of six internal control indicators:

(1) Time keeping and payment separate from payroll preparation (26.2%)

(2) Payroll preparation and payment separate from bank reconciliations (25.2%)

(3) Names checked to personnel files (6.7%)

(4) Procedures used for changing names, rates and deductions (7.1%)

(5) Payroll audited by internal auditors (8.5%)

(6) Internal control satisfactory on previous audit (6.6%)

OBJECTS

– Goodness of internal control of the payroll function of a hypothetical manufacturing firm.

Figure 5.2 Study of internal control judgements (Ashton, 1974). The figures in brackets represent the percentage of the variance (S^2) in judgements accounted for by each cue.

Two cues dealing with separation of the tasks involved in the payroll process accounted for 26.2 percent and 25.2 percent respectively of the total variation in judgement (see Figure 5.2). The other four items were statistically significant but accounted for only 6–9 percent of the variance. Separation of duties, then, was judged again to be the dominant criterion for internal control. This is consistent with generally accepted payroll auditing practices which stress the need for separation of duties:

> The personnel department plays the role of providing an independent source for interviewing and hiring qualified personnel. The department is also an independent source for records for the internal verification of wage information. As a part of these controls, segregation of duties is particularly important.
>
> Controls over the preparation of checks include preventing anyone who is responsible for preparing the checks from also having responsibility for summarizing the records of signing or distributing the checks.
>
> The actual signing and distribution of the checks must be properly handled to prevent their theft. The controls should include limiting the authorization for signing the checks to a responsible employee who does not have access to timekeeping or the preparation of the payroll, the distribution of payroll by someone who is not involved in the other payroll functions, and the immediate return of unclaimed checks for redeposit. (Arens and Loebbecke, 1976, pp. 410–411.)

The study also examined judgement consistency across auditors and consistency over time for the same auditor. The average correlation between ratings of all pairs of auditors was high ($r = 0.70$, $p < 0.01$) indicating a great deal of consensus among the auditors. A test of each auditor's ratings at two different points of time indicated a good deal of judgement stability ($r = 0.71$, $p < 0.01$). Finally, tests were made for configural use of the cues by examining the interaction effect of various combinations of cues. These proved to be small, indicating a strong tendency for auditors to process information in a linear fashion.

Another study employed the lens model to investigate auditors' judgement in planning audits of accounts receivable and credit approval practices (Joyce, 1976). The experiment is summarized in Figure 5.3. Sixteen different sets of internal control situations (for accounts receivable by a hypothetical wholesale tire firm) were created by random selection of the five items of internal control listed in Figure 5.3. Each of the five items contained two levels such as 'approved' or 'not approved'. The judges, thirty-five professional auditors from four large CPA firms, reviewed each hypothetical situation and developed a summary audit program by selecting any or all of five preselected standard audit procedures. They also estimated the number of manhours required to perform each audit procedure selected.

The results were analyzed to determine the extent to which each of the five cues influenced the judges' selection of audit programs. This was accomplished by calculating (with straightforward analysis of variance (ANOVA) statistical tests) the amount of variation in the audit programs accounted for by each of the five cues. Items dealing with separation of duties accounted for the largest part of the variance in audit program selections (see Figure 5.3). This result reinforces the conventional notion of the critical need for separation of duties and supports the other studies outlined above.

The next most important cue, accounting for 18.2 percent of the variance, was 'approval of credit by responsible officer before shipments'. This also is consistent with generally accepted auditing procedures for accounts receivable, 'Before goods are shipped, a properly authorized person must *approve credit* to the customer for sales on account. Weak practices in credit approval frequently result in excessive bad debts and accounts receivable that may be uncollectable' (Arens and Loebbecke, 1976, p. 235). A change in accounts receivable write-offs, although not as critical as the other two, was also important. These results are consonant with those of professionally trained, experienced auditors.

The study made several other interesting tests. Four duplicate sets of internal control cue sets were judged by each subject. Comparison of these with original sets indicated a very high level of subject reliability over time. Two tests of inter-judge consistency proved contradictory. Canonical correlation analysis indicated it to be high, while a product moment correlation coefficient test indicated some, but less, consistency. The reliability across auditors within and across firms proved to be relatively high. Interestingly, the level of consensus with other auditors decreased in relation to their years of experience. Presumably, the older auditors would be further away from their professional training and so had developed their own 'tried-and-true' methods which may not have mirrored current conventional practice. Yet, on the whole, judgement consensus and consistency were high.

Considerable differences emerged, however, in both the number of hours estimated for each audit procedure and for the entire audit. The average estimate for total time ranged from eighteen to 120 hours. One explanation for this wide variation is that a great deal of difference exists in auditors' judgements of how much work to perform in a given situation. Another suggests that, since the judgements were being made for a hypothetical firm, it was very difficult for the auditors to estimate reliably the time required. In a real situation, especially after the first audit, one would anticipate a good deal of convergence in both plans and time.

The experiment included a 'self-insight' test. The auditors were asked to rate the five items of internal control in terms of how important they felt each was in arriving at their time estimate. Self-insight, in general, proved to be high, although auditors underestimated the extent to which they relied

OBJECT

– 16 Different control subsystems for accounts receivable in a hypothetical tire wholesaler

CUES

– items of Internal Control:

(1) Sales approved (not approved) by credit manager before shipment (18.2%)

(2) Bad debt expense/sales ratio is significantly less (more) than previous year (5.4%)

(3) Write-offs of receivables are reviewed and approved by controller (credit manager) (10.1%)

(4) Accounts receivable subsidiary ledger is maintained by a clerk other than (who also) prepares and mails monthly statements to customers (28.1%)

(5) Accounts receivable turnover is significantly greater (less) than for last year (12.0%)

JUDGES

– 35 Professional auditors

JUDGEMENTS

– Selection of any or all of 5 tests to be applied to each of the 16 internal control subsystems and manhours allocated for each test selected:

(1) Confirmation of accounts receivable

(2) Review of accounts written off as uncollectible.

(3) Review of collection subsequent to balance sheet date.

(4) Determination of adequacy of allowance for uncollectible sales cutoff.

(5) Review of year end cutoff.

Figure 5.3 Accounts receivable audit program judgement (Joyce, 1976)

on minor cues. Finally, statistical tests of the degree of configural versus linear information processing patterns indicated that very little, if any, configural judgement took place.

In another auditing experiment, Hofstedt and Hughes (1977) also used the lens model to test materiality judgements. The judges were fifteen MBA students majoring in accounting. The task involved a decision as to whether or not a loss from the write-down of a subsidiary should be disclosed as an extraordinary item. Of the three cues used 'loss as a percentage of income' emerged as dominant; 'loss as a percentage of all investments in unconsolidated subsidiaries' was also important. The third cue, 'loss as a percentage of the net book value of the subsidiary' was little used. Differences were noted among the subjects in their judgement process. While most responded in a linear fashion, a few indicated a configural pattern of processing information. Some had lower materiality thresholds than others and so tended to disclose the loss in less serious situations than did others. Tests of cue usage across judges indicated a high level of consistency for major cue usage but less consistency for lesser-used cues. These results are consistent with the previous lens model auditing studies.

The net result of the lens model studies of professional auditors is not unexpected. On the whole, a significant degree of judgement consensus is indicated, and the judgements of individual auditors are consistent over time. Separation of duties is the most important cue for auditing and the relationship of the item to earnings levels is a critical cue for materiality judgements. Little evidence emerged to support configural information processing. These results stem, undoubtedly, from the gross over-simplification of the experimental tasks. Against this background, consensus would be expected.

But consider, in contrast, the monumental job of auditing organizations such as General Motors, IT&T, Mitsubishi, Philips, Royal Dutch Shell, IBM, or the federal government of the USA. These are vast organizations with tentacles reaching every corner of the globe. The sales of General Motors, for example, are greater than the gross national product of all but a handful of countries. The task of verifying balance sheet items (such as inventories, accounts receivable, and machinery and equipment, for example) is momentus, if not overwhelming. One would expect a good deal of variance across professional auditors from different firms and countries when faced with the task of planning audit programs for General Motors. The high degree of consensus across auditors in the experiments discussed above must be considered only against the background of the very simple experimental tasks. In actual situations one would anticipate much less consensus.

These studies, then, should stimulate more research into the nature of the professional auditing judgement process (Kennedy, 1977). The lens model has also been used to study the investment analysis process. These studies proved more interesting and controversial than the auditing experiments and are reviewed next.

LENS MODEL STUDIES OF INVESTMENT SECURITY EVALUATION

The investment analyst is the archetype lens model expert judge. Advertisements picture him as a neatly attired, thirty-year-old MBA graduate with close-cropped hair, horn-rimmed glasses, shirt and tie, but no jacket. The office, which resembles a medical clinic, includes a prominently displayed CRT terminal and voluminous computer printouts on top of a modern stainless steel desk. The impression is of a well-trained professional carefully gathering and weighing the appropriate information to arrive at a sound and thoughtful judgement of the potential of various investment opportunities. A typical description by an investment broker of the process involved in reaching a decision is as follows:

> I looked first at Industry to determine the possible range of price swing and then used Near Term Prospects along with P/E Ratio Comparison to determine the play the P/E would have in price action. After a decision was made here, I combined Profit Margin Trend and Earnings per Share Trend to get a feeling for the impact earnings direction would have on price. Then I would combine judgements of P/E Ratio and Earnings per Share to decide the fundamental condition of the company, and I applied my judgement to the company's fundamental condition to the three technical factors. I would then arrive at a decision regarding price movement. (Slovic *et al.*, 1972, p. 293.)

This type of judgement process is ideally suited for lens model research and, in fact, several well-designed lens model experiments have been conducted to investigate the nature of securities assessment.

One of the first applications of the lens model to the accounting area was a descriptive study of the stockbrokers' decision process (Slovic, 1969). The experiment, outlined in Figure 5.4, had two brokers rate the growth potential of 128 hypothetical stocks. Cues consisted of eleven pieces of financial information provided in Standard and Poor's reports. Each cue took one of two levels such as 'low–high' or 'poor–good'. The hypothetical stocks varied considerably since they were created by combining different levels of the eleven cues. The brokers rated each stock by evaluating the probability that the market price of the stock would increase substantially in the subsequent six to twelve months. They used a nine-point rating scale ranging from 'strong recommendation not to buy' to 'strong recommendation to buy'.

The results are noteworthy. Four cues (see Table 5.2) dominated the ratings—near-term prospects, price/earnings ratios, earnings yearly trend, and earnings quarterly report. This was as expected, since near-term political, economic, and product prospects are normally key considerations; and earnings ratios and trends traditionally have been thought to be key information for assessing stock values. Three cues—profit margin, resistance level, and support level—were also used, but to a much lesser extent. Four

OBJECTS

– 128 Hypothetical stocks

CUES

– Eleven pieces of financial information for each stock

(1) Yield

(2) Near term prospects

(3) Earnings quarterly report

(4) Past year's performance

(5) Profit margin trend

(6) Earnings yearly trend

(7) Price/earnings ratio

(8) Shares outstanding

(9) Resistance trend

(10) Support trend

(11) Sales volume trend

JUDGES

– 2 Stockbrokers

JUDGEMENT

– Growth potential of each stock

Figure 5.4 Lens model study of stock evaluation (Slovic, 1969)

cues—yield, past year's performance, shares outstanding, and sales volume trend—were little used; such information is not stressed in the financial analysis literature and it proved redundant to the evaluation process. (Unfortunately, the researcher did not include a measure of the reputation of key managers, a factor commonly mentioned by security analysts as a key consideration.)

Table 5.2 Main linear effects of each cue (Slovic, 1969)

	Percentage of variance explained		
Cues	Broker A	Broker B	Average
1. Yield (the cash dividend price)	0.00	0.00	0.00
2. Near-term prospects	0.33***	0.08**	0.21
3. Earnings quarterly trend	0.16**	0.01**	0.08
4. Past year's performance	0.01*	0.00	0.01
5. Profit margin trend	0.01*	0.13**	0.07
6. Earnings yearly trend	0.00	0.30**	0.15
7. Price/earnings ratio	0.19**	0.19**	0.19
8. Shares outstanding	0.00	0.00	0.00
9. Resistance trend	0.00	0.06**	0.03
10. Support trend	0.02**	0.03**	0.03
11. Sales volume trend	0.00	0.00	0.00
Sum of the effects over the statistically significant effects	0.72	0.79	

* $p < 0.05$;
** $p < 0.01$.

Tests were also undertaken to determine the extent of configural information processing during the judgement task. The normal ANOVA statistical interaction test indicated that about 6 percent of the total variation in judgement was accounted for by interaction effects, while the separate effects of the individual factors accounted for 76 percent. It was argued, however, that straightforward analysis of interaction effects may not reveal the true amount of configural thinking. An index of the influence of each factor on the mean judgement was proposed as a better test of its individual influence. This test revealed considerably more configural thinking—27 percent and 19 percent respectively for the two brokers. Further, as some argue, if a significant interaction exists between two factors, the variance explained by each, alone, should also be treated as configural variance (Hayes, 1968). Following this logic, configural use of information was predominant for Broker B (85 percent) and substantial for Broker A (36 percent).

Significant differences emerged in cue utilization between the two subjects (see Table 5.2). This finding proved fortuitous. The two brokers had been selected because it was believed they would have a similar approach to the task. Their responses to cues, however, differed markedly. Upon further investigation the researcher found that Broker A considered himself to be a 'chartist', that is to say, an analyst who relies heavily on trends shown by support and resistance charts of price and volume trading. Broker B, by contrast, considered himself to be a 'fundamentalist', an analyist who relies heavily on the underlying value of the company as revealed by ratios of key information in income statements and balance sheets. It is noteworthy, then, that the lens model is powerful enough to pick up such differences in information utilization.

There are several lessons in this test for accounting and information system managers. They could, for example, employ lens techniques to assess the way different people process information. Once the patterns are identified, the information system could be designed to suit differences in judgement style. A chartist, for example, would be better served by a system featuring charts and graphs of stock price and volume, while a system designed for a fundamentalist would feature traditional ratios and trends for income statement, balance sheet, and funds flow data. Lens analysis could also alert the designer to certain key information going unused or underutilized. Discussion of such phenomena with users might help them to better understand why such information is included. Lens analysis thus appears to hold great promise for designers who wish to adapt their information systems to suit users' judgement styles more effectively.

Even though the companies in the experiment were hypothetical, and only two brokers were surveyed, Slovic's study has proved to be a milestone. It was the first application of the lens model to an accounting and information systems setting, and it confirmed the importance of accurate earnings figures to financial statement users. It indicated the power of the linear regression model as a way of describing information cue usage in investment analysis. It offered evidence to support the idea that the stock evaluation process is, in reality, configural. It readily identified chartists and fundamentalists; and, most importantly, the study demonstrated that the lens model is admirably suited for investigating the investment analysis process. Other security evaluation lens studies soon followed.

Slovic, along with two other researchers, engaged in a more comprehensive stock evaluation experiment (Slovic *et al*, 1972). They employed a larger sample of investment analysts and used eight of the eleven ratios in the previous study. The experiment is outlined in Figure 5.5. The subjects, thirteen stockbrokers and five MBA students, evaluated the common stocks of sixty-four hypothetical firms, using a nine-point scale ranging from 'expectation of a substantial decrease in the value of stock' through 'expect no significant change' to 'an expectation of substantial increase in value'. Subjects were instructed to judge each stock for possible inclusion in the $10,000 portfolio of a middle-aged businessman.

As in the previous study, the results confirmed that information about earnings and near prospects are heavily relied upon in stock evaluations (see Table 5.3). The brokers also tended to use cues related to support and volume more frequently than did the students. Presumably, students receive a great deal of training in analyzing earnings but little in assessing stock

OBJECT

– 64 Hypothetical stocks

CUES

– Eight factors provided in Standard and Poor's *Standard Listed Stock Reports*

(1) Industry outlook (stable *vs.* dynamic)

(2) Resistance level (up *vs.* down)

(3) Support level (up *vs.* down)

(4) Volume trend (up *vs.* down)

(5) Near-term projects (good *vs.* poor)

(6) Profit-margin trend (up *vs.* down)

(7) Price/earnings ratio comparison (good *vs.* poor)

(8) Earnings per share yearly trend (up *vs.* down)

JUDGES

– 13 Stockbrokers and five MBA students

JUDGEMENT

– Rate each stock on a nine-point scale in terms of its potential capital appreciation over the next 6–18 months

Figure 5.5 An experiment in the use of information investment decision-making. (Slovic *et al.*, 1972)

volume and short-term price changes. The brokers, by contrast, use such information in their daily monitoring of price movements. Otherwise, cue usage was very similar between the two groups.

Table 5.3 Importance of individual cues (Slovic *et al.*, 1972)

Cue factor	Brokers		MBA students	
1. Industry outlook	0.07	(0.14)	0.09	(0.12)
2. Resistance level	0.09	(0.09)	0.05	(0.03)
3. Support level	0.11	(0.09)	0.04	(0.03)
4. Volume trend	0.10	(0.14)	0.05	(0.11)
5. Near-term prospects	0.18	(0.14)	0.10	(0.11)
6. Profit margin trend	0.12	(0.08)	0.14	(0.14)
7. Price/earnings ratio trend	0.11	(0.13)	0.17	(0.18)
8. Earning per share trend	0.22	(0.18)	0.36	(0.28)
	1.00	1.00	1.00	1.00

Note: Figures in parentheses represent the mean score for the judges' subjective weights of how they thought they used each cue.

The study also investigated aspects of judgement reliability. Since the firms were hypothetical, judgement accuracy could not be assessed. Consistency of judgement across subjects, however, was low. Further, there were substantial individual differences in the use of the various cues, although the brokers exhibited more disagreement than did the students.

Subjects also ranked each cue in order of its importance in making their judgements so that a 'cues-usage index' could be calculated for each subject by relating perceived to actual cue utilization. For the brokers, subjective weights for the importance of cues did not relate closely to their actual usage, but for the students it did. Presumably the brokers' training and experience was more varied than that of the students.

Following this lead, the researchers posited that years of experience might tend to reduce insight into the perceived versus actual cue utilization relationship. A test across all thirteen brokers indicated a negative relationship between experience and cue utilization insight ($r = -0.43$, $p < 0.01$). More experience would seem thus to produce untrustworthy rationales of individual information-processing habits. The researchers speculated that skilled behaviors become more automatic and require less attention with increasing experience. Another explanation is that more experienced experts may be less sensitive to available information and so may easily ignore critical pieces of new and important information. Perhaps systems designers could spotlight such instances for experienced experts. More important, designers should be wary when they ask users what information they need—since the cue insight test indicates that designers could be easily misled.

Comparisons of how individual brokers made judgements again revealed different patterns of information use. Two illustrations were cited. One broker's ratings were highly sensitive to earnings yearly trends and support and resistance levels. (Support level is a key chart used by technical chartist investment analysts to reveal the price band where there has been a lot of trading. So the band, it is argued, supports the current price when the price is above that level. Resistance level reveals the price at which enough stock is placed on the market either to halt upward price movement temporarily or to prevent any further upward movement.) This broker also relied almost entirely on linear information processing. No configural combinations of the eight cues had a significant influence on his ratings. He was, it appeared, a technical chartist.

By contrast, the second broker relied heavily on near-term prospects and earnings yearly trend and, but to a lesser extent, on price/earnings ratio and profit margin trend. Statistical analysis also revealed a significant amount of influence for seven configural variables, including combinations such as: industry outlook + near-term prospects, volume trend + near-term prospects, and resistance level + support level + price/earnings ratio trend. In fact, the configural variables accounted for about one-third of the variation in his average judgement. The separate effects of the eight individual variables accounted for the other two-thirds. Considering the inherent power of the linear model to swamp configural effects, this result can be interpreted as revealing a large degree of configural thinking on the part of this broker, who would be categorized as a fundamentalist.

These findings suggest two distinct styles of processing information for the same task. Some investment analysts, particularly chartists, process information linearly, while others, particularly fundamentalists, do, in fact process information configurally. Designers, then, should be ready to identify different styles and adjust information systems to suit the individual users.

These results led the researchers to reflect on the entire process of stock evaluation. The vagueness and complexity of the process, as indicated by differing verbal descriptions of the way the subjects believed they processed information, and by the wide variation across the sample in judgements and actual cue utilization, led them to speculate that quantitative models of stock evaluations may well outperform individual expert judgement. Thus, the issue of the statistician versus clinical expert surfaces once more in the context of stock evaluation. As it turns out, these conjectures were not far off the mark. We will discuss this in more detail later. Suffice it to say for now that this is an exciting speculation.

This study, then, proved to be an interesting and valuable follow-up to the previous one. Earnings and near-term prospects once more proved to be key cues. Consensus across judges was low. For the brokers, their subjective notion of how they process information differed significantly from their actual patterns; and this discrepancy increased with years of experience. The study also revealed that experts tend to develop rather distinct styles of information processing as characterized by the 'technical chartist' and the 'fundamentalist'. Some brokers also processed information configurally while others adopted an almost pure linear approach. Designers, then, should be sensitive to different styles of information processing—even for the same task—and tailor appropriate systems to suit the different needs.

In a later experiment, thirty-nine MBA students used seven pieces of information and some general data about the economy to estimate the price of sixty common stocks over the coming year (Wright, 1977). The stocks represented real companies competing in industrial and construction machinery and metal products. They were selected from sources such as the Compustat and Data File. All companies had sales over $20 million. The experiment is outlined in Figure 5.6.

The results were revealing in that judgements across subjects varied significantly. Average estimates for price changes ranged from minus 21 percent to plus 42 percent. These estimates did not differ from a computerized random selection. There were conspicuous individual differences in judgements, and wide differences in judgement accuracy as shown by comparing estimates to actual prices. Forty percent of the subjects, however, were able to estimate price changes significantly better than a random selection. (Some experts, it seems, can outperform stock selection by throwing darts at the stock listings.)

As for information use, subjects relied most heavily on earnings data and then on debt to equity ratio in making judgements. Other information, including the beta ratio, accounted for little, if any, of the differences in estimates.

An interesting phenomenon that emerged from the study was that while no systematic bias showed up for the high-priced stocks, subjects consistently overestimated the prices of low price/earnings ratio stocks. The researchers offered no explanation for this. Hindsight, however, indicates that the student judges did not, in fact 'overprice' the low price/earnings ratio stocks. In the period 1970 to 1972 (the judgement period of the experiment), a curious phenomenon—known later as the 'two-tier market'—began to take shape.

The market had been stung in the late 1960s by a host of small electronic and other 'concept' stocks. Experts retreated en masse from a strategy of following concept stocks to the old principle of investing in blue-chip companies with proven records. Four dozen premier growth stocks (such as Sony, IBM, Xerox, Avon, Kodak, Polaroid, and Hewlet Packard) with high price/earnings ratios captured the fancy of the institutional investors. The prices of these stocks rose nicely during this period. At the other end of the spectrum, the opposite phenomenon occurred. The stocks of low price/earnings multiple companies fell disproportionately as analysts 'assigned them to the rubble heap'. In the experiment the MBA students were not aware of the historical market psychology of that period. Traditional fundamental analysis, then, would lead them to 'overprice' the low price/earnings stocks in relation to actual events. In this respect they mirrored many investment analysts who were themselves caught by the two-tiered market. Thus, the

OBJECT

- Actual price changes in the security prices of 60 common stocks over a year

CUES

(a) A description of the actual general macroeconomic conditions over the 12-month period.

(b) Financial information:

(1) closing price at the beginning of the year

(2) earnings per share for the prior year

(3) earnings per share for the current year

(4) average changes in earnings per share for the prior four years

(5) cash dividends for the current year

(6) long-term debt to equity ratio at the end of the current year

(7) beta ratio (estimate of the ratio of the covariance of a security's rate of return with a market average divided by the variance of the rate of return of the market average)

JUDGES

39 Second year MBA accounting and financial major students

JUDGEMENT

- Estimate the security price of each company's common stock after 1 year

Figure 5.6 Predicting stock prices from economic and financial information (Wright, 1977)

students priced the low price/earnings stocks 'correctly' in terms of conventional fundamentalist analysis.

There is a lesson here for accounting and information systems designers. In some cases qualitative and 'soft' information is much more valuable than hard quantitative information of the normal kind. Designers would do well to include important but soft data in their systems.

Statistical tests were performed to assess the way individuals made their judgements. Although the linear model explained a good deal of the variation in cue usage, there were also indications of some configural use. Conspicuous differences also emerged among individuals in the extent to which they processed information configurally.

Finally, the results suggested that four basic types of information-processing models were used. A sophisticated statistical test, known as cluster analysis, indicated that individual subjects employed one of four different decision-making styles to complete the task. It may be that experts do not merely process information in a linear or a configural way. They may also employ different 'styles' when processing information. This is an exciting prospect. Identification and classification of these styles could prove of great value to accounting and information systems designers in introducing systems into their organizations. Systems designed to suit particular decision styles should have a much better chance of success than general-purpose ones. Developments along these lines are the subject of the next chapter.

In sum, the study indicated substantial differences in the use of cues, type of information processing, judgements, and accuracy. Forty percent of the judges, however, did much better than chance, which indicates that some experts can outperform random selection of stocks. The linear model predicted the use of cues rather well, although it appeared that some judges used considerable configural thinking in completing the task. Finally, four distinct decision types were used by the judges.

Limitations of the research

A surprisingly large number of lens model accounting studies have been undertaken; so many that space limitations prevent us from outlining each of them here. The studies discussed above are merely a sampling from amongst the earlier efforts. Subsequent lens studies, although numerous, parallel the earlier ones in terms of findings. Although we have learned a great deal from these efforts, there are limitations which must not be overlooked.[2]

Often measurement of decision achievement is an insuperable problem. Bankers, for example, do not keep track of the success or failure of rejected loan applicants; and the mere decision to give a loan obviously affects the future outcome. So only if the bank accepts some applicants who are judged to be rejections can the decision achievement be properly measured (Libby, 1981). The experiments also place the decision-maker in the possible role of responding to a predetermined set of accounting information (Einhorn, 1976). In reality the expert is much more involved in gathering his or her own information, and the decisions they face are considerably less structured (Gibbins, 1977).

LESSONS FOR ACCOUNTING AND INFORMATION SYSTEMS DESIGNERS

The Brunswik lens model has been used to advantage to further our understanding of how experts actually use accounting and related information to make important decisions. Much has been learned: not about accounting *per se*, but about how information is utilized by experts who rely on it. Yet these experiments represent only a beginning.

Nevertheless, although further studies are needed, several lessons for accounting and information systems designers have already emerged. One important finding is that the judgement of experts is remarkably unreliable, especially for the more complex tasks. Thus, in spite of soundly designed information systems, decisions often prove faulty. Individual experts, however, are consistent in their judgement over time. Taken together, these two findings imply that accountants and other information systems people should take a more active role in the judgement process, especially in helping decision-makers take maximum advantage of the available information. The passive role of provider of information and scorekeeper will no longer do. Information systems designers should become involved in the interpretation of information, which would not be unreasonable as they have a better grasp of the messages inherent in the information than do users. Designers can no longer ignore the fact that their systems do not automatically result in accurate judgements.

The implication is not that the accounting and information system designer should usurp the decision-maker. In fact the politics and power broking common to most organizations would make it unfeasible. Rather, the information system designer could effectively play a key consultative role. This role has been summed up neatly by Townsend, the former President of Avis Car Rentals Inc.:

> From management's side, the important thing about getting the most out of the controller is to tell him about plans enough in advance so he can provide his input. Controllers are professionals. They don't gossip. Treat them as full members of the inner council. Save lots of agony by letting the controller have a good look at new ideas before they're implemented. If controllers are elected to insidership, they'll be valuable. If they're treated like plumber's helpers, they'll get their kicks making ends instead of means out of their reports and their systems—and you can't blame them. Yes, Virginia, accountants *are* people. . . . There abideth accuracy, time-

liness, understanding, and unflappability in the controllers' office—and the greatest of these is all four of them. No accounting system is very good, and all of them are infinitely variable. The controller will frequently be asked for figures in a hurry. He must never lose his head—that's what management do, not controllers. If he does prepare a hurried report, he should label it for what it is. Prepared under pressure and not understood. (Townsend, 1970, pp. 23–25.)

The important point is that, as accounting and information systems are, even at the best of times, difficult to understand, experts, especially top management, need the active involvement of the systems designers in the interpretation of information. Without them we will likely get the worst of both worlds.

Another lesson to emerge from the lens studies has to do with the amount and timeliness of information. Considerable evidence emerged to indicate that experts rely on only a small number of information cues and, further, that they process these cues separately in a linear fashion. Information systems designers, then, could do well to highlight these key pieces of information on a summary page and relegate the remainder to supplementary pages. Where information cues actually do combine into a new, configural piece of information which contains relevant messages, the accounting and information system expert should feature them, even going so far as to produce a concise qualitative interpretation for the manager who, after all, is not the information expert. A great deal of information and the configural messages may prove too complex and illusive for the manager to grasp without help. All of this, then, suggests a more active, but not a usurping, role for the accounting and information systems designers.

The lens studies also provide a strong reminder of the great reliance placed upon earnings information, especially by investment analysts. It behooves the accountant, then, to be extremely diligent in calculating earnings figures.

The lens studies also suggested that both the timing and amount of information provided is important. More information, after a point, does little to increase the accuracy of judgements. Conversely, it merely makes the user more confident in his initial judgement. Thus, the timing of information provision is critical. This, of course, is recognized widely in accounting textbooks, but the reason for it has never been satisfactorily explained.

Finally, these studies suggest that no general patterns of human information processing exist. Different individuals rely on different information cues, and they seem to process information in quite different styles. Designers, then, should be sensitive to these differences. Research and theories investigating this phenomenon are the subject of the next chapter.

In sum, the lens studies have given us new insights into the way information systems are used in organizations. Accounting and information systems designers can no longer ignore the fact that their systems do not result automatically in sound judgements and decisions. These studies have alerted us to some of the important realities of how information actually is processed by the experts making the decisions. A great deal has been learned. More lens studies undoubtedly would continue to add to these insights.

INFORMATION ECONOMICS AND THE LENS MODEL

An issue arising from the lens model is that while it is admirably suited for describing the expert judgement phenomenon, it does not encompass the total decision-making process, particularly with respect to decision rules, outcomes, and ultimate payoffs. Consequently, it is difficult to use it to derive principles for information systems selections (Ashton, 1974), since judgement does not necessarily correspond to decision and action.

In order to overcome these limitations, a synthesis of the lens model with the information economics model has been proposed (Mock and Vasarhelyi, 1978). As shown in Figure 5.7, it was developed with the limitations of both the lens and the information economics models in mind. The major feature of the combined model is the way it links environment, cues, and judgements with actions, outcomes, and payoffs. This means that the entire process can be assessed in cost/benefit analysis. This model also provides for a feedback loop from outcomes and payoffs to states of the world. Thus, it is a dynamic representation of the entire process.

Although the combined model was suggested only as a preliminary proposal, it holds promise for providing new insights into human information processing. The idea of bringing two quite different perspectives of human information systems together is tantalizing. No attempts have been reported as yet directed towards its use in empirical research. When, as is bound to happen sooner or later, it is picked up as a research paradigm, exciting

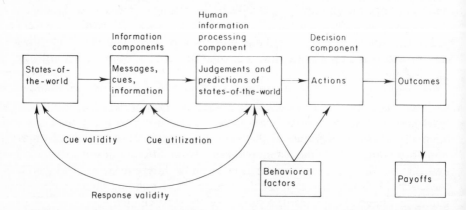

Figure 5.7 An integrated information–decision model (Mock and Vasarehelyi, 1978, p. 418. Reproduced by permission of the *Journal of Accounting Research*, Institute of Professional Accounting, Graduate School of Business, University of Chicago)

insights should emerge. In the meantime, the descriptive lens model and the normative information economics model complement one another in a highly valuable way.

MATHEMATICAL SIMULATION VERSUS THE EXPERT

The final aspect to arise from the accounting and information processing lens studies is the controversial 'statistician versus expert clinician' issue. An important study investigating this issue successfully simulated the bank officers' judgement process (Libby, 1975), suggesting that a model of the loan judgement process held great potential for replacing loan officers. Moreover, such models might help increase our understanding of the effects of different information usage patterns on the prediction of success.

The study involved forty-three commercial bank loan officers who used five financial ratios as cues, to judge the likelihood of failure within three years of sixty real industrial firms. The experiment is summarized in Figure 5.8. The loan officers were able to predict the failed firms with a high degree of accuracy. (Unfortunately the loan officers' information processing patterns were not reported.) More important, a model was constructed, using discriminant analysis, which provided highly accurate predictions of subject responses. It also successfully indicated the point where individual loan officers would switch from a failure to a non-failure judgement.

The successful simulation of this complex process has widespread implications. It indicates that these, and other similar types of judgements based upon accounting information, can be mathematically modelled and that experts can be replaced by these models. Almost any financial institution, for example, could build such a model, locate it centrally, and make it accessible to computer terminals scattered around the country.

This line of reasoning, of course, brings us back to the issue involved in Meehl's box analogy. Development and use of mathematical models would represent a shift to statistical judgement. It would appear that such an approach holds as much, if not more, potential in the field of financial analysis as it does for clinical psychology. Undoubtedly, the argument will be raised that the 'better' financial analysts can outperform mathematical models; and doing better means outperforming other competing financial institutions. Given this possibility, financial institutions will undoubtedly stick with their expert analysts, at least for the foreseeable future. Some of the more progressive ones, however, may well develop statistical models to complement the judgement of the loan officer. In fact, Value Line, a very successful security analysis service, has been using mathematical models for many years with outstanding success.

Value Line has employed four different models in the recent past. Each one represented a more sophisticated model than the previous one. The first, used in the 1930s and 1940s, was in reality a visual fit of stock price to reported earnings and book value. More specifically, Value Line analysts

OBJECT
Sixty actual large industrial firms

CUES
Five accounting ratios based on certified financial statements:

(1) Profitability (net income ÷ total assets)

(2) Activity (current assets ÷ current liabilities)

(3) Liquidity (current assets ÷ current liabilities)

(4) Asset balance (current assets ÷ total assets)

(5) Cash position (cash ÷ total assets)

JUDGES

– 43 professional loan officers from commercial banks

JUDGEMENT

(1) Evaluate the likelihood of failure (YES–NO) of the firm within three years

(2) Give confidence in prediction on a three-point scale

Figure 5.8 Loan officers' use of accounting ratios to judge likelihood of failure (Libby, 1975)

fitted a constant earnings per share multiplier and a percentage of book value per share to a constant multiplier of earnings per share. The analyst estimated a stock's future value from the formula simply by plugging in estimated book value and earnings for the next year. The formula for General Electric, for example, was stock price = 0.8 × book value per share + 18 × earnings per share. Over the long run the model predicted accurately, but it did not discriminate well on shorter-term price movements.

The next model, used in the 1950s, was a straightforward time-series multiple-regression analysis model. The dependent variable was the average stock value over the past twenty years. The independent variables included per share dividends, earnings, book value, and a lagged average stock price. This model, while more sophisticated than the first, encountered the same problem as had the earlier one. It did not discriminate among winners and losers in the short-term holding period. The problem lay in the fact that the model required twenty years of historical data and thus it was not, needless to say, representative of current stock market conditions. The model ignored relationships of similar variables amongst other stocks—it merely related a particular firm's stock price to its own financial information.

A third model was developed in an attempt to overcome these limitations. (As the reader will note, these techniques and their explanations are necessarily technical. It is assumed, perhaps naively, that the reader has some fundamental knowledge of financial analysis and descriptive statistics.) This model combined a technique known as cross-sectional analysis with time-series multiple-regression techniques. The cross-sectional analysis involved dividing all stocks into five groups based on quality ratings. A random selection of twenty-five stocks was made within each group. Earnings and dividends were combined in one variable for each of the 125 stocks. Next, a simultaneous multiple-regression analysis was conducted for the logs of each of the twenty-five stock groups across all 125 stocks over the immediately preceding twenty-one years. This produced an earnings–dividends ratio. Then, a market sentiment variable was created by calculating, for each stock, an average market yield over the twenty-one years. These two variables—the earning dividends ratio and the market sentiment ratio—along with the lagged average annual price, were used as the independent variables. The dependent variable was the current year average price. Multiple-regression analysis then developed a predictive model for each of the five quality groups. Finally, to get the average 'justified' price for each individual stock, an adjustment factor converted the rating from the group formula to the average price for each particular stock. The justified price for the coming year was then compared to its own moving average over the previous fifty-two weeks. The percentage difference was used to rank each stock. This third model, however, had a flaw. It predicted accurately if, and only if, accurate predictions of future earnings and dividends could be made. This proved a key limitation and the model was abandoned in 1966.

A fourth model attempted to overcome the problem of estimating future earnings and dividends. It required only data known at the time of the prediction. The model combined three types of analysis—relative-value fundamental analysis, relative-value trend analysis, and individual stock trend analysis. It consisted of four distinct ratings which Value Line labelled 'nonparametric value position', 'magnitude of over- or under-valuation', 'earnings momentum', and 'earnings surprise factor'. Such euphonistic labels were selected, no doubt, to impress Value Line's clientele. The specific methodology for each of these ratings is rather technical and will not be discussed here. The interested reader is referred to the excellent exposition by Black (1973). Suffice it to say that Value Line developed a single predictive multiple regression equation for each stock in the form of

$$Y = a + b_1x_1 + b_2x_2 + b_3x_3 + b_4x_4.$$

where x_1 is a stock's earnings rank, x_2 is price rank, x_3 is lagged price rank, and x_4 is price momentum. The resultant Y for each stock is used to rank it amongst 1500 stocks. Each stock also is ranked by an over- or under-valuation score.

The performance of Value Line's models has been impressive, to say the least. They consistently performed well in contests in which Value Line and thousands of stock analysts each year selected a portfolio of twenty-five stocks. Average price gains by Value Line-selected stocks were remarkably higher than the average of the stock analysts. Academic studies verified the superior performance of the Value Line models (Black, 1973). These models, then, outperformed the average security analysts who relied on traditional approaches to stock evaluation.

The idea of replacing human experts with mathematical models seems, at least at first glance, to be well founded. Presumably such models could be used in many situations where professional experts use accounting and economic information to make important judgements. A list of such judgements includes: auditing programs, financial accounting presentation decisions, materiality decisions, stock predictions, loan evaluations, interpretations of management accounting information, and sundry managerial decisions ranging from market planning to capital budgeting. The possibilities of accounting and information systems designers incorporating statistical models into their information design is both exciting and vast.

The argument is compelling. After all, models, especially those linked to computers, seem almost human or even superhuman. Such models manage refineries and freight yards, provide upper management with overnight global sales analysis, direct a staff of robots which run entire warehouses, diagnose heart ailments, beat most people at chess, compose music, and even write obscure poetry.

Yet for all its potential, there are problems with this idea. In the first place the reasoning is circular. We cannot have the models without the experts. The models are constructed by sampling the manner in which the experts utilize relevant information to form opinions. If the experts are replaced with mathematical models, it will not be long before there are no longer any experts making judgements. After a time, then, there would be no way of knowing whether or not the models are successfully mirroring the collective judgements of the experts because there would no longer be any experts to compare them against. In short, no experts–no models.

There are other problems. The models are, after all, parsimonious representations of the actual professional judgement process. The better professionals do more than merely process pieces of information and made decisions. They attack a problem by developing at least two competing explanations of the phenomenon under review. Then they test these competing views on colleagues and other respected professionals. Individuals with the possibility of making thoughtful contributions are consulted over lunch, during coffee breaks, in phone calls, or in formal meetings. (It even has been said, albeit facetiously, that the most valuable colleagues are those who are always wrong—you simply ask them which solution is best and then proceed quickly to do the opposite.) The two competing views are debated and shaped until one emerges as dominant. The whole process is accomplished in the atmosphere of an evolving dialogue.

The possibility of a computerized mathematical model duplicating this organic process seems remote. If we stop to think about it, how can a mathematical model capture the nuances of a wink, a snort, a knowing glance, or even a laugh. Yet these kinds of information are critical; and the prospects of developing a computer model that can be of two minds about a hard problem seems unlikely. For the near future, at least, the professional expert would appear to be safe.

In the final analysis, then, it is here at the collective level that human behavior is most mysterious. Most of us continually send out 'messages' to each other through talking, listening, writing, reading—almost at the same time. We constantly exchange information in what seems to be an urgent biological fashion. The richness of this process defies our own comprehension, let alone our ability to render it into mathematical language. An eminent and insightful biologist aptly described this dynamic process as follows:

> There are no closed, two-way conversations. Any word you speak this afternoon will radiate in all directions, around town before tomorrow, out and around the world before Tuesday, accelerating at the speed of light, modulating as it goes, shaping new and unexpected messages, emerging at the end as an enormously funny Hungarian joke, a fluctuation in the money market, a poem, or simply as a pause in someone's conversation in Brazil.
>
> We do a lot of collective thinking, probably more than any other social species, although it goes on in something like secrecy. We don't acknowledge the gift publicly, and we are not as celebrated

as the insects, but we do it. Effortlessly, without giving it a moment's thought, we are capable of changing our language, music, manners, morals, entertainment, even the way we dress, all around the earth in a year's turning. We seem to do all this by general agreement, without voting or even polling. We simply think our way along, pass information around, exchange codes disguised as art, change our mind, transform ourselves. (Thomas, 1975, p. 132.)

This whole affair evolves in a highly organic manner. In biological terms, fallibility and mutation are the hubs of evolutionary progress. All professional fields are growing and changing continuously—mostly for the better. Compare today's knowledge of accounting or psychology with that of the 1930s or even the 1950s. If the process were turned over to the mathematical models this wondrous evolutionary process would likely grind to a standstill. The future is too interesting and important to be entrusted to mathematical models. We need the differences in opinion and judgements to progress in those difficult areas facing our society.

Even if we could, would we relegate this wonderful process to mathematical models? Not likely—it is simply too interesting and too much fun.

Notes

1. Discriminant analysis is a form of linear multiple-regression. It is used to distinguish (or discriminate) statistically between two or more groups of cases—such as the failed and non-failed firms—in the sense of being able to tell them apart. The researcher selects a collection of discriminating variables that measure characteristics on which the groups are expected to differ. The mathematical objective of discriminant variables is to weigh and linearly combine the discriminating variables in some fashion so that the groups are forced to be as statistically distinct as possible. Whereas the linear multiple regression model *minimizes* the sum of the squared deviations of all cases from the least-squared regression function, discriminant analysis *maximizes* the sum of the squared deviations of *each group* of cases from the least-squared discriminant function. The discriminant function takes the form

$$D_i = d_{i1} Z_1 + d_{i2} Z_2 + \ldots d_{in} \times n$$

where D_i is the score on the discriminant function, the ds are weighing coefficients on each variable, and the Zs are the standardized values of the n discriminating variables used in the analysis. The discriminant function maximizes the separation of the groups. Once the set of variables and their weights are found which satisfactorily discriminates cases with known group memberships, a set of classification functions can be derived which permits classification of new cases with unknown memberships. The adequacy of the discriminant function is checked by classifying the original set of cases to see how many are correctly classified by the variables used (see Nie *et al.*, 1975).

2. For an excellent if technical review of the lens model accounting studies and their related methodological problems the reader is referred to Chapter Two of *Accounting and Information Processing: Theory and Applications*, by Robert Libby.

References

Arens, A. A., and J. K. Loebbecke, *Auditing: An Integrated Approach*, Prentice-Hall, Inc., New Jersey, 1976, pp. 410–411.

Ashton, R. H., 'Cue utilization and expert judgements: a comparison of independent auditors with other judges', *Journal of Applied Psychology*, Vol. 59, No. 4, 1974, pp. 437–444.

Black, F., 'Yes, Virginia, there is hope; tests of Value Line ranking system', *Financial Analysts Journal*, September–October 1973, pp. 10–14.

Boatsman, J. R., and J. C. Robertson, 'Policy-capturing on selected materiality judgements', *The Accounting Review*, April 1974, pp. 342–352.

Einhorn, H. J., 'Synthesis: accounting and behavioural science', *Studies on Human Information Processing in Accounting*, Supplement to *Journal of Accounting Research*, Vol. 14, 1976, pp. 196–206.

Gibbins, M., 'Human information processing in auditing: the lens model and auditors' judgements, a critique', unpublished manuscript presented at the CICA Auditing Research Symposium, Laval University, Quebec, November 1977.

Hayes, J. R., 'Strategies in judgemental research', in B. Kleinmuntz (ed.), *Formal Representation of Human Judgement*, John Wiley & Sons Inc., New York, 1968.

Hofstedt, T. R., and G. D. Hughes, 'An experimental study of the judgement element in disclosure decisions', *The Accounting Review*, April 1977, pp. 379–395.

Joyce, E. J., 'Expert judgement in audit program planning', *Studies in Human Information Processing in Accounting*. Supplement to the *Journal of Accounting Research*, Vol. 14, 1976, pp. 29–60.

Kennedy, H. A., 'Human information processing in auditing: the lens model and auditors' judgement', unpublished manuscript presented at the CICA Auditing Research Symposium, Laval University, Quebec, November 1977.

Libby, R., 'The use of simulated decision makers in information evaluation', *The Accounting Review*, July 1975, pp. 475–489.

Libby, R., *Accounting and Information Processing: Theory and Applications*, Prentice-Hall, Inc., New Jersey, 1981.

Mock, T. J., and M. A. Vasarhelyi, 'A synthesis of the information economics and the lens model', *Journal of Accounting Research*, Autumn 1978, pp. 414–423.

Nie, N. H., C. H. Hull, J. G. Jenkins, K. Steinbrenne, and D. H. Bent, *Statistical Package for the Social Sciences*, McGraw-Hill, Inc., New York, 1975.

Slovic, P., 'Analyzing the expert judge: a descriptive study of a stockbroker's decision process', *Journal of Applied Psychology*, August 1969, pp. 255–263.

Slovic, P., D. Fleissner, and W. S. Bauman, 'Analyzing the use of information in investment decision making: a methodological proposal', *Journal of Business*, Vol. 45, 1972, pp. 283–301.

Thomas, L., *The Lives of a Cell*, The Viking Press, New York, 1975.

Townsend, R., *Up the Organization*, Alfred A. Knopf, New York, 1970.

Wright, W. F., 'Financial information processing models: an empirical study', *The Accounting Review*, July 1977, pp. 676–689.

CHAPTER 6

Individual Differences and Information Systems

We usually think of managers as thoughtful, reflective people who judiciously plot secure futures for their organizations, or that part of it for which they are held responsible, by meticulously interpreting available information for clues about the consequences of sundry courses of action. The process is similar to chess where strategies, such as controlling the center of the board with a phalanx of pawns, and tactics, such as harassment by knights, unfold in accordance with a master plan. The unfolding events are assessed carefully and strategies are fine-tuned in light of new information. This may be a comfortable view, but evidence is mounting that the comparison with the game is not at all correct.

It now seems more likely that individual managers have quite distinctive ways of processing information and making decisions and further that these differences are more striking than any similarities. In fact, we now are able to pigeonhole managers into various categories, known as cognitive styles, by systematically identifying their patterns of processing information and making decisions. Managers, it seems, carry their own cognitive style with them from situation to situation just as they do the color of their eyes and their manner of speaking. These styles result in different ways of utilizing accounting and information systems. As a result, the utility of any particular system depends to an important extent on the cognitive style of the user (Dermer, 1973). Individual differences can expand or dampen the possibilities of human information processing.

This realization may be disturbing for it implies that systems should be tailor-made to the personality of the individual manager. At first glance it presents a formidable task for accounting and information managers who, by and large, are technical experts in accounting and computing—not in personality theory and cognitive psychology.

Yet, as it turns out the problem may not be so difficult. Wherever we go we leave traces of ourselves. Some of these are physical, such as our own distinctive odor. An intelligent dog with a good nose can track any man across open ground by his smell. Similarly, managers leave distinct personality characteristics behind them as they go about managing the affairs of their organizations; and some of the tools of cognitive psychology can be used to identify and distinguish any manager almost as surely as the dog identifies the man.

Indeed, a prime target of psychological study for some time now has been the understanding of the way in which people transform information into thought patterns and subsequently into decision and action. The individual is bombarded constantly with information in various forms—light, sound, smell, touch, and taste—all of which undergoes a series of transformations whereby part of it is lost while some is carefully preserved. In fact, we spend nearly all our time sending messages, talking, listening, and exchanging information. From the perspective of cognitive psychology, the human being is a complex information-processing organism.

In fact, the study of human information patterns dominated the theoretical movement of personality theory and experimental psychology for several decades. Many issues were and still are being addressed. What is the nature of the physiological process of information translation? How is information preserved and discarded? How are information patterns received and matched with stored patterns? How is meaning attached to information input? What are the characteristics of the human memory storage system? What is the nature of information decay? What is the nature of memory search and retrieval? How are memories structured? What parts of processing strategies are available for both familiar and novel problems? These are but a few of the areas that have been carefully studied.

Yet the results of these efforts remain largely obscure to accounting and information systems managers. This chapter aims to redress this by reviewing some of the major works and ideas which relate individual differences to accounting and information systems.

COGNITIVE STYLE

Much of the research into the relationship of cognitive style to information processing has investigated the ways in which people learn to combine and structure information for adaptive purposes. Cognitive style, it is important to note, is not the same as personality. Personality is the combined effect of sundry traits such as: emotional stability, cautiousness, vigor, ascendency and responsibility. Cognitive style is but one aspect of personality.

A valuable definition of cognitive style comes from Doctor and Hamilton (1973), who define it as the characteristic, self-consistent way of functioning an individual exhibits across perceptual and intellectual activities. It determines the way each individual processes, transforms, and restructures the stimulus information from the environment to shape the resulting behavioral response. In other words, cognition regulates the expression of drives into realistic accommodations of the perceived demands of the situation at hand.

It was only natural, then, that a branch of behavioral accounting and information systems should spring up around cognitive style and grow to become a major force in understanding the functioning of these systems in organizations. Although the field is relatively young, a surprisingly large amount of activity has ensued in experiments and theory-building. Even though the net result of these efforts to date has not matched the promises, they have spawned a number of fascinating findings and some very practical implications.

High- and low-analytics

The most straightforward cognitive style scheme employs a one-dimensional perceptual component whereby an individual is classified as either high-analytic (field-independent) or low-analytic (field-dependent) as in Table 6.1. According to this scheme, individuals can be classified according to their ability to differentiate an object from its context. High-analytics experience parts of a perceptual field as discrete from the organized background rather than fused with it. They have the ability to break up a basic configuration. For them, the field is structured and its organization dictates the way in which its parts are experienced. They reduce problems to a set of underlying relationships which they use in the form of an explicit model to choose among alternative courses of action.

Table 6.1 High- and low-analytic cognitive styles

High-analytics (field-independent)	Low-analytics (field-dependent)
Parts of a perceptual field are discrete from the original background	Perception is dominated by the overall organization of the field
Experience is delineated and structured	The organization of the field dictates the way the parts are experienced
Have the ability to break up a basic configuration	Perceives the field as a structured whole
Approach a problem by structuring it in terms of a planned method which will generate a likely solution	Approach problems by developing and testing hypotheses, feed-back and trial and error

Low-analytics, by contrast, have difficulty perceiving parts of the field as discrete. They have little capacity to orient objects independently of the contexts in which they appear. The field is perceived as a structured whole; and when the field lacks structure, experience tends to be ill-organized. In short, for the low-analytic, the organization of the entire field dictates the way the parts of the field are experienced (Witkin, 1969).

One of the first experiments using the high–low-analytic cognitive style concept proved to be a study by Doctor and Hamilton (1973), who were primarily concerned with uncovering why proven operations research information systems generally tended to be rejected by managers. This problem, of course, has perplexed management scientists ever since Churchman and Schainblatt's (1965) experiments unearthed this phenomenon. The researchers speculated that the problem might lie, at least in part, with the cognitive style of the management scientist, and that the degree of task structure in the work environment might be a crucial element in shaping cognitive style.

Specifically, they speculated that management scientists generally work with highly structured tasks and tend to design highly analytic reports; whereas managers work with less structured tasks which favour a low-analytic cognitive style and a preference for a general report format.

The researchers classified subjects as either field-dependent or field-independent on the basis of Witkin's (1964) embedded figures instrument which tests an individual's ability to differentiate an object from its context. Subjects then read a simple business case and, assuming the role of top management, decided whether or not to accept the recommendations contained in a 'consultant's report' about the case problem. The consultant's report came in two different formats—analytic and general. The analytic report began with a problem review and an outline of the major alternatives. The body of the report contained the actual formulae used in the numeric analysis, including a regression model. Data tables, however, appeared in the appendix. The general report, following the style preferred by most management consultants, began with a summary of recommendations and benefits. The body of the report contained no formulae or other technical material. All mathematical details, data tables, formulae, and numeric analysis, were relegated to the appendix.

The researchers anticipated that the high-analytics would favor the general report. The results, however, as can be seen in Figure 6.1, did not support these expectations. Rather, the high-analytics did not favor either report style and, in fact, had a high rejection rate for both. By contrast, the low-analytics had a significantly higher acceptance rate and, contrary to expectations, favored the analytic report style over the general one. Report style differences, however, did not make any difference in acceptance rates.

The researchers do not comment on the unexpected pattern which

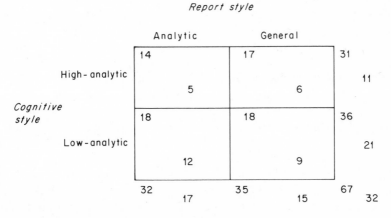

Figure 6.1 Cognitive and report style and acceptance of recommendations. The figures in the corners are the number of subjects in each cell; the figures in the centers are the number of report acceptances. (Source: compiled from Doctor and Hamilton (1973), pp. 890–891.)

emerged. What may be happening is that the high-analytics like to see the problem structured according to their preferred method and if it is not, they become dubious of any solution. Alternatively, they may simply be more thorough and critical in their review of reports. Or it may be that low-analytics are somewhat overawed by thorough analysis backed up by impressive quantitative analysis and so are prone to accept it. Either way, the study indicates that cognitive style does have some influence on the acceptance of management science reports and, importantly, that this has a stronger influence than the format of the report.

In another study, Benbasat and Dexter (1979) investigated the influence of analytic cognitive styles and different types of accounting information systems on decision-making performance. Subjects were categorized as either high- or low-analytic on the basis of the Witkin embedded figures test. Most of the subjects—students, professors, and practitioners of accounting—proved to be high-analytics. Each subject operated a computer-simulated plant by making decisions, for each of fifteen periods, about purchases and production levels. Half the subjects had at their disposal a data base containing twenty data elements including: demand levels, inventory quantities, order quantities, production levels, sales revenue, and cost information, as well as profit margins and levels. The data were not aggregated in any way and so subjects had complete access to every piece of raw data generated during the simulation. The other half of the subjects had access to a data base consisting of aggregated accounting information including: raw materials and finished goods inventory levels, sales, cost of goods sold, expenses, and net earnings.

The general results showed that cognitive style influenced profit performance, decision time and report request behavior. The type of accounting information system seemed to have less impact, although it proved to be significantly associated with decision time but not profit performance or report request behavior.

Several interesting specific results emerged with respect to the effect of cognitive style. To begin with, high-analytics outperformed low-analytics, outstripping them in profit performance and taking less time (see Figure 6.2). This was expected; after all, high-analytics should be good at an analytic task and should perform it efficiently, whereas low-analytics are not so well suited to an analytical task and would struggle with it and take more time. Also, and of more significance for our purposes, the structured–aggregated accounting information seemed to suit the high-analytics better than did the raw data base system (see cell 3 in Figure 6.2). The outstanding performance of this group supports the idea that analytics prefer problem-solving approaches which emphasize basic relationships, perceive the field as structured, reduce problems to a set of underlying relationships which are used in the form of an explicit model to make decisions, and break up a basic configuration to advantage in problem-solving situations. It follows that structured—aggregated accounting information (such as income statements, balance sheets, cost reports, and funds flows) are well suited to high-analytics. After all, such statements and reports are, in effect, models which structure the complicated set of underlying economic relationships into an organized form.

For the low-analytics the type of accounting information system had the opposite effect. The group in cell 1 in Figure 6.2 performed the worst of any group. It would seem that structured–aggregated accounting information is a hindrance, perhaps even anathema, to them. This finding accords with the theory. Low-analytics are said to lack the ability to perceive parts of the field as discrete and so rely on an intuitive global sensing of the entire field when making decisions. What might be happening is that the propensity of accounting models to aggregate and structure the field would obstruct their views of the details of the field and impede them in intuitively grasping the entire field. The net effect would be poorer performance.

This interpretation is supported by the performance of the low-analytics in cell 2. Although this group took longer than their counterparts in cell 1, they considerably outperformed them. In fact, their profit performance was not far off that of both groups of high-analytics. Apparently a raw data base is better suited to low-analytics. For them structured and aggregated information, such as that found in accounting reports, may even be a major deterrent to performance.

These two studies, then, provide evidence to support the idea that aspects of cognitive style are important factors in determining the appropriate type of accounting information system. High-analytics, with their structured and organized manner of processing information and making decisions, are better served by traditional accounting systems and models. Low-analytics, by contrast, rely on a global sensing of the total field and perform best when supported by a data base with detailed and raw information. The cognitive style of the decision-maker, it seems, can have a substantial impact on the way in which accounting and information systems function. Designers, therefore, should provide accounting information to decision-makers in a format which is compatible with their cognitive style.

Accounting information system

	Structured–aggregate	Raw data base
Low-analytic (field-dependent)	$202,100; 78 minutes 1	2 $305,700; 91 minutes
High-analytic (field-independent)	$334,700; 57 minutes 3	4 $321,000; 84 minutes

Cognitive style

Figure 6.2 Average profit and decision time per period. (Source: summarized from Benbasat and Dexter, 1979.)

Heuristic–analytic cognitive styles

Other researchers employed a slightly different cognitive style construct. They categorized individuals as either 'heuristic' or 'analytic' depending on how they process information and how this difference affects both decision outcomes and actions taken. The analytical dimension is retained but is contrasted with a quite different cognitive style—the heuristic—rather than merely categorizing individuals as either high or low on the analytic continuum.

Heuristics, sometimes referred to as globals, are persons who are unaware of the means by which they process information. They do not develop explicit plans for collecting, storing, and using information. Rather they absorb it in an *ad-hoc* fashion, processing it as it comes along and using it in a spontaneous, intuitive manner. Their decision process is characterized by common sense, intuition, and feelings about what might transpire in the future. They appear to be distinctly haphazard in the way they process information.

In working through problems, heuristics do not seek to uncover a causal system of underlying relations. Instead they rely on analogies with similar or familiar problems and look for satisfactory rather than optimal solutions. They tend to grasp situations in their totality rather than building them up from distinguishable parts. The emphasis is on arriving at something that will work, not on uncovering the precise underlying relationships and finding the optimal solution. Although they may appear to be unsystematic in the way they process information, their decisions are usually in harmony with the prevailing circumstances.

Analytics are almost the antithesis of heuristics. Sometimes called systematics, they develop explicit plans to acquire and process information. They use the information, so carefully acquired, to uncover fundamental underlying relationships amongst the variables of the problem situation and to arrive at an optimal solution in terms of explicit objectives. They employ quantitative data to guide decisions at the expense of neglecting or ignoring factors and information that cannot be quantified, or that do not fit their model. Analytics, in short, take a formal, rational, and studied approach to analysis, carefully building up an understanding of the problem and situation from its clearly identifiable parts.

Heuristics and analytics, then, are seen to be the two archetypical extremes on a continuum. They represent the dominant style an individual uses to process information, reason, and make decisions. Heuristics rely on the practical aspects of the situation, experience, and common sense; whereas analytics rely on systematic processes and abstract models (Zmud, 1979). It is recognized, however, that individuals are not locked in to one extreme or the other, and may even exhibit different styles depending on the context and demands of the situation.

One of the first experiments using this approach classified subjects as either heuristic or analytic and tracked their performance during a computer-based business simulation game (Huysmans, 1970). The investigator supplied one half of each group with an explicit and detailed operations research analysis, including formulae, of the underlying relationships of the simulation, expecting this approach would appeal to analytics. The rest of the subjects received a similar analysis, but stated in more general terms and without formulae. Surprisingly, both heuristics and analytics accepted both information systems almost without reservation. Heuristics who were supplied with the operations research analysis, however, advocated a lower degree of actual use of such systems.

Along similar lines, Mock *et al.* (1972) investigated the effect of two different information systems on the performance of both heuristics and analytics during a business simulation game. The information system consisted of financial accounting statements and supplemental information about advertising expenditures, order quantities, and production levels. Half the subjects received the information system after each period and before they made the next set of decisions. The rest received it only after a lag of one period. Their task was to maximize profits and to minimize costs.

The results, summarized in Table 6.2, support the general proposition that differences in cognitive styles and information structures influence the performance of a complex task. As anticipated for this analytic type of problem, analytics had higher profits and lower costs and outperformed heuristics in ten of the fifteen decision periods. This coincides with expectations as the task, although complex, was structured and in fact could be mathematically optimized. The heuristic group, however, outperformed the analytics in the early rounds and took less time to make decisions. This would suggest that a heuristic cognitive style is better suited to learning a new and complex task when time is at a premium; but that an analytic cognitive style is better suited to a complex but structured and repetitive task.

Table 6.2 Profits, costs, and decision time for cognitive styles and information structures

Average performance for fifteen periods	Cognitive style		Information structure	
	Analytics	Heuristics	Real Time	Lagged Time
Profits	$178,640	$170,360	$170,430	$159,910
Unit product cost	$788.00	$791.00	$795.00	$803.00
Decision time (minutes)	5.21	4.67	4.74	4.41

Source: summarized from Mock *et al.* (1972).

Subjects receiving the real-time accounting system, as shown in Table 6.2, outperformed those with the lagged one. This conforms to the conventional management accounting principle which calls for timely information. The experiment also monitored learning rates to see if differences could be attributed to either cognitive style or information structure; however, no differences emerged. Nevertheless, the study demonstrated that cognitive style and information structure can have an important effect on decision performance, as well as on the time taken to make decisions.

Another major investigation along these lines established an even firmer link between psychological type and accounting systems (Vasarhelyi, 1977). The experiment involved a financial planning case study of the Phillip Morris Corporation, including ten years of financial and qualitative information stored in a computer data base. The information was available through an interactive planning simulator (IPS) by means of a computer terminal. The fifty subjects, all of whom had business experience and some exposure to accounting, developed formal financial plans for Phillips by 'conversing' with the data base through the terminal. The subjects were tested and classified as either analytic or heuristic. Their formal plans were ranked for quality by a panel of hand-picked expert judges. Information utilization was measured both through an automated system which traced IPS usage and through a questionnaire on information utilization.

The results are impressive. As expected, analytics used the structured part of the IPS more than did heuristics, but used the unstructured part less. Analytics also used more information and made more use of the computer. Heuristics made decisions faster and expressed concern over the rigidity of the IPS. Interestingly, as the experiment unfolded, both groups became more favorably disposed towards man–machine planning systems such as the IPS. Level of education also influenced performance. These results, however, must be treated tenuously as many of the statistical significant levels were weak, due in part, as the author points out, to the difficult measurement problems.

An interesting but unplanned aspect of the experiment sprang up when the computer system proved extremely unreliable. System breakdowns and delays were the order of the day. The disruptions and irritations, heightened by software problems which made the IPS overly verbose, eventually necessitated elimination of several subjects from the data base and the experiment nearly turned into a technical nightmare. Inadvertently, then, the experiment captured a part of the reality of computer-based information systems that designers will have no problem recognizing. These events led to a great deal of 'noise' in the experimental data. Yet, in spite of these problems, most subjects seemed to enjoy the IPS. Many even stayed on the system longer than necessary simply to 'play' it. Information systems, it seems, can be fun!

The study produced several guidelines for accounting and information systems managers. Interactive systems for analytics should emphasize quantitative data and they should be allowed plenty of time to interact with the system. By contrast, systems for heuristics should emphasize qualitative data and have some capacity for using the system in a flexible way. The study also revealed that managers experienced in computers are predisposed to use interactive systems. More importantly, some managers who had slightly negative attitudes towards computers before using IPS-type systems later become converts. The study also highlights the fact that new information systems are seen as controversial. They require 'public relations' efforts, as well as careful cultivation of the manager users. These factors are often overlooked—even by the most diligent accounting and information systems managers—as efforts focus on the technical aspects of the system. In spite of technical breakdowns, or perhaps because of them, the study proved to be a milestone, serving notice that cognitive style can be a critical clue for designers seeking to increase the success of accounting and information systems in their organization.

These analytic–heuristic cognitive style experiments have demonstrated that, in general, cognitive style differences can have an important effect on the use of accounting and information systems, as well as on decision performance. Although a great deal more research is required before specific prescriptions can be formulated, the general idea that accounting and information systems can be tailored to different cognitive styles with resultant improvements in decision-making performance remains a tantalizing prospect.

In another study along similar lines, Lucas (1981) investigated the influence of heuristic versus analytic cognitive styles and two different information systems media on performance, satisfaction, and learning. The subjects, nearly one hundred executives, participated in a simulation of the ordering task for a whiskey importer where demand was uncertain, but inventory and holding costs were known. The objective was to minimize costs. The computer data base, available to different subject groups in different media, consisted of data on historical demand, as well as simulation capability for pre-testing the results of decisions.

The results suggest that both cognitive style and information system medium affect performance and learning. Heuristics using the CRT with graphics performed best in terms minimizing costs; while heuristics with tabular output recorded the highest costs. For the analytics, the type of information system had no influence on cost performance but CRT graphics proved best for them in terms of learning. What may be happening is that heuristics, lacking any *a-priori* models, and not being prone to analyzing tabular data, would rely more on the graphic displays than would the analytics, who would have some sort of a preconceived model that might hinder them in the search for the best solution.

These, and other similar experiments, provide general support for the idea that cognitive style influences information processing and performance; and, importantly, they suggest that information system structure can be tailored to advantage to the cognitive style of the user–manager.

THE MINNESOTA EXPERIMENTS

In a related and important series of experiments, researchers at the University of Minnesota investigated the effect of computer-based accounting information systems on managerial decision-making. Some of these experiments also studied the impact of personal characteristics on system utilization and decision performance. The studies, which later came to be known as the 'Minnesota experiments', used computer simulations of routine production, inventory, or purchasing decisions to investigate the effect of different forms and contents of accounting reports on decision performance. While the results suggested that decision-making is affected by information system structure, evidence to support the idea that cognitive style is also important proved to be mixed.

The initial experiment had participants interact with a computerized operations management simulator to make decisions for production scheduling, labor force levels, and raw material ordering (Chervany and Dickson, 1974). Half the participants (RDs) received accounting reports about costs and qualities of production, labor, and inventories in detailed raw data reports. The reports contained over a thousand pieces of data. The other participants (SSDs) received the same information in reports which presented the data in statistical form, including means, ranges, and standard deviations. The two groups were then compared for cost performance, decision time, and confidence in decisions made.

The results are fascinating. The RD group outperformed the SSD group in six out of seven cost performance categories; but the SSD group performed significantly better in the seventh and pivotal category—stock-out costs. As it turned out, stock-out costs amounted to nearly 30 percent of total costs, so participants who caught on to this performed much better than those who did not. An important result was that the participants in the SSD group triggered to this key aspect to a much greater extent than did those in the RD group. What seemed to have happened is that RD subjects were not able to transform the large amount of raw data into any useful summary form that would lead them to the critical variable. This result is consistent with findings from experimental psychology, indicating that humans have limited information-processing capabilities and can be overloaded.

The experiment also indicates that detailed, raw data reports are well suited to the routine and well-understood aspects of production decisions, but that summarized information is more valuable for identifying critical, but obscure, decision parameters. This strongly suggests that the appropriate format for an accounting and information system depends upon the nature of the task at hand.

Participants in the SSD group took more time to make their decisions but had less confidence in them than did those in the RD group. Perhaps they did not realize they had cracked the important stock-out problem; or maybe they were not used to receiving accounting information in the form of means, ranges, and standard deviations and, feeling uncomfortable with it, spent more time working through the decisions and, as a result, identified the critical stock-out problem. Or perhaps participants in the RD group felt more confident knowing that they had access to complete data. There are lots of possibilities; but either way, the experiment demonstrated that the format of accounting information can be crucial for decision-making.

The other Minnesota experiments continued in the same format. The next experiment provided the SSD reports to one group through a CRT computer terminal and to the other group in traditional hard copy form (Kozar, 1972). The CRT group had better cost performance but took longer to make decisions. Differences in subjects' quantitative and verbal skills did not influence performance. In another experiment, critical decision-making information was positioned together in the reports for half the subjects while the others got an information system where the critical information was mixed in with non-critical data (Barkin, 1974). The report format, as well as cognitive style, influenced the amount of data selected. Next, Senn and Dickson (1974) simulated a purchasing decision environment and found that users with summarized data on CRTs made decisions faster, and requested less information, than either users with summarized or detailed data from line printers. Neither mode, however, affected purchasing costs performance nor decision confidence. Another experiment employed an interactive decision support system for a commodity buying study and found that the setting of performance goals improved performance (Wynne and Dickson, 1975). It also appeared that the use of the interactive system, along with psychological variables, enhanced expected, but not actual, performance; and, importantly, subjects became more enamored of the interactive system as they gained experience with it. Then Benbasat and Schroeder (1977) employing an elaborate inventory management simulation, found that graphic output and decision aids, but not cognitive style, influenced performance, although cognitive style and the type of information system did affect the amount of information used and requested. The final experiment investigated the consequences of decision aids, business background, attitude to risk, and attitudes to computers and quantitative data on a warehouse expansion decision (Chervany and Sauter, 1977). Attitudes, business background, and decision aids did not affect the decision to expand, although the business background did influence confidence in decision-making.

The Minnesota experiments are hard to summarize. Undoubtedly they are important. They demonstrate the critical nature of variations in accounting and information system structure and media to decision-making, productivity, confidence, and attitudes (Dickson et al., 1977). They also suggest, although the evidence is only modest, that in some circumstances cognitive style influences the way information is used and, but to a lesser extent, performance. The inconclusive results may be due to the fact that the experiments used different task environments and different cognitive style constructs. In summing up the experiments, Chervany and Dickson (1978) conclude that information use may well be determined not so much by cognitive style, as by (to a very large degree) task characteristics. Yet it seems far too early to relegate cognitive style research to the behavior accounting archives. Future studies are needed which are designed to control for differences in both task and cognitive style differences before we can conclusively resolve these issues.

PERSONALITY AND HUMAN INFORMATION PROCESSING

A major reason for the disappointing overall results, some argue, stems from the use of different cognitive style constructs and measuring instruments employed by different researchers (Zmud, 1978). Further, many of the constructs used capture only a small part of the cognitive domain. These limitations led many experts to advocate widespread adoption of a single personality construct for future research—Jung's personality typology.

Jung held that the wide variation in human behavior can be explained in terms of four basic differences in the way individuals function mentally (Jung, 1923). These differences are summarized in Table 6.3. We prefer to perceive the world in either a sensing or an intuitive way. We prefer to make judgements about what we perceive in either a feeling or a thinking fashion. We also have a basic preference for either the perceiving or judgement mode. Finally, some people, the extroverts, prefer to focus on the external world of people and events while others, the introverts, prefer the abstract world. As our personality develops we develop strong preferences for one mode or the other in each of the four basic functions and then rely on them, often to the neglect of the others.

Table 6.3 Jungian typology of personality

Cognitive constructs	Cognitive characteristics		
1. Dominant cognitive reality	*Extroverted* Prefers the external world of people and events	versus	*Introverted* Prefers the internal world of archetypes, ideas and concepts
2. Dominant cognitive mode	*Perceiving* Prefers perceiving and understanding over judging	versus	*Judging* Prefers judging over perceiving and understanding
3. Dominant cognitive process for perceiving	*Sensing* Relies on known facts, concrete data, and actual experience	versus	*Intuition* Relies on concepts, theories, ideas, and hypothetical relationships
4. Dominant cognitive process for judging	*Feeling* Judgements based on personal values and feelings	versus	*Thinking* Judgements based on impersonal analysis and logic

These personality traits, many experts believe, should influence the way individuals utilize accounting and information systems. The following sketches of the Jungian personality are taken from Jung (1923) and Myers

(1980). The connections with information processing are suggested in the works of Mason and Mitroff (1973), Zmud (1978), Henderson and Nutt (1980), Wade (1981), and Keen and Bronsema (1981).

Perception—sensing versus intuition

Perceiving is the process by which we become aware of events, people, and things. It is done in two distinctly different ways—sensing and intuition—and each individual has a strong preference for one or the other. Sensing types become aware of their environment directly through the five senses. That which is experienced directly can be counted on, and understanding comes from solid agreement of facts and actualities with conclusions. Sensing individuals do not skip in reading and conversation and they are careful, accurate, and take a lot of time when calculating. They see the shapes of numbers but their meaning must be learned by rote.

These persons, however, are ill at ease with abstractions and general principles. They are uncomfortable with the symbolic world and do not score well on intelligence tests, nor do they make good scholars. Indirect sensing, from the unconscious or from other people, is not to be trusted as is direct experience. So abstractions, general principles, and symbols must be translated carefully before they convey meaning.

Sensing types are likely to be friendly users of accounting and information systems. They like concrete, objective, hard facts and details. They enjoy problem-solving and go at it in a slow, methodical way, processing information very carefully, going over it again and again before arriving at a conclusion. They are said to make excellent accountants and navigators. Fearful of extrapolating further than the facts allow, however, they are prone to become data-bound and will continue to collect information rather than risk a generalization. Although they process a great deal of information, they have trouble understanding the message buried in the data and struggle to get meaning from summaries and models.

Sensing types, then, present a paradox for accounting and information system designers. They have a great affinity for information, especially in detailed and concrete form, but they lack the aptitude for using models and abstractions to advantage. Computerized decision support systems, then, should be helpful to them in overcoming this drawback, but only after a long struggle. In sum, sensing types should be friendly users but require coaching and guidance when using accounting and information systems.

Individuals who prefer intuition contrast sharply with sensing types. Intuitives are more taken with possibilities than actualities. They admit to consciousness only the sense impressions related to the inspiration of the moment. They take off from the known and established, leaving intermediate steps to the unconscious, to arrive in a twinkling at an advanced point. They listen for intuitions to pop up from the unconscious with tantalizing visions of possibilities. Problems are referred automatically to the unconscious and answers which spring forth are pounced upon with enthusiasm. They are excited by inspiration.

These attributes lead intuitives to be independent of their physical surroundings. They are inventive and original, although at the expense of careful observation. They are by nature initiators, inventors, and promoters. They seek enterprise and achievement, paying little attention to the present; and yet they are neither fickle nor lacking in persistence and they often develop a sound judging process. Inventiveness, initiative, and enterprise are the trademarks by which they contribute to society.

Intuitives pose a unique challenge to accounting and information systems designers. They live in the future, paying little attention to the current situation. They are less interested in facts than they are in hunches and intuitions. They see objects and events in their totality with properties not derivable from their parts; and they admit to consciousness only impressions that relate to their present interest. Consequently, they are prone to neglect or ignore important pieces of information, prefering to churn out hypothetical conclusions not necessarily based on available data. With their gift of creativity they dominate intellectual fields but, except for senior marketing jobs, they are uncommon in managerial positions. Not surprisingly, they dominate the management consulting field where their ability to make lightning connections between data and imaginative solutions serves them well (Wade, 1981).

Intuitives, then, are not likely to be good users of formal accounting and information systems. They do not pay much heed to routine detailed reports even though they need them, more so than their sensing counterparts, to balance their propensity to leap to conclusions not based on facts. This weakness means that designers must put special efforts into connecting up intuitives with formal systems in a meaningful way. Thus they are ideal candidates for sophisticated decision simulation models, especially those that link computer-based models to data bases. Importantly, however, neither sensing nor intuitive types are superior for managerial positions. Smooth administration of daily operations is the forte of the sensing type; while strategy formulation and planning for the future are the gifts of the intuitive.

Judging by feeling versus thinking

While perceiving is the process of becoming aware of our world, judging entails coming to conclusions about what we perceive. Judging is carried out in two distinctively contrasting ways. Some people rely on a logical, impersonal thinking process, while others use a personal, subjective, and feeling approach. Both styles are equally reasonable, but each of us prefers one over the other. We use the preferred one more often, trust it more implicitly, and obey it more readily, to the neglect and disregard of the other.

Feeling types take a personal approach to life. They are tender-hearted, naturally friendly, and good at social graces. For them, feeling is the effective instrument for the sympathetic handling of people and is the bridge between human beings. They become very good at handling human relations. Feeling types, however, are prone to suppress and undervalue thinking, especially when it is in conflict with feelings. They find it hard to know where to start a statement, or in what order to present their position. Consequently, they may give more detail than necessary, repeat themselves, and ramble. They value sentiment over logic and are good at selling, teaching, counselling, and family life.

Thinking types, by contrast, take an impersonal approach to life. They value logic and objectivity over sentiment. They will suppress, ignore, and undervalue feeling when it is incompatible with their thinking judgements. Yet they are not necessarily sound thinkers, it is just that their mental powers run on a logical track. Thinking types come across as brief and businesslike, even as lacking in friendliness. They are stronger in executive ability and more adept in the organization of facts and ideas than they are in the social arts. They contribute to society through intellectual criticisms, exposure of wrongs, solution of problems, and the enlargement of human knowledge and understanding.

Neither feeling nor thinking, of course, is necessarily the better judging process. Thinking types judge on a true–false dichotomy, while feeling types work from the agreeable–disagreeable perspective. Each has its appropriate field but to use feeling where thinking is required, and vice-versa, can lead to trouble. Individuals who prefer thinking grow more adept in the organization of facts and ideas; whereas those who prefer feeling are more adult in handling human relationships. Both types, naturally, are happier and more effective in activities that call for the judgements they are better equipped to make.

Feeling types are not good candidates for effectively using accounting and information systems. They respond to their feelings, not to logical abstractions, in making evaluations and reaching conclusions. Their judgements depend heavily on how they personally feel about the event or issue—whether they find it pleasant or unpleasant. They do, however, respond to information in art form, such as poetry and paintings, but formal accounting and information systems leave them cold. While research results are sparse, Ghani (1980) found that feeling types prefer and do better using graphic displays, in contrast to thinking types who prefer and perform better with tabular output. De Waele (1978) reports that feeling types enjoy the execution stage in marketing over the design and decision phase. Feeling types, then, are not likely to use information systems to advantage. For them, sentiment overrides data and logic.

Thinking types, by contrast, make the best and most friendly users of accounting and information systems. They value logic over sentiment and truth over tact. They like to categorize everything, follow a formal system of logic, and use a true–false type of reasoning to arrive at conclusions (Mason and Mitroff, 1973). For them, judgement should be impersonal as the goal is to arrive at the objective truth independent of either their own or others' feelings and desires. They like information and use it well. They are zealous proponents of formal information systems. Nevertheless, they are prone to overutilize models and rules and consequently they may not really understand the problem situation; also, they will rely on information even when it is ambiguous.

Judging versus perceiving preference

Individuals differ in the way they perceive and judge. These two aspects of cognition, however, do not usually occur at the same time. Perception goes on until all the evidence is in and all new developments have been considered. Then the time arrives for a verdict and perception must be shut out for a time, while the judging takes over. New information and developments are immaterial and irrelevant. These two processes, however, compete for attention and so individuals come to prefer and rely on one or the other. The important consequence is that the preference makes a difference.

Individuals who prefer a judging attitude believe life should be willed and decided, and so are forever coming to conclusions. They like to dispose promptly of matters and issues, both for themselves and others. They are systematic in doing things, they like planned schedules, and prefer an orderly life. Consequently they are quick to decide the best way to do something and then consistently do it that way, willingly accepting the routine involved. This type of willpower can lead to impressive results, like the legendary tortoise who won the race against the hare.

Judging types are clear about their standards but want others to conform to them and are quick to advise them to do so. Yet due to their organizing abilities, penchant for deciding, and acceptance of routine, they make good executives. They are self-regimented, purposeful, exacting, and take pleasure in getting things done and out of the way. Without an adequately developed perceptive side, however, they will be narrow, rigid, and incapable of seeing the views of others. They can also be impervious to perception and so prone to prejudice. They need order in their lives and the judging attitude accomplishes this.

Individuals who prefer a perceiving mode treat life as something to be understood, not something to pass judgement upon. They hope they can solve a problem by seeing it from all sides, penetrating it to the bottom and understanding it better. They are spontaneous, adaptive, welcome new experiences, and amass storehouses of information. They take in new ideas, facts, and proposals, keeping opinions and decisions open, so no valuable experience, information, or insight is overlooked. Not surprisingly, they do not come to a conclusion until it is forced on them and will even open up previous decisions for reconsideration. They have an inexhaustible interest in the what and why of life, and are much more interested in understanding than in judging and deciding. Whereas judging types order their lives perceptive types just live them.

When individuals are in a perceiving mode they are prone to accept and use information. Consequently, people who prefer the perceiving mode over the judging one will have a greater infinity for accounting and information systems and should be friendly users. Systems with a good deal of accurate and detailed information will be appreciated. They will massage the information carefully, sifting through it for understanding. Judging types, by contrast, will not be antagonistic to information; but they will look to it for quick answers and are likely to ignore or misuse accounting and information systems which do not have clear-cut messages. Systems for judging types, then, should highlight key pieces of information, feature summaries, conclusions, and even commentaries about their meaning.

Preference for the outer versus the inner world

The final basic difference individuals exhibit is a preference for either the outer world of people and things or the inner world of concepts and ideas. Extroverts, basing their conduct on the outer world, are governed by what others think and by objective conditions, even to the extent of being unsure of themselves without external reference. They are vocal, expansive, understandable, accessible, and sociable, unloading their emotions as they go along. They enjoy life and understand it only as they experience it. They learn through direct experiences rather than from abstract principles. They are prone, however, to be intellectually shallow, understanding life only on a superficial basis, without pausing long enough to see its deep and underlying meaning. Extroverts are highly esteemed, outnumber introverts by three to one and, importantly, their perspective dominates western civilization.

Extroverts, then, are receptive to information, especially if it keeps them informed of the current situation. They prefer verbal and video media over hard copy and tabular information media. They process information quickly but are prone to interpret it superficially. Consequently, they need help from system designers in interpreting formal accounting and information systems; and, since their conduct is governed by external conditions and other people, they respond automatically to financial control systems, accepting messages in the information without questioning. They tend to use information systems superficially. This, of course, can be very dangerous.

Introverts, engrossed by the internal world of ideas and concepts, cannot live life until they understand it. Consequently, they have an affinity for information. They massage it carefully to develop a deep understanding of the problem or decision at hand; and they are at home with accounting and decision models. Introverts also have a great capacity for ignoring what they see as distracting outer stimuli, such as financial control systems. In general, however, they are good at processing information, which they use to find its underlying meaning. They like to puzzle through messy problems until they find a unifying meaning.

The Jungian personality typology is only beginning to be used by accounting and information systems researchers but it looks as if it may become the dominant concept for the next decade of research. A major attraction, of course, is the availability of the widely used and validated instrument—the Myers–Briggs Type Indicator (MBTI)—to measure subjects' traits. A few pioneering studies have already surfaced.

Keen and Bronsema (1982), for example, documented the extensive research using the MBTI. Their review brought to light some interesting personality differences among professional groups. These are summarized in Table 6.4. Accountants ranked high on sensing for perceiving and thinking for judgement. This is consistent with the professional attributes required of accountants—attention to detail, propensity for concrete action, and judging on the basis of impersonal analysis and logic. Professionals in operations research, data processing, and office automation rank high on intuition and thinking and prefer the judging mode to the perceiving one. Interestingly, middle managers have a similar profile. This finding puts in doubt the widely held belief that computer and operations research systems fail because information systems people design towards their own, rather than the manager's, cognitive style. Upper managers, small businessmen, and courtroom judges, however, do differ significantly. Their profiles feature sensing, thinking, and judging preferences. These are consistent with the need in their professions for clearing the air, collecting the facts, and translating them into practical action. Keen and Bronsema conclude that previous research employed cognitive style concepts, such as the heuristic analytic scheme, that are too narrow. The Jungian typology they propose is richer: and it can be captured readily with the MBTI instrument.

Table 6.4 General profiles of personality type differences

Technical field	Perceiving	Judging	Preferred mode
Accountants	Sensing	Thinking	Not available
MIS and O/R specialists	Intuition	Thinking	Judging
Middle managers	Intuitive	Thinking	Mixed
Marketing managers and management consultants	Intuition	Thinking	Judging
Sales and customer relations	Sensing	Feeling	Not available
Senior executives, small business owners, and judges	Sensing	Thinking	Judging
Court judges	Sensing	Thinking	Judging
Intellectual fields	Intuition	Feeling	Perception

Source: summarized from Keen and Bronsema (1981).

In another study, Henderson and Nutt (1980) demonstrated the potential of the Jungian typology for understanding decision processes and information processing. In a creative and well-designed study they linked decision styles, based on Jungian personality concepts, to organizational characteristics and information system dimensions. Sixty-two executives, from both private and public corporations, were classified into one of four decision styles according to their preferred modes of perception and judgement (see Table 6.5). The participants assessed each of eight hypothetical capital budgeting proposals in terms of the likelihood they would adopt them, and by their perceived risk. The results provided general support for the relationships proposed in Table 6.5, although information source (either interactions with trusted colleagues or a computer-based model) proved to be only marginally important. The study demonstrates the potential for rich experiments based on Jung's personality constructs. The near future, without doubt, will witness a great number of accounting and information systems experiments using the MBTI.

From a practical point of view the potential for designers seems highly promising. Some types, say intuitive, thinking, perceiving individuals, will make maximum use of any system even if poorly designed; whereas sensing, feeling, judging managers, especially if they are extroverts, are not likely to utilize effectively our traditional types of information systems. They use information in a cursory fashion, rely primarily on sense data, react to feelings instead of logic, and ignore information that does not quickly provide a clear-cut answer. For these types, however, information systems which feature pictures, sounds, graphs, and verbal media, yet highlight concrete facts and stress relationships, would be of considerable help in getting them to utilize information systems. There are lots of possibilities. With some imagination and creativity designers should be able to give each manager the kind of information systems he or she is psychologically attuned to and will use most effectively (Mason and Mitroff, 1973).

CONCLUSION

We will now review our discussion and hazard some conclusions. The central thesis of this chapter is that individual differences influence the way managers gather, process, and utilize information in making decisions; or, to put it another way, individuals with different cognitive structures should prefer and work better with different types of accounting and information systems. It follows that prudent matching of system characteristics with cognitive styles should lead to more effective utilization of these systems and ultimately to more effective decision-making and better task performance.

This is an appealing line of reasoning and it holds great promise for accounting and information system designers; and yet the cumulative results of the research carried out so far have been inconclusive and at times contradictory (Huber, 1983). A great deal of the difficulty, of course, lies with the inconsistencies among the various experiments. They tested different cognitive characteristics; they employed a variety of task environments; and they controlled for different accounting formats and reporting media. So we

Table 6.5 Preferred information and environmental features by decision style

| | Decision Styles | | | |
	ST (Sensation-Thinking)	SF (Sensation Feeling)	NT (Intuition-Thinking)	NF (Intuitive-Feeling)
Preferred features of the environment				
(a) Performance appraisal	Objective cost center measures	Objective measures of the cost center manager	Compare cost center's performance with perceived potential	Compare cost center manager's performance with perceived potential
(b) Structure	Centralized well-defined authority	Participative decision-making and clear-cut roles and rules of work	Liaison to power centers	Delegation to decentralized units
(c) Goals	Profitability	Multiple (profit, stability, growth, service, people-oriented, etc.)	Competitive with peers and/ or increasing market share	Dual (growth and profit)
(d) Leadership style	Push for results	Rapport with co-workers	Leadership via example	Charisma
Preferred information for capital project decision				
(a) ROI projections based on:				
Interaction	Experienced managers who understand investment decisions, project accounting, and financial data to predict ROI	Trusted and respected colleagues review accounting and financial data and unique project features to estimate ROI	Experienced consultants review cost and revenue data and estimate ROI, considering possible demand changes	Trusted and respected colleagues consider cost estimates and unique aspects of the project and state their ROI beliefs
Analysis	A computer-based planning model, predicted ROI	Computer-based model used to stimulate discussion among trusted and respected colleagues who estimated ROI	Computer-based model was used to ask 'what if' questions about demand to predict ROI	Computer-based model was used to elicit beliefs about ROI
(b) Validation	Checking details of calculations and data acquisition	Acceptance by key groups	Consider in light of external factors	Enhances organization's prestige or visibility

Source: Henderson and Nutt (1980), p. 375. Reproduced by permission of The Institute of Management Science.

should not be surprised that we have yet to bring closure on the issues raised by the general thesis. All the same, at least we have come to realize that we need consensus amongst researchers on which cognitive style constructs to focus on, which psychological instruments to employ, and which accounting and information systems attributes to control.

In spite of these limitations we have learned a great deal. We know that cognitive style has a strong influence on the acceptance of, and preference for, accounting report formats and media. We also know that different styles lead to different performance on complex tasks. Most importantly, agreement seems to be developing that the Jungian personality typology, as measured by the MBTI, provides a rich theory upon which to base a comprehensive framework of personality and information processing.

So it would be premature, even wrongheaded, to discard the general insight that systematic patterns of human information processing can result in predictable ways of utilizing formal accounting and information systems and, ultimately, to quite different decisions stemming from identical information. The problems seem to lie more in conducting careful and rigorous experiments than with the general premise. At this stage we have merely scratched the surface.

The potential of this approach is captured by the history of a large community nursing program, where designers evaluated the cognitive style of the key users and then designed a new financial reporting system accordingly (Bariff and Lusk, 1977). The center was experiencing severe problems in evaluating and controlling its services, and wished to design a new accounting system. During the design phase the researchers administered various cognitive style tests, resistance to change indicators, and tolerance for stress measurements to key administrators and nursing supervisors. The results were used to develop behavioral profiles of two key groups—field supervisors and key administrators.

Both groups turned out to be relatively flexible and have a high tolerance for ambiguity. The administrators were the least flexible and so more attention was paid to them during design and implementation stages. Also, the stress level for both groups turned out to be lower than the national norm. The tests also revealed that both groups could be categorized as low-analytics. Neither group differed from national norms in terms of defense mechanisms; and importantly, the user behavioral profiles indicated that simple reports which minimize complexity would be most suitable for the cognitive structures of the users, and that resistance and anxiety should not be obstacles during implementation.

Armed with these clues, the designers developed three report sets with different combinations of raw versus percentage data and tabular versus graphic formats. Every report was evaluated by each manager for readability, completeness, amount of detail, and ability to locate and abstract data. The managers also gave their opinions about the relative importance of the four dimensions. An analysis of the responses indicated that both administrators and supervisors alike preferred disaggregated reports with raw rather than transformed data. As a result, the reports were disaggregated and the reporting frequency was increased. The managers, pleased with the new accounting system, believed it helped them considerably with their jobs. The new system proved to be a great success.

This case history sounds the appropriate note upon which to close this chapter. It provides a concrete example of how scientifically developed user behavior profiles can be used to advantage for the design and implementation of accounting and information systems. The general idea of matching individual differences to information system characteristics seems highly practical and well within the grasp of designers. In its simplest form it is merely a systematic way of carrying out user needs assessments, which in the final analysis, is the 'name of the game'.

References

Bariff, M. L., and E. J. Lusk, 'Cognitive and personality tests for the design of management information systems', *Management Sciences*, April 1977, pp. 820–829.

Barkin, S., 'An investigation into some factors affecting information system utilization', PhD thesis, University of Minnesota, 1974.

Benbasat, I., and A. S. Dexter, 'Value and events approaches to accounting: an experimental evolution', *The Accounting Review*, October 1979, pp. 735–749.

Benbasat, I., and R. G. Schroeder, 'An experimental investigation of some MIS design variables', *Management Information Systems Quarterly*, March 1977, pp. 37–50.

Chervany, N. L., and G. W. Dickson, 'An experimental evaluation of information overload in a production environment', *Management Science*, June 1974, pp. 1335–1344.

Chervany, N. L., and G. W. Dickson, 'On the validity of the analytic–heuristic instrument utilized in "The Minnesota Experiments"': A Reply', *Management Science*, June 1978, pp. 1091–1092.

Chervany, N. L., and R. F. Sauter, 'Analysis and design of computer-based management information systems: an evaluation of risk analysis decision aids', Management Information Systems Research Center, Monograph 5, University of Minnesota, 1977.

Churchman, C. W., and A. H. Schainblatt, 'The researcher and the manager: a dialectic of implementation', *Management Science*, February 1965, pp. B69–87.

Dermer, J. D., 'Cognitive characteristics and the perceived importance of information', *The Accounting Review*, July 1973, pp. 511–519.

Dickson, G. W., J. A. Senn, and N. L. Chervany, 'Research in management information systems; The Minnesota Experiments', *Management Science*, May 1977, pp. 913–923.

Doctor, R. H., and W. F. Hamilton, 'Cognitive style and the acceptance of management science recommendations', *Management Science*, April 1973, pp. 884–894.

Ghani, J. A., 'The effects of information representation and modification on decision performance', PhD Dissertation, Wharton School, University of Pennsylvania, 1980.

Henderson, J. C., and P. C. Nutt, 'The influence of decision style on decision making behaviour', *Management Science*, April 1980, pp. 371–386.

Huber, G. P., 'Cognitive style as a basis for MIS and DSS designs: much ado about nothing', *Management Science*, May 1983, pp. 567–582.

Huysmans, J. H. B. M., 'The effectiveness of the cognitive style constraint in implementing operations research proposals', *Management Science*, September 1970, pp. 92–104.

Jung, C. C., *Psychological Types*, Harcourt Brace, New York, 1923.

Keen, P. G. W., and G. S. Bronsema, 'Cognitive style research: a perspective for integration', The Proceedings of the Second International Conference on Information Systems, Cambridge, Mass., December 1981, pp. 21–52.

Kozar, K. A., 'Decision making in a simulated environment: a comparative analysis of computer display media', PhD thesis, University of Minnesota, 1972.

Lucas, H. C. Jr., 'An experimental investigation of the use of computer-based graphics in decision making', *Management Science*, July 1981, pp. 757–768.

Mason, R. O. and I. I. Mitroff, 'A program for research on management information systems', *Management Science*, January 1973, pp. 475–486.

Mock, T. J., T. L. Estrin, and M. A. Vasarhelyi, 'Learning patterns, decision approach and value of information', *Journal of Accounting Research*, Spring 1972, pp. 129–153.

Myers, I. B., *Gifts Differing*, Consulting Psychologists Press, Inc., Polo Alto, Calif., 1980.

Senn, J. A. and G. W. Dickson, 'Information system structure and purchasing decision effectiveness', *Journal of Purchasing and Materials Management*, August 1974.

Vasarhelyi, M. A., 'Man–machine planning systems: a cognitive style examination of interactive decision making', *Journal of Accounting Research*, Spring 1977, pp. 138–153.

Wade, P. F., 'Some factors affecting problem solving effectiveness in business, a study of management consultants', PhD Dissertation, McGill University, 1981.

de Waele, M., 'Managerial style and the design of decision aids', PhD dissertation, University of California Berkeley, California, 1978.

Witkin, H. A., 'Origins of cognitive style', in C. Scheerer (ed.), *Cognition: Theory, Research, Promise*, Harper & Row, New York, 1964, pp. 172–205.

Witkin, H. A., *Professional School Psychology*, Vol. III, Grune & Stratton, New York, 1969.

Wynne, B., and G. W. Dickson, 'Experienced managers' performance in experimental man–machine decision system simulation', *Academy of Management Journal*, March 1975, pp. 25–40.

Zmud, R. W., 'On the validity of the analytic–heuristic instrument utilized in the Minnesota experiments', *Management Science*, June 1978, pp. 1088–1090.

Zmud, R. W., 'Individual differences and MIS success: a review of the empirical literature', *Management Science*, October 1979, pp. 966–979.

TWO. Impersonal Forces and Accounting and Information Systems

CHAPTER 7

Organizational Sociology and Accounting and Information Systems

The previous chapters reviewed the results of many years of research concerning the effect of several personal factors on accounting and information systems. We concluded that this impact is more complex than was at first realized and that some of these factors may even have unanticipated negative consequences for our organizations. Undoubtedly future research will continue to examine the processes of participative budgeting, expert utilization of financial cues, and cognitive traits. These topics are important and conclusive findings are needed urgently. These studies also suggested that the personal factors approach to the study of accounting and information systems may be too narrow. Many impersonal forces also are at work and we need systematic ways of understanding their impact as well.

One neat way to do this is to follow the approach taken by organizational sociologists. Investigations of this sort focus on social interaction and decision-making in organizations within the broad framework of impersonal forces such as uncertainty, interdependencies amongst organizational components, specialization arrangements, integrative mechanisms, and technology. It is argued from this vantage point that the structures of these forces influence organizational arrangements and their enduring patterns of behavior. It seems to follow naturally that, if these contextual variables influence the design of our organizations, they should also influence the shape and characteristics of our accounting and information systems.

Speculation of this sort may not be far off the mark. Several organizational theorists have included accounting and information systems in their studies; yet their efforts remain largely unknown to management accounting and information systems designers. This is unfortunate; for if system designers do not create thoughtful ways of analyzing how our systems fit into the grander scheme of things, we may never get beyond the debits–credits and bits–bytes. That would be a pity. Accounting and information systems are an institution in their own right—influencing and being influenced by other macro-organizational structures. It may be time we looked beyond the trees. After all, we work in the forest.

Following this line of reasoning, we review here some of the major macro-organizational studies which are especially relevant to management accounting and information systems designers. Some of these studies stress the uncertainty of the work environment. Others center on the nature of the work being performed. Still others focus on the structure of goals and power; but all deal in a general way with the impersonal forces which shape our organizational management systems. More importantly for this book, they all touch on the appropriate configuration of accounting and information systems, given the state of uncertainty or the nature of the organization's task. The first of these that we shall review is the classical, milestone study by Burns and Stalker.

Environmental circumstances

Burns and Stalker (1961) conducted one of the earliest studies of this nature. It proved to be a seminal effort. They paid particular attention to the relationship between a firm's external circumstances and its social technology, as they aptly label its management systems. External circumstances refers to markets served, production techniques developed, and scientific knowledge available. Social technology pertains to the flow of formal authority, lines of communication, division of tasks, and arrangements for co-ordination of effort. Social technology, they conclude, is determined largely by external circumstances.

As evidence for this thesis, Burns and Stalker observed that some of the firms they studied operated in relatively stable environments. These firms had a well-defined social technology. They divided tasks and problems into distinct slots. They defined precise duties for each function. They allocated power unambiguously amongst managers. They relied heavily on vertical hierarchial arrangements; and they co-ordinated the entire operation from the top, the only place where overall knowledge of the firm resided. Burns and Stalker labeled these kinds of management systems 'mechanistic'.

Other firms, however, existing in relatively more fluid environments, had a quite different social technology. Because of this, problems and actions could not be precisely defined. Nor could they be assigned to distinct specialist departments. Nor could individual tasks be performed without a knowledge of the goals and tasks of the entire organization. So a manager's methods, duties, and power arrangements had to be continually negotiated and redefined. They accomplished this through frequent and intensive interaction with other managers throughout the organization. Lateral, rather than vertical, relationships dominated. Formal definitions of hierarchy melted. Complete knowledge of the organization was no longer ascribed to top management. Burns and Stalker called this sort of management system 'organic'.

From this, Burns and Stalker concluded that the most essential part of a top manager's job is to interpret correctly both the degree and kind of instability in the market circumstances, production techniques, and scientific knowledge facing their firm. Only then are they in a position to decide on the appropriate social technology. In some of the firms studied, top management had failed to make this analysis and consequently their systems were often inappropriate and ineffective. In other cases, where the environmental circumstances had been identified, the appropriate social technology was adopted. In still other firms, even when the environment–management system mismatch was recognized, the clash of politics and managerial careerism prevented suitable action being taken. It seems that the one best management system for all firms does not exist.

Burns and Stalker's work holds special interest for management accounting and information systems designers because they also theorize about the appropriate type of accounting and information system for each of the mechanistic and organic types of firms.

In mechanistic firms, operating in stable environments, overall knowledge is available only at the top of the hierarchy, resulting in a simple but forceful management control system. Superiors govern operations and work behavior by issuing strong, clear commands. Unilateral instructions flow downward and become more explicit with each successive layer of hierarchy. Upward-flowing information, however, is successively filtered out on its way to the top. As this process continues it loses its impact, accuracy, and force. This unilateral, autocratic style of control, Burns and Stalker argue, is uniquely suited to the mechanistic management system. These ideas are depicted in Figure 7.1.

In organic systems, by contrast, the management control pattern is remarkably different. All-encompassing information is no longer available at the top and often critical knowledge exists only at the tentacles of the firm. Each functionary seeks out and interprets for himself the information needed to perform his part of the overall task. Much back-and-forth exchange of information ensues. Communication patterns resemble lateral consultation more than vertical command. These systems seem almost to be self-designing.

So, according to Burns and Stalker, environmental circumstances which shape management systems also influence the shape of the appropriate accounting and information systems. The organization of the accounting and information system department, as well as form of the system itself, should be consistent with the overall organizational design. In centralized mechanistic firms the management accounting and information system should be centralized and unilateral. In décentralized–organic firms, horizontal flows of information should be featured. A great deal more participation and discussion with line managers is required at all levels; and decentralization of responsibility to management accounting offices down the line is a necessary aspect of successful design in organic systems. Accounting and information systems need to match both the external circumstances and the social technology.

Once articulated, of course, all of this seems eminently logical—even self-evident. Yet this is always the most difficult step. Burns and Stalker, however, were the first to articulate these relationships.

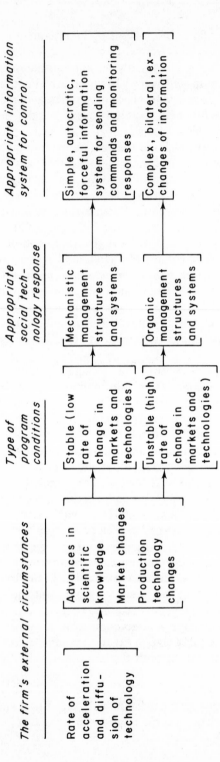

Figure 7.1 Burns and Stalker's model of external circumstances and management systems

Uncertainty and market mechanisms

Not long after Burns and Stalker's pioneering work appeared, Arrow (1964) wrote a short but excellent paper on organizational control and information flows in large firms. Arrow, of course, approached the problem with an economist's lens. Yet he finished with a theory strikingly similar to Burns and Stalker's. Unfortunately, at least for management accountants, Arrow's paper remains inadequately recognized. He is, of course, better known for his Nobel Prize-winning work on welfare economics.

Arrow bases his theory of control and information in large organizations on the effect uncertainty has on organizational decision-making and relationships. The manager, he argues, receives 'signals' from the environment and from other managers. These signals modify his perception of all the possible states (conditional probability distributions) of his job-related world. Modifications are made in light of his accumulated knowledge from both learning and experience. In addition, of course, to receiving messages, managers transmit them to each other and the decisions made are based upon their revised, current assessment of the various factors at work, within the framework of the 'operating' and 'enforcement' rules laid down by the organization. Operating rules instruct the members of an organization how to act, and enforcement rules persuade or compel them to act in accordance with the operating rules.

The process, Arrow argues, is dynamic. When decisions are made they generate further information which is transmitted in one form or another, and which leads to new decisions and signals. At the same time, new signals are coming in to the managers. Operating and enforcement rules are consequently modified in accordance with the messages transmitted. This process is depicted in Figure 7.2.

So when the upper echelons have low-cost access to the sundry conditions prevalent throughout the organization, Arrow argues, a centralized organization system can be employed to advantage. The key factor here is the availability of omniscient information to top management. This permits centralization and co-ordination of the complex flows of products and services through the various activity centers. The vitally needed co-ordination is achieved via a structured vertical hierarchy and general acceptance of plans made at the highest level. Control is exercised through specific and detailed operating rules. These are followed up with enforcement rules designed to detect and report violations of operating rules to upper management. Top management then have only to reward compliance and sanction deviations. Management accounting and information systems are an integral aspect of both the operating and enforcement rules. Thus conceived, the centralized management system seems logical, internally consistent, and complete.

But perfect transmission and assimilation of knowledge by top management, Arrow argues, is not only costly, but usually an infeasible path to pursue, in most if not all of our complex organizations. A major reason for

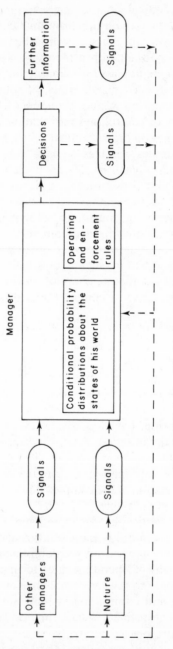

Figure 7.2 A simplified information economics model

this, he explains, is that managers are information channels of decidedly limited capacity since information, especially that received lower down in the organization, is not necessarily transmitted to the next step up the hierarchy. Another reason is that the absorption of every piece of information would, in all likelihood, lead rapidly to information overload on the part of the sundry managers in the hierarchy. But perhaps most importantly, in large organizations with their complex flow of products and services, lower-level managers will always know much more about their own spheres of activities than will higher officials. The net effect of all of this is that the centralized management system, so theoretically well-suited to the context of 'omniscient' upper management, breaks down.

A widespread response to these breakdowns, Arrow continues, is for organizations to adopt a decentralized approach to managerial arrangements. This is accomplished by rearranging the enterprise into many small, widespread, but related organizational sub-units which trade amongst themselves and with the external market as if they were independent units. A sort of quasi-miniature free market economy featuring free-wheeling economic sub-units is the result.

The operating and enforcement rules are the nervous system of this decentralized organizational arrangement. The major operating rule for each subunit is: 'maximize profits of your own activity center'. The enforcement rules here are designed to encourage each manager to increase profits as much as possible in his sphere of responsibility. In order to make these arrangements work, however, a system of incentives must be established to provide motivation for these managers to act in such a way as to enhance the overall corporate well-being. This creates new demands for information about the economic performance of each autonomous sub-unit.

These arrangements, of course, are not perfect. One problem with them, some would argue, is that if each sub-unit vigorously pursues its own profit, the various parts of the organization may work against the common organizational purpose. Goal-incongruent behavior might prevail. Goal-incongruent behavior refers to actions taken by individual managers that are in their own best interests as far as sub-unit profit maximization is concerned, but are not in the best interests of the overall firm. The organization may, as a result, even fly apart. Some mechanism is required to hold the separate pieces together.

The answer, Arrow argues, lies in market mechanisms. External market prices and negotiated internal market prices provide the necessary information which, in a sense, replace perfect knowledge. Even when the internal market prices are not available, or seem inappropriate, as is often the case, they can be approximated with the aid of mathematical programming techniques. So, actual and simulated market-based information eventually reveals to upper management those managers who are capable of prospering. By the same process the less-fit managers are exposed. The marvelous, but invisible, organization of the market-place works to provide the required information.

Thus, Arrow's theory of control in a large organization is based on the role of uncertainty in shaping organizational design, including the management control system. The nature of the information available to top management determines the relative state of uncertainty, which in turn determines the selection of either centralized or decentralized organizational arrangements. In the decentralized firm real or quasi-market prices replace the perfect information of the centralized firm. Accounting and reporting systems vary, depending on which of these arrangements is adopted. Table 7.1 summarizes these ideas. The relative state of knowledge of top management, it seems, is the key factor in the choice of organizational arrangements, including those of accounting and information systems.

Table 7.1 Arrow's model of uncertainty and information systems for control

Top management environments	Organizational structure	Information system for control	
		Operating rules	Environment rules
Relative certainty of economics of the various sub-units	Centralized system	Specific behavior instructions issued	Detect violation of instructions and administer appropriate punishment
Relative uncertainty of the economics of the various sub-units	Decentralized system	General instructions to maximize a certain objective function	Encourage managers to increase the value of the objective function as much as possible

Task uncertainty, information, and organizational design

The next model for review combines elements of the work of both Burns and Stalker, and Arrow. But while these authors suggested that the configuration of accounting and information systems are shaped by environment, Galbraith (1973) argues that the disparity between the information needed and that available determines the degree of uncertainty, which, in turn, can be dealt with from a repertoire of strategic organizational responses. Information and organizational design are the central variables of this model.

The amount of information required to be processed, according to Galbraith, is a function of three independent factors: (1) output diversity (that is the number of different services and products); (2) the number of different input resources (such as machine centers and staff groups); and (3) the difficulty of the level of performance required (such as tolerance limits of machines). The difference between the amount of information required and the amount available for processing determines the level of task uncertainty.

Organizations respond to the level of task uncertainty by following one, or even both, of two strategic alternatives. Either they reduce their need for information; or they increase their capacity to process information; and, Galbraith continues, information needs may be reduced in two ways. The first involves creating slack resources. In place of information, slack or excess resources are used to alleviate immediate problems. Excessive inventory levels, long delivery times, extra machine capacity, overtime, and staff departments are examples of areas where slack is created rather than increasing the amount of information processed. The amount of slack required, of course, depends upon the extent of uncertainty in relation to the task.

The other strategy to counter insufficient information is to create self-contained tasks. This could take the form of a shift from an interlocking responsibility for all products to responsibility for a segment only of the organization's total products. Galbraith cites the case of airplane manufacturing firms as an example. These firms have two main choices in their organizational arrangements. The first is to allocate responsibility to product engineers, design technicians, process engineers, fabricating, assembly, and test units, and so on, with each unit having responsibility for the entire aircraft. The second choice is to organize around self-contained units by airplane sections (such as a wing or the tail).

The creation of self-contained units reduces the amount of information processing needed in two ways. First, it reduces output diversity. Each self-contained unit deals only with *one* body section, whereas the functional response would require each unit to deal with *all* body sections. Second, creation of self-contained units reduces specialization. Rather than sharing, for example, process engineering across all aircraft section units, the engineers in each unit would be involved in process engineering as well as product design and quality engineering. This reduces the need for information processing *across* functional departments.

Two major strategies also exist for increasing an organization's capacity to process information. The first involves investing in vertical information systems. It is advantageous, then, to develop new annual operating plans and budgets, rather than making incremental changes to the old ones, when, for example, uncertainty levels become intolerable. This entails collecting information and new plans at appropriate times and places instead of overloading the organizational hierarchy by forcing it to cope with a vast number of budget exceptions.

The second strategy for increasing the capacity to process information involves the selective creation of new lateral relations. This move lowers the level of decision-making to the point where the information is located, instead of transmitting it to high echelons who then make the decision. This strategy decentralizes decision-making; but it does so without calling into existence new self-contained groups.

The creation of new lateral relations can be accomplished by several means. These include: direct contact amongst those who share a problem,

122

establishment of new liaison positions (such as project or product administrations) to manage interdepartmental contacts, formation of task forces such as product or project teams, or in the extreme case employment of dual reporting relations and matrix organizational structures. New lateral relations, however, are not a free good. They lead to an increase in the time managers must devote to the processing of horizontal information. This cost in time can be offset by moving decisions to the level where the information is located, rather than centers high up in the organization. This has the added advantage of guaranteeing that all relevant information is included in the decision processes. The result should be sounder decisions.

Galbraith emphasizes that these moves are not called for because of incompetent management but because the information processing and computational capacity is insufficient to deal with the complex and interdependent co-ordination requirements of an organization. Galbraith's model of information and organizational design is summarized in Figure 7.3.

A major strength of the model seems to be its perspective that information needs are a central factor in organizational design. Information and uncertainty are treated simultaneously; unlike Burns and Stalker, and Arrow, who treated them sequentially. Another strength is the insight the model provides into resolving organizational problems by judicious selection from a repertoire of strategies, rather than by relying on a narrow alignment of strategies that stem from the belief that organizational arrangements must be taken to match specific environments with a particular design.

Thus, Galbraith's model may be more realistic than those we looked at

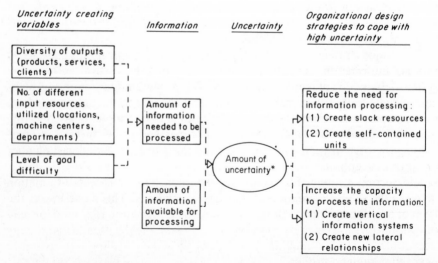

Figure 7.3 Galbraith's model of information and organizational design strategies.
*The amount of uncertainty, then, is the difference between the amount of information needed and the amount available

earlier in this chapter. Burns and Stalker argued that a mechanistic social technology is most appropriate for a stable environment, whereas organic management suits unstable settings. Arrow argued that the centralized structure is required for situations where upper echelons had available perfect information, but decentralized, quasi-market arrangements best suited situations where imperfect information prevails. By contrast, a strength of Galbraith's model is its ability to frame the problem in terms of a repertoire of responses. So instead of redefining authority, responsibility, and accountability every time a storm of uncertainty passes through the environment, organizations can weather the storm by selecting the appropriate response from our repertoire and then replacing it again when the storm passes. This would avoid a series of substantial realignments from centralized to decentralized structure—a phenomenon we see often—perhaps too often, many argue—in our organizations. A change in information systems is an alternative to organizational redesign.

Galbraith lends vividness to his theory by citing in detail the case history of a firm which produced different assembled mechanical devices for the aircraft industry. Work in this firm ranged from acquisition of raw materials to forging and stamping, to machining and the assembly of units in an orderly fashion. A conventional type of functional organizational structure was employed. Costs were under control; growth was adequate; and profits were good.

In spite of these favorable conditions, management were dissatisfied with the prevailing state of affairs. Their impression was that their time was spent in dealing with short-term problems, 'fighting fires', and neglecting the longer-run tooling and capital investment programs in the process. Of course, the lack of attention to longer-run problems eventually fed more fuel to the short-term 'fires'.

In due time a management task force was formed to study the problem. The task force produced an historical analysis of the firm's development. Members of the task force were surprised when they documented the changes that had taken place in the previous decade. The product line had doubled. The number of individual parts produced had increased by more than half, as had retooling. The number of machining and assembly stations had expanded. Quality specifications and tolerance limits had risen significantly. The production department had acquired a new expertise in dealing with exotic metals; and in order to keep up with expanding volume the number of shifts had increased from one to three. The firm had increasingly met delivery dates, while at the same time reducing inventory levels. Remarkably, until formation of the task force, the magnitude of these changes had remained almost unnoticed; but the information processed had not kept pace with production. The result had been a large increase in uncertainty and a preoccupation with 'fighting fires'.

Viewed over a suitable time period, the firm had experienced substantial changes in product diversity and volume, the number of parts produced, and the requirements for retooling. In Galbraith's terms, output diversity had increased significantly. Almost simultaneously, the number of input resources also increased, as witnessed by the expansion in the number of machining and assembly stations. At the same time, the goal levels required for quality, tolerance, delivery, and new metal technology had risen sharply. These changes in output diversity, input resources, and difficulty in maintaining the new goals meant that the amount of information in need of processing had grown by leaps and bounds.

Once the problem had been diagnosed, management moved rapidly. They selected two of Galbraith's strategic responses. First, they created more self-contained units, such as separate departments to concentrate on new products and processes. Second, they formed liaison units, including both line and staff people to handle the multi-functional interdependence at low levels in the organization. In Galbraith's terms, they brought into existence new self-contained units, and they created new lateral arrangements. These strategic alignments ameliorated the immediate problems, and management was able to concentrate on the long-run situation.

Production technology and control information

The next model from organizational sociology to be reviewed is that of Joan Woodward (1965). Her comprehensive study examined the formal organization and reporting procedures in 100 of the largest manufacturing firms in south Essex. Her research team gathered data on several organization structure variables and they obtained assessments of each firm's business success.

Her first attempt to analyze these data turned out to be disconcerting. There appeared to be a remarkable lack of connection between the measurement of success and such factors as degree of functional specialization, span of control, number of hierarchical levels, and staff–worker ratios. Then, in a remarkably insightful move, one which paid off handsomely, she grouped the firms according to their typical mode of production. Only then did the data indicate a pattern that was not random. Woodward had discovered the existence of a connection between production technology and social structure. Firms with similar manufacturing equipment and systems had similar organizational structures. Furthermore, firms within each grouping which were closest to the mean on a particular organizational variable were the most successful firms. Woodward had struck a rich vein of ore.

More specifically, she was able to link production technology to differences in span of control, communication methods, and levels of hierarchy. She observed that how a person reacts on the job depends as much on the demands of the role and circumstances as on personality; and since production technology influences the roles defined by formal organization, it must, she reasoned, also influence the individual's industrial behavior. Formal organization, she concluded, depends more on technical considerations than we had previously realized.

Woodward's work precipitated a long list of further research including the well-known Aston studies which, for over a decade, expended enormous effort attempting, ultimately in vain it seems, once and for all either to support or to falsify Woodward's central thesis that production technology strongly influences organizational arrangements. Her study, in spite of this, proved to be a milestone in the field of organizational sociology. Witness to this is the fact that James D. Thompson, the venerable organizational theorist, dedicated his celebrated book to her.

Often overlooked in her work, but of vital interest to management accounting and information system designers, is her main conclusion that the control system furnishes the key to organizational relationships. Woodward spelled out specific and distinct differences in the nature of accounting and information reporting for different production technologies (see Table 7.2). For process production technologies, she found clear-cut task definition and a close association of planning, execution, and control. The entire production process ran with perpetual, real-time process controls. Continuous evaluation of plant performance seemed mandatory since immediate corrective action is needed should plant performance deviate from programmed levels. Most of the communication flows were verbal, rather than written. Reporting systems were minimal. Accounting and control reports, arriving after the fact, merely confirmed what was already known and, if called for, adjusted.

Table 7.2 Woodward's typology of production technology and information systems for planning and control

Production technology	Characteristics of information systems for planning and control
Process	Planning and control built into process control Extensive use of verbal communication
Batch and intermediate	A series of simultaneous control systems Lack of clear-cut operationalizable standards Conflicting objectives Weakened accounting and information system role
Assembly line	Large quantity information systems Emphasis on formal and written communications Large and comprehensive data base

The situation differed for intermediate batch production technologies where large numbers of orders were handled simultaneously. Control procedures were complex. Precise definitions of objectives were often missing. Evaluation of production performance became much more difficult than for process technologies. Managers in these firms talked in vague and nebulous ways of their criteria for performance, including maximizing profits, excellent customer service, high quality standards, and as much output as possible.

These imprecisely defined factors posed severe problems for the accounting and information systems. Attempts to co-ordinate and control by a master-plan resulted only in setting a series of often impossible and contradictory targets such as the 'highest quality' and the 'lowest cost'. The response of the accounting and information system was to include a series of controls which operated simultaneously, each with subsidiary objectives for costs, quality, and service. These reports were little used. The first-line supervisors relied on their own judgement and experience rather than on the formal accounting and control systems. Planning and control departments, attached to the line just above the first line of supervision, were separated and distant from the executive function. As often as not, these units were considered to be merely useless, paper-producing mills.

For assembly line technologies, the quantity of formal accounting and information flows increased dramatically. Here Woodward noticed that the discretion of line supervisors was reduced and that of the staff groups enlarged as compared to batch and intermediate production situations. Line-staff conflicts were frequent, and managers relied on formal reports and written communiqués to protect themselves. Further, large quantities of detailed and accurate information seemed necessary to rationalize large, complex assembly line production operations such as those found in an automobile plant. Assembly lines had to be kept moving to reap the economies of large scale. Accurate, reliable, timely, and appropriate information was essential.

So it seems that the nature of a firm's production technology has a great deal of influence over role definition and organizational structures. This comparative study suggests that there is no 'one best way' of designing accounting and information systems to suit all organizations. Traditional explanatory variables, like good personal relationships and close identification of managers with the firm's goals, fell by the wayside in her study. Only when the researchers began to categorize organizations and look at the differences between their production technologies did they begin to realize that different types of organizations required different accounting and information systems. Systems which were well suited to process technology firms were ill suited to mass-production firms. Logical and patterned connections exist, it seems, between the nature of a firm's production technology and the accounting and information systems designed to serve them.

ORGANIZATIONAL MODELS AS ANALYTICAL TOOLS

These ideas suggest that impersonal forces such as environment, uncertainty, information availability, organizational design, and production processes have important relationships with accounting and information systems. Such relationships often come across as lifeless abstractions and may seem remote when compared to personality, leadership styles, and participation. In order to breathe some life into them, we shall present excerpts from a couple of practical examples and then discuss them against the background of the models outlined in the previous chapter. The models are used as analytical devices to provide insights into the workings of accounting and information systems in real-life situations.

The case of a national finance company

Our first situation, a national finance company, is relatively straightforward.

Consumer Acceptance Company (CAC) was one of the largest finance companies in the nation with hundreds of branch offices across the country. Its primary business was the acceptance of conditional sales contracts from customers who had purchased consumer goods. Usually customers could not get loans from chartered banks and so turned to commercial loan companies for finances. The company paid the retailer while the customer paid CAC in monthly instalments. It operated nationally and had several regional offices located in major cities. Branch offices were located in most cities and towns including downtown areas and suburb shopping centers. The branch offices varied in size from three to forty personnel depending on the market served and the amount of money loaned. Branch offices received money for loans from the Central Office and at the end of each working day all branch bank accounts were closed out to a Central Office bank account. Branches, however, reported through one of five district offices to the Central Office.

The Central Corporate Office, located in a large city in the center of the nation, functioned as a central policy-making and administrative center. The Central Office established specific policies and procedures regarding every aspect of branch operations including: loans, collections, record-keeping, branch control and reporting methods, personnel policies, and detailed job descriptions for all branch positions and office administration procedures. These standard operating procedures, designed to ensure consistent branch operations across the nation, were contained in procedures manuals located in each branch. They emphasized that branch managers should aggressively seek new profitable accounts, make sure payments were received on time, and run a neat, tidy and efficient office with all records and reports continually up-to-date.

On the third working day of the month each branch submitted to the Central Office, as well as to its District Office, a report for the previous month. The report contained the essential statistics about branch operations including: the number and dollar value of all loans, details of collections, branch expenses by line item category, and a detailed aging schedule which stressed overdue accounts and delinquency rates. These reports were sent to the Central Office for computer analysis of branch operations including a multiple regression analysis which analyzed office expenses and personnel levels according to the number of branch transactions for the month. The computer also compiled this information into a district report which compared all branches in the district and ranked branch performance for each district. These reports, of course, were provided to each branch so they could compare themselves with other branches in their district. Branch managers, very sensitive about their relative performance, eagerly awaited this report each month. Interestingly, budgets and long-range plans are noticeable by their absence.

More recently, CAC had installed an on-line computer system which connected each branch to a large computer at the Central Office. Branch transactions were entered each day, and a summary of operations by branch, district, and for the entire company was submitted early the next morning to the President. Branch managers could also call for an update on their branch operations for the month to date.

The district managers closely monitored the monthly reports, scrutinizing them for anything that appeared out of line, especially new loans and accounts which were over thirty days overdue. If a branch seemed out of line, the district manager and a staff member paid a quick visit to get to the bottom of the problem; and, if warranted, a staff expert was assigned to the branch until performance reached a satisfactory level. In addition, each district manager conducted a thorough, on-hand inspection of each branch at least once a year. During the visits, which were made on a surprise basis, the district manager and his staff performed a comprehensive audit of all loan and collection records as well as inspection of employee performance evaluation and pay rates. At the end of this visit the district manager conducted the annual performance evaluation review of the branch and assistant managers. The review included setting objectives for the next year regarding any aspect of branch operations needing attention.

Branch managers operated their branches with some autonomy, hiring and training their own staff personnel and taking full responsibility for loans, collections, and expenses. Branch managers could earn an additional 30 percent of their annual salary in the form of a bonus based on branch performance. In addition, company-wide contests were a regular feature where the best-performing managers won, say, a free trip for two to Mexico. Branch managers were highly satisfied with these arrangements, including the controls and reports, and particularly the autonomy and responsibility that they perceived with the job.

At first blush, the accounting information and control system at CAC seems excessively comprehensive. Standard operating procedures cover all aspects of branch operations. Every nook and cranny is monitored, reported on, and scrutinized on the spot. Surprise visits and spot checks are the order of the day; and branch performance is reported daily to the president's office. It would seem to be a prime illustration of the very kind of oppressive and punitive control system observed by Argyris as described earlier.

Analysis of CAC's accounting, information, and control systems with the models in the previous chapter, however, yields a different perspective. In terms of Burns and Stalker's model it is apparent that CAC has a well-defined social technology. Tasks are divided into distinct slots. Precise duties are defined for each branch position. Power and authority arrangements are unambiguously allocated to corporate, district, and branch managers. Heavy reliance is placed on vertical hierarchial arrangements; and operations are co-ordinated from the top, the only place where overall knowledge of the firm resides. The simple but forceful management control system reinforces this pattern. Instructions flow downward through the hierarchy, becoming more explicit at each successive layer in a unilateral and autocratic control style. CAC seems almost the archetypical mechanistic firm.

This social technology, nevertheless, is well suited to the firm's circumstances. Markets are well defined. Procedures for operating a branch are well understood. Scientific knowledge is minimal. So with the exception of the short-term money market, the environment is stable. (CAC, like most consumer financial companies, had a precarious financial structure consisting mainly of short-term money market notes, some long-term debt, and very little equity. They turned a profit on the margin between short-term borrowings and interest rates charged to customers. Consequently, it is absolutely essential that the branches are tightly controlled and responsive to calling in or expanding loans depending upon short-term fluctuations in the money market.) CAC's mechanistic social technology, then, is consistent with its operating environment.

Turning to Arrow's model of uncertainty and control systems, CAC mirrors the centralized prototype. Top management have at their disposal, at a low cost, omniscient information about nearly every circumstance anywhere in the organization. Centralized co-ordination is achieved through specific and detailed operating rules contained in the standard operating procedures. These are complemented by enforcement rules which detect and report violations from the procedures to upper echelons. The branches are monitored closely, and visits by district managers follow quickly if anything untoward is detected. So uncertainty is low; in fact, it cannot be tolerated because of the precarious capitalization, and the centralized management system fits perfectly the top management environment.

Analysis of the CAC situation using Galbraith's ideas confirms the above conclusions. Output diversity is low, goals are reasonably achievable. The branch offices are self-contained and highly homogeneous. Consequently, the amount of information requiring processing is relatively small and most if not all of it is available to top management. Formal control information is simple, low in quantity, and handled readily with a straightforward but forceful vertical information system. CAC, then, has made an appropriate response to its uncertainty-creating variables.

The case of Aluminium Extruders (U.K.)

Our second illustration traces the evolution of the information system for control through a corporate reorganization. The organization, Aluminium Extruders (AE), is a recently acquired U.K. subsidiary of a large, widely diversified, integrated, global, metal producing company headquartered in North America. Recently the company had acquired several metal firms in Europe. AE specialized in new technology for special aluminium applications to customer order. AE's products had a wide variety of possible applications, new applications were being developed all the time, and engineering technology changed rapidly. Products also required specialized engineering work with close co-ordination of manufacturing, field sales personnel, and engineering on production schedules and delivery deadlines.

The old situation

> The new managing director of AE concluded that the present organizational design was ill-suited for exploiting new product opportunities. The different functional people simply were not working together. Many reasons were suggested for this. The managers did not know who held the responsibility and authority to develop new products. Upper management did not pay enough attention to this activity. Delays occurred as information travelled up and down the proper functional channels. R&D efforts appeared to be disproportionately allocated among product lines due to the personal influence of a few product specialists; and squabbles continually erupted amongst the functional managers over designs and production schedules. These disputes had to be sent up the line to top management and so were delayed, postponed, or even left unresolved. These symptoms underlined the difficulties encountered by the various functional groups as they wrestled with new product development. In a few instances, however, engineers, marketing managers, and manufacturing personnel had formed informal work groups and successfully worked out common problems for specific products.

According to Burns and Stalker's model in Figure 7.1, AE operated in an unstable environment. There is ample evidence for this conclusion. Engineering technology changed rapidly. Products required a high degree of engineering competence. AE custom-manufactured products according to the needs and whims of customers; and the market for the products had grown rapidly. Program conditions were characterized by a high rate of change in both markets and technologies.

Turning to AE's social technology, we see evidence that they were employing a mechanistic management structure. The organization was essentially functional with different executives assigned responsibility for manufacturing, marketing, engineering, and finance. Vertical hierarchical arrangements predominated for issuing orders. Conflicts went up the hierarchy for resolution and decisions were passed down. Top management attempted to co-ordinate the various function units from on high. The management structure, it would appear, was mechanistic.

Now, according to the model, AE has a serious mismatch in that a mechanistic structure does not suit an unstable environment. In fact, signs of conflict had begun to appear. Continual squabbles occurred between departments. Decisions on differences moved very slowly up and down the vertical hierarchy. R&D efforts were inefficiently allocated among product lines. Attractive market opportunities had been neglected. The mechanistic structure seemed to be under considerable stress. An organizational design study group had already begun to identify the mismatch.

It may be protested by some that if we look more closely, AE's management systems are less mechanistic than it seems at first glance. There is no quarrel with this. A partial division of executive responsibilities had been established. The functional jurisdictions had begun to melt; the controller had instituted monthly product line profit and loss statements; and a few small, informal groups, composed of engineers, plant people, and marketers had sprung up to work out common problems. The informal social technology, it seems, was moving towards more organic arrangements; and top management had begun to sense that the degree and kind of instability in markets and scientific technology facing the firm was not well served by the present organizational arrangements.

Arrow's model in Table 7.1 leads us to a similar conclusion. Top management seemed to lack information about the state of affairs, events, and problems at the lower levels and at the boundaries of the organization. Enough information was not being transmitted upwards to top management. Messages traveling through the transmission channels bogged down. As a result, operating rules issued by top management were often inappropriate, and their efforts to co-ordinate the complex flow of products through the functional departments to customers were ineffective. The use of the vertical channels, and attempts to follow higher-level plans, meant delays which cost market opportunities. The centralized style of management arrangements was inappropriate to the amount of information available at the upper strata of the organization and top management's ability to assimilate it.

Galbraith's model in Figure 7.3 hinges on the difference between the amount of information required for processing relative to the amount already processed by the organization. The amount required is a composite of output diversity, input resources utilized, and the difficulty of the level of performance required. For AE's mix of activities it seems clear that the level of both output diversity and input resources utilized was high. The difficulty of the level of performance required also seems high. The highly technical nature of the product lines bears witness to this conclusion. A high degree of engineering competence was required for most products.

Obviously, then, the amount of information required for processing was great, if not vast. Although we have no direct documentation of the amount of information already processed by the organization, several factors indicate that it was much lower than required. Co-ordination of the functional departments, particularly on new product development, was not adequate. A comprehensive plan did not exist. Sensing the need for more communication and information, informal product groups began to appear; and the works accountant had begun to produce financial information relating to product line. All this suggests that a strategic organizational response was badly needed in order to close the gap between the amount of information required and the amount available.

Let us return to the case for a description of AE's response.

The new situation

A new profit-centered organization design was instituted featuring several decentralized profit-responsible product groups assisted by staff departments including R&D, Sales, and Finance. Several product departments were established within each product group. These were headed by department managers in charge of marketing, engineering, and production units for their assigned products. Their main responsibility was to co-ordinate all activities of their product lines, including the sales force and R&D efforts which were not under their command, and assure that the products were profitable. The marketing unit worked on marketing strategy, pricing, contacting customers on special requests and factory problems, promotion, and new product development. The production unit was responsible for efficient manufacturing, meeting delivery dates, and production costs. The engineering unit designed new products, devised new production processes, and worked on special customer requests. A production control manager looked after scheduling of work, supervised expediting, shipping and delivery, inventory, and purchasing clerks. The product department managers were the king-pins of the new organizational arrangements.

These changes correspond closely to the prescriptions of our theoretical models. They would, for example, prescribe a shift to organic management structures to suit the high rate of change in the external circumstances of their scientific knowledge, markets and, in all likelihood, their production technology. This seems to mirror the actual events. Powers and duties shifted from functional–vertical responsibility to product–lateral accountability. The product department managers became responsible for managing the lateral relationships involved in the design, marketing, production, and selling of the products assigned to them. So they had to have considerable understanding of the various overall goals and tasks of the entire AE organization. Matters such as R&D and the sales force, however, were not under their jurisdictional authority. Duties and powers in these areas would be in a state of continual negotiation and flux. Top management was no longer in a position to know everything about the various product centers. The new management structure, then, had shifted from mechanistic to organic organizational arrangements.

We also see that AE no longer attempted to co-ordinate their complex flow of products from the top of the hierarchy by issuing clear, firm commands based upon omniscient information, and following up with punitive enforcement rules and sanctions. Rather, they reorganized around quasi-independent, miniature, free-market product groups—each with responsibility, if not the entire authority, for profitable survival in their own market sphere.

Previously, the company faced a gap between the amount of information required for processing and the amount available. The response followed two major strategies. First, it created slack resources by some duplication of manufacturing resources and by investing in inside marketing personnel. Second, it created self-contained units in the form of profit-responsible product departments. These two moves reduced the need for information processing.

At the same time, AE also increased their capacity to process information. The new product–profit responsibility required a vertical accounting information system that provided information on financial performance for product groups; and to manage the new product departments the product group managers needed to be involved in a significant amount of lateral communication, negotiation, and building of reliable relationships. They were required to 'manage' the product flow from R&D through engineering, sales, manufacturing, delivery, and customer service. The company, then, employed all four coping responses: creation of new self-contained units, employment of organizational slack, development of vertical information systems, and creation of new lateral relationships. The new organizational design seems better suited to the amount of information processing required than was the old.

We shall next look at the new management accounting and information system and its workings in some detail. It also will be assessed in terms of our organization design models.

The new management accounting and control information system

The performance of the new profit centers was measured to a large extent by the actual profits they earned. Each profit center manager formulated a detailed one-year and general five-year profit plan for top management to review and adjust if necessary. During the year, actual performance was continually evaluated against this plan. The structure of this control system, then, was straightforward—planned profits versus actual. Formulating and use of this control device, however, proved to be a rich and elaborate process.

For example, in the aluminium rolled product department (ARP) the new department manager began preparation of the next year's plan in October. First, he put together a detailed sales plan by obtaining sales estimates from his own marketing personnel, with assistance from central marketing staff, as well as from the field sales force. The two estimates served as a double check and also served to induce widespread participation in the plan and, consequently, top management hoped, help insure its effectiveness. Both groups went about the task thoroughly. The sales force built up their estimates on a customer-by-customer analysis while the marketing personnel worked down from general economic conditions and overall product line estimates. When the sales force estimate proved larger than that of the marketing personnel, he selected the latter figure and began estimating manufacturing costs.

In order to accomplish this he estimated direct material costs and consumption factors based on the sales estimates, and called on the production personnel to estimate other direct product costs, supervisory salaries, and overhead expenses. Next he had all his managers detail their personnel and other indirect costs. After gathering all this information he estimated a profit-volume-cost plan which top management reviewed in relation to profit and sales goals for the entire subsidiary. It became clear to the new managing director that the combined plans of all departments would not meet the overall AE goal. After an analysis of market penetration, new product development, and other factors, the planned sales volume for the ARP department was discussed by upper line management with the profit center manager and revised upward significantly. All agreed, however, that the new plan was attainable but tough.

Every week the ARP manager received a detailed statement of actual profit performance compared to plan, as well as manufacturing expenses by cost centers. He then devised a profit cost–volume report which isolated fixed and variable expenses. These reports were used to analyze expenses and as the basis of meetings with shop hands and ARP managers to discuss variances.

Although the precise relation of profit performance to promotion and salary decisions had never been explicitly stated, the department manager knew that the EA managing director and controller met frequently to review the performance of each profit center to identify unsatisfactory performance. Each month the profit center managers went before the managing director to review progress and explain variations from the annual profit plan. The ARP profit center manager also knew that he was given a formal appraisal review every four months by his superior at which time his department's performance in relation to its plan was evaluated. Furthermore, he knew full well that the managing director's performance in relation to his plan was being constantly monitored by the corporate controller in headquarters overseas in North America. The ARP profit center manager knew he was to take the steps necessary to meet the profit objective. During periods when he was below plan, there was considerable pressure to increase sales efforts, meet with R&D to develop new products, and to reduce asset levels.

The philosophy of control that pervaded the firm's global operations had been developed by the corporate controller in North America. The main feature was complete decentralization of profit responsibility but with built in tough targets. This way profit center managers were limited in the degrees of freedom available for building in organizational slack in operating budgets. As well the pressure was kept on them for growth. The corporate controller believed this was an excellent way for managers to develop business acumen. Those that did were readily identified and rewarded while those that did not were quickly relegated to technical jobs.

Uncertainty and managerial accounting and control information systems

It was established earlier that AE operated under highly uncertain circumstances. So, according to Arrow, it is best served by decentralized managerial arrangements which feature a free-market economy. The reason for this is that knowledge of environmental conditions, such as market prices and customer idiosyncrasies, were in the hands of the product department managers at the tentacles of the organization, rather than with upper management. These managers, being closer to customers, could then respond quickly and accurately to market-place changes. The sundry product-based, profit centers employed by AE were, in effect, an attempt to effect a miniature free-market economy. Responsibility for the profit of a cluster of products was decentralized to each product group manager, who had command over most of the resources and people involved in his cluster of product–market relationships.

The new operating rules at AE for the product group managers were to maximize the profits of their responsibility centers. Profit was the mandate. As for enforcement rules, they knew that the upper management group met frequently to review the performance of each profit center. This group also used profit performance to pinpoint trouble spots; and every four months each profit center manager was given a formal appraisal which included a review of profit performance. So actual profit performance was constantly being evaluated against planned levels. These enforcement rules, it seems, would encourage the product group managers to increase profits as much as possible in their sphere of responsibility. Managers who made profits would be recognized and appreciated. The new management control system, along with the new organizational decentralization and the revised operating and enforcement rules, conform closely to the theoretical prescriptions for organizations that operate in relatively uncertain environments.

The characteristics of the new management control system also follow Burns and Stalker's prescriptions for firms operating in relatively unstable circumstances. Much critical environmental information about customers, technology, and markets is known only by the product department managers at the firm's lower levels. The new management control system highlights the effectiveness of the flow of product through the organization to the customer. So lateral consultation and exchange of information, especially about products and product performance, ensued. An important part of these exchanges took place both during the formulation of the profit budget and later when profit performance was reported against plan.

In the perspective of Galbraith's model, the creation of the new self-contained profit center departments reduced the need for information processing. Each unit processed the information it needed for profitable operations but did not transmit this detail to anyone outside the department. Upper management relied on a very simple and general accounting information system—the measurement of profits—for controlling the sundry units. Thus the amount of information processed vertically through the hierarchy was reduced considerably. The new arrangements brought the amount of information processed in line with the amount required.

We also see that the department manager designed his own variable budget information system to track expense performance of his department and to understand the effect of sales volume on allocated, non-controllable costs of other groups such as outside marketing, administration, and engineering. He sought out and interpreted for himself the expense patterns of his profit center. He also held meetings with his managers and foremen to analyze the causes of budget variances. These parts of the information system for control were self-designed. All in all, the characteristics of the new management control system closely followed the theoretical prescriptions.

These models of the fit among environment, organizational design, and the new management accounting and information systems indicate that the new management control system is well suited to its situation. There are, of course, other ways to look at this example. Some might argue that the management control system is inappropriate. They would point out that the system seems to have created some tension. The motivational force in the system to meet the profit budget is strong—perhaps too strong; and the pattern of participation, where top management have the last word on the profit and sales budget levels, seems unfair. The Management Committee's informal weekly review of profit performance might be excessively frequent. To some these could be worrisome aspects of the new management accounting and control information systems.

Yet some tension was required to make the new concept of product profit centers work. The frequent review of performance provided the necessary motivational force; and participation in the budget setting was widespread even though top management, with their broader view of the total scheme of things, should be entitled to have the final say in setting budget levels. Delegation of profit responsibility without some way of providing motivation, and without a means of monitoring results, and without recourse to make obvious adjustments to inappropriate budgets, would seem to be both impractical and imprudent.

Either way, the macro-perspective of the organizational model does put the organizational design, and the function of management accounting and information systems, into a broader perspective. The models seem capable of giving us new insights into problems of designing accounting and information systems.

CONCLUSIONS

This chapter has introduced management accounting and information system managers to the idea that organizational structure and management systems might vary according to the type of environment faced, the production technology employed, and the nature of the actual work done. The general thesis of the various models reviewed is that these factors, which shape organizational arrangements, may also account for differences in our accounting and information systems.

This chapter has sought to outline some of the macro-aspects of organizational life that the personal factors approach either neglected or assumed. The contribution to management accounting and information system design of this way of thinking has not been to approach accounting and information design as a problem in social psychology, but rather as one of seeking a congruence in the characteristics of accounting and information systems with those of the organizational setting; characteristics such as environment, technology, available knowledge, type of work, and uncertainty. This line of reasoning is different from, but not contradictory to, the views about accounting and information systems in previous chapters.

But perhaps even more important than its contribution to our thinking about the design of accounting and information systems is what this approach

138

offers for the analysis of the problem of system design. We have argued, for example, that environmental circumstances—including the degree and kind of instability in market, production, and scientific technologies—are key factors shaping management accounting and information systems. We also have new insights into the appropriate characteristics of management accounting and control systems—particularly the nature of operating and enforcement rules—for both the centralized and decentralized structures. We have shown how management accounting and information processing are inextricably intertwined with issues of organizational design, that the basic activity of any organization is to process information, and that organizations should be designed according to their information processing needs. We have also seen how management accounting and information systems vary according to the type of production technology. An unanticipated but pleasing consequence of all this is that some neat conceptual schemes have already come to light for analyzing the complex problem of accounting and information system design.

Conceptual apparatuses like these, which link impersonal forces with organizational processes, would seem to hold great potential for explaining the design and use of accounting and information systems. For when we have learned how these systems can be rearranged in various settings so that they are no longer random, we may develop a clearer notion of how systems designers should proceed. Then we need not concern ourselves so much with the individual traits and idiosyncratic behavior of the managers involved. For it may well be, as Horngren (1971) suggests, that it is an impossible goal to try to tailor accounting and information systems to the quirks and personalities of individuals. The commitment of research in behavioral accounting, Horngren argues, should be to discover patterns which are relevant to information processes generally, rather than to the question of autocratic or democratic management and the personality differences of individual managers. More likely, however, both are crucial.

References

Arrow, K., 'Control in large organizations', *Management Science*, Vol. IV, No. 3, 1964.
Burns, T., and G. M. Stalker, *The Management of Innovation*, Tavistock, London, 1961.
Galbraith, J., *Designing Complex Organizations*, Addison-Wesley, Reading, Mass., 1973.
Horngren, C. T., 'The accounting discipline in 1999', *The Accounting Review*, January 1971, pp. 1–11.
Woodward, J., *Industrial Organization: Theory and Practice*, Oxford University Press, London, 1965.

CHAPTER 8

Organizational Theory and Management Accounting and Information Systems

The sociological perspective has firmly established that an organization's accounting and information system is affected by particular forces in each setting. This realization set the stage for a small but important series of studies that adopted an organizational theory approach to understanding the patterned variations so readily observable in accounting and information systems across organizations. The arena of organizational theory includes investigations of the way organizations in the round arrive at their goals and strategies, as well as how they go about selecting their organizational structures and their management systems. From this perspective, organizations are only 'intendedly' rational, since their limited capacities prevent anything near complete rationality (Perrow, 1972). The interest is more in their natural history than in their rationalistic pursuits.

This chapter reviews several major accounting and information studies adopting the organizational theory perspective. It may come as a pleasant surprise for many readers to learn that a rich store of knowledge is slowly but surely falling into place as a result of these investigations.

Role specialization and accounting systems

In one of the earliest studies adopting an organizational theory approach, Golembiewski (1964) related role specialization to the way management accounting systems are used in organizations. The way an organization divides up its work, he argued, leads to different ways of using internal accounting information. Organizations featuring responsibility centers specializing in a small number of activities will use accounting information extensively for score-card-keeping. Specialization, of course, encourages separatism and so the critical organizational problem is the need for a delicate integration of the work of the various specialized units into a common and smooth flow without encroaching on the prerogatives of the speciality units. But when things go awry, and a coherent flow of work does not ensue, upper management are prone to place undue emphasis on the scorekeeping data provided by the management accountant.

Management accountants, of course, will spy the underlying problem immediately. Over-emphasis on one segment in the flow of work through an organization does not square with the widely accepted management accounting principle, that individuals should be charged only with costs over which they have control. Yet in the highly specialized organization, score-card information must stem from subjective allocation of common costs to the various specialized units. This in turn leads the accountant to assign the cost of an error arbitrarily to one unit or another. And to make matters worse, upper management often use score-card data in a blunt fashion to force integration. Conflicting demands placed on management accounting reports is the unhappy result. They are used not only to establish goals for co-operative efforts, but also as a means of identifying unco-operative efforts, but also as a means of identifying unco-operative and unproductive units. Balancing these conflicting roles, even under the most amicable conditions, is a difficult and delicate task.

It is because of this that management accounting reports become the focal point in the battlefield of sorting out responsibility for both good and poor performance. Department heads naturally wish to appear in a favorable light and strive mightily to have their own departments look good. So they are quick to wage political warfare when they feel disadvantaged in the assignment of costs; and they are keenly aware that the ability of any particular department to disrupt the total flow of work can be used as a lever for a more advantageous assignment of costs.

As a result, accountants are pressured to unearth crucial data about the warring department and to get the managers to agree with the allocation methodology. In order to do this the accountant must have enough power to be taken seriously by the organization and to counteract those line managers who question the legitimacy of the management accounting office. The management accounting office is pitted against the line managers and, consequently, becomes preoccupied with jostling for power and focusing on the score-card-keeping role. This, in turn, leads to defensive attitudes, self-preservation reactions, separatist dispositions, jurisdictional disputes, and duplication of efforts by the line organization. When this occurs the effectiveness of the management accounting effort is diminished not only for scorekeeping activities, but also for the important attention-directing and problem-solving roles.

By contrast, some organizational designs feature self-contained units responsible for all the elements necessary to produce the entire product or service. The line organization, which has considerable power and minimal dependence on other line units, includes management accounting personnel who report on a solid-line basis to the unit manager and on a dotted-line basis to the headquarters accounting staff office. Providing accounting information about performance measurement is a relatively simple task, mainly because the problems associated with the allocation of common costs and the pinpointing of errors are minimized since status conflicts no longer depend on the assignment of costs over which the line managers have only partial or no control, and for which they have only ambiguous responsibility. This is a considerably more favorable situation for the management accountant. Reports are not used as a goad to superior performance so the pressure is taken off both internal reporting and accountants. The line units can be compared in terms of simple, yet meaningful, measures of performance, such as return on investment. Natural competition ensues as each line unit strives to outperform the others. Score-card information is no longer so crucial, nor is it subject to arbitrary allocations. As a result, accounting information receives more telling emphasis. These circumstances are congenial to the three scorekeeping, attention-directing, and problem-solving roles of internal reporting and, importantly, to the accountant.

Golembiewski, then, sketches out two contrasting organizational designs and relates them to the management accounting job. Even though these ideas have not been verified by empirical research, and while the two scenarios may exaggerate the problems of the functional–specialist organizational structure and stress only the positive arguments for the self-contained organizational design, they do, nevertheless, demonstrate vividly the profoundly different consequences that a simple structural variation can have for the management accountant.

Environment and accounting systems

Hofstede (1967) produced the next important work linking organizational theory to accounting and information systems. The study, aimed at determining how to live with budgetary standards and yet be motivated by them, consisted of an exhaustive investigation of the budgeting systems in six large manufacturing plants in five different industries—printing, metal products, textiles, electronics, and food. He gathered data by examining company records and interviewing 70 line manufacturing managers, controllers, management accountants, and work-study engineers. It is noteworthy that while he directed his research towards linking human relations aspects such as leadership style, participation, attitudes, satisfaction, and motivation to budget-related behavior, he concluded that economic, technological and sociological considerations have a more important impact on the way budgeting systems function.

In the printing company, for example, customer service was paramount. Managers and workers alike seemed impressed with the necessity to pay close attention to the whims of customers. Emergency orders and customer impulses took precedent over preset production plans, budgets, and standard cost accounting systems. By contrast, in the metal products, textile, and electrical components plants, an engineers' climate prevailed; rationality of manufacturing, the dominant requirement, was aided considerably by a smoothly functioning management accounting system. In the fifth plant, a food and tobacco processing firm, manufacturing held secondary importance to purchasing; so much so that the top purchasing executive ranked above the top manufacturing manager. The standard cost accounting system for manufacturing functioned as an internal affair of that department, not as an integrated part of the company-wide budgetary control system which, in fact, had little or no influence on managerial behavior. Key competitive factors, Hofstede concluded, have a substantial impact on the use and influence of management accounting and control systems.

These results have been supported by later studies. Otley (1978), for example, studied the use of financial control systems in a coal-mining firm. In 'tough' operating environments where making a profit is difficult, upper management used budgetary information to keep the pressure on lower-level managers. But in 'liberal' operating environments, where profits come easily, upper management used budgetary information more for problem-solving purposes. Good companies, it seems, match their organizational design to the demands of their circumstances. Environment, technology, and markets, as well as internal human relations, go a long way in explaining the way budgets work in organizations, but external causes seem to be more fundamental.

Competition, internal variables, and the use of sophisticated controls

The idea that markets and competition might have an important influence on management accounting and control systems was the focus of a thorough and well-designed study by Khandwalla (1972), who found that the intensity and type of competition accentuates the need to determine whether or not organizational subunits are operating as expected. The study included 97 large firms distributed over a wide range of industries and manufacturing technologies. The president of each firm rated three types of competition—price, marketing, and product—for intensity and for its importance to profitability. Similar ratings by marketing executives about competition served as an independent check on the validity of the presidents' ratings. The presidents also rated their firms on the extent to which each of nine management accounting and control devices (standard cost systems, marginal cost data, flexible budgets, internal auditing, performance audits, discounted cash flow analysis, statistical quality control techniques, operations research modeling for inventory, production scheduling, and systematic evaluation of managers) were used in their company. The three competition indices were combined into an overall index of competition and the nine control devices were combined into an overall index of the degree of sophistication of controls. The two scales proved to be statistically related. This result supported the general premise that competitive conditions tend to increase the use of sophisticated controls.

In addition, a number of interesting specific relationships emerged. Product competition, for instance, had the greatest impact on the usage of controls. What may be happening, the study speculates, is that competition stimulates a great deal of new product activity which, in turn, leads to more complex organizations. Different markets are sought out, R&D is required, new products are market-tested, and advanced production processes are adopted. As a result, a highly technocratic organization evolves, featuring decentralization, differentiation of subunits, and a requirement for a great deal of integration and co-ordination. The response is to use sophisticated controls as a powerful integrative device to enforce standards across interdependent departments and furnish firm-wide norms of performance. Product competition, it seems, triggers a host of reactions, including greater use of sophisticated controls.

These speculations seem highly plausible. After all, bringing new products on the market requires a great deal of planning and co-ordination, an important function of management accounting systems. It also seems likely that information regarding performance of the new products would be of vital interest to managers at all levels. So the performance measurement function should loom large. Further, new product development entails problem-solving, a function that is well served by accounting systems since they provide vital information for rate of return analysis, make-or-buy decision analysis, and new-product pricing decisions. So new-product activity should lead to greater use of management information and control devices which help, not only for integration and co-ordination, but also for the problem-solving and performance measurement requirements of new-product activity.

By comparison, marketing competition, including both distribution and promotion, had only a modest impact on the usage of management controls. Only one control, the use of statistical quality control of production, emerged with a significant correlation. Product quality is likely a key factor in winning customers under conditions of heavy promotion and distribution competition. The obsession with quality of Japanese automobile firms is a case in point. They overtook US and European competition at a time when price and product loomed less important to customers than quality and reliability. In the highly competitive world car market, promotional promises and dealer networks are important; but they must be backed up by reliable, quality vehicles. It seems only reasonable, then, that statistical quality control information is critical under conditions of heavy marketing competition.

Price competition proved not to be associated with the degree of usage of sophisticated controls. The overall level of price competition in the sample was high and its impact, Khandwalla speculates, might be great at lower levels in the organization where managers are directly on the firing line. Unfortunately, data were not collected at this level. Interestingly price competition proved to have the highest correlation with the presidents' perception of the extent to which raising their firms' profits was frustrated by the competitive acts of rival firms. What might be happening is that under severe competition organizations become cautious and are reluctant to invest in risky projects such as control systems where payoffs are indirect and uncertain. An alternative explanation is that when price is the critical competitive factor, information and controls on aspects other than price are of only marginal interest.

This is an important study. It establishes that competition influences both the type of financial controls employed and the way they are used. It also points to the potential for systematic measurement, perhaps through the use of structured questionnaires, of different forms of competition to supplement the usual management accounting reporting system—expanding its scope to monitor environmental variables systematically is a tantalizing possibility. A better understanding of the way external variables affect the need for information could well enhance the effectiveness of control systems.

Khandwalla (1974) also investigated the relationship of internal organizational variables, including size, mass-output orientation of technology, vertical integration, and decentralization of top-level decisions with the use of sophisticated controls. The technology variable consisted of a continuum of production uniformity ranging from custom fabrication for customer's specification at one end, to large-scale mass-production assembly line or continuous process at the other. The vertical integration variable represented the degree of ownership of factors of production and channels of distribution. The results indicated that the use of sophisticated controls is positively associated with size, vertical integration, and decentralization. What may be happening is that in order to cope with the complexity resulting from vertical integration and size, organizations decentralize decision-making to conditionally autonomous subunits and then turn to sophisticated controls to co-ordinate their activities and keep track of their performance.

Then, in an insightful and rewarding move, Khandwalla divided the sample into high- and low-profit firms. The results revealed a strikingly different pattern between the two groups. The more profitable firms responded quite differently to the problems posed by size and mass output. For one thing, they were more vertically integrated. Control of sources of raw materials and distribution channels protects the large investment in mass-production technology but it also leads to greater complexity. The response is to decentralize decision-making power to autonomous subunits. This in turn calls for an increase in the use of sophisticated controls in order to co-ordinate the diverse set of activities and to provide top management with the means to review and judge the effectiveness of the decentralized sub-units. Controls, then, proved to be the critical link which enables these large, complex firms to follow the principle of 'decentralization with co-ordinated controls', an organizational adaptation which proved so successful for decades for firms like Dupont, General Motors, Sears, and Standard Oil of New Jersey (Sloan, 1963).

The low-profit firms, by contrast, exhibited a quite different pattern. Rather than decentralize and use more sophisticated controls as the degree of mass-production of technology increased, they attempted to co-ordinate and control through centralizing decision-making. The low-profit group did, however, increase their usage of controls in the face of increases in size and vertical integration. By contrast, the high-profit group increased their usage of controls along with increases in decentralization and greater mass-production technology orientation. The two groups also differed in their response to increased vertical integration. The low-profit group increased the use of controls, whereas the high-profit group did just the opposite. Khandwalls speculates that the latter firms look more to direct integrating and co-ordinating devices, such as project teams, link-pin roles, and the creation of a climate of co-ordination. The significant point is that these different responses appeared to have a major impact on profitability.

The message that emerges is important. Controls are an important dimension of a wider 'gestalt' of organizational factors. They must be integrated, along with other organizational design factors, into a functional whole with properties not derivable from the summation of the parts. It would appear that the high-profit firms are more sensitive to this and select controls appropriate to their wider gestalt. Realizing the correct configuration is by no means straightforward; but it seems to be crucial.

Organizational complexity and control and information systems

Khandwalla (1977) also investigated the association of organizational structures and processes, including control and information systems, with factors such as technology, economic conditions, decentralization, and participation. He conceived of control and information systems as a scale ranging from 'small and rudimentary' at one end to 'extensive with delivery by advanced computer and MIS experts' at the other. The controls in the scale included: quality control of production, internal audit, personnel evaluation, standard cost systems with variance analysis, operations analysis with accounting ratios, break-even analysis, cost center accounting, inventory control by operations research tools, sophisticated capital budgeting analysis, and the extent of formal staff activity gathering market and prospects intelligence. These elements were combined into an aggregate control and information system scale in order to investigate its association with sundry situational variables.

The results indicated that the use of sophisticated control and information systems increases with the complexity and intricacy of their organizational setting. The control and information scale was positively associated with several impersonal factors including: environmental sophistication and heterogeneity, automated and mass-production technology, vertical integration, and size. It was also positively associated with personal factors including devolution of decision-making and the pursuit of optimum resource utilization. Diverse, complex, competitive, and innovative organizational settings, it seems, make co-ordination and control difficult. So it is not surprising that, in these circumstances, control and information systems emerge as a key aspect of organizational infrastructure.

Other impersonal factors did not prove to be associated with the use of such systems. What may be happening, Khandwalla speculates, is that in turbulent settings, where outcomes are difficult to predict, sophisticated financial controls and information systems may not be cost-effective. Firms do better by playing it 'by ear' rather than 'optimizing based on historical information'. They cope by keeping their options open and reacting to events as they occur.

Although Khandwalla did not speculate on the matter, the above results might be generalized in terms of complexity in the organizational setting. The relationship of the usage of sophisticated controls with complexity seems to be an inverted 'U' shape rather than linear. When complexity is low, sophisticated controls are little needed. As complexity increases, however, their utility increases sharply at first and then levels off. Beyond that point their utility begins to decline as complexity becomes so great that the best posture for organizations is to fall back to a point where they merely adopt a 'react to events' strategy. In this case reaction replaces information and controls as the appropriate organizational response.

The results also indicated that two strategic mechanisms—coercion and standardization—are not associated with the use of sophisticated controls. Coercion involves the control of participants through orders, warnings, justification, arbitration, and the use of outsiders to propose change and force decisions. Standardization occurs when activities are subject to standard procedures and rules. It neither complements nor supplements control and information systems; rather it is used in lieu of them. Under conditions of certainty, organizations tend to rely heavily on standardization and bureaucratic coercion. As complexity increases, however, decisions made at the top, forcing the acceptance of, and the standardizing of, the behavior of subordinates will no longer do. These mechanisms give way to the information and analysis available from sophisticated information and control systems. Yet as complexity grows even more, the utility of these systems fades and organizations retreat to a simple 'react and survive' stance.

Contingency factors and effectiveness reporting

Another important research effort adopting an organizational theory approach to accounting and information systems is the innovative and provocative study by Hayes (1977), who investigated the appropriateness of management accounting systems for measuring the effectiveness of different departments in large industrial organizations. Departmental effectiveness, Hayes proposed, is a function of three major contingency factors—internal, interdependency, and external. Internal factors include aspects such as productivity, cost behavior, manpower utilization, supportive relations, and work-group cohesion. Interdependency includes aspects such as interdepartmental reliability, co-operation, flexibility, and procedures for co-ordination amongst departments. External or environmental factors include share of market, dealer and customer opinions of products, stability, and diversity.

The research focused on the appropriateness of management accounting information for measuring the performances of production, R&D, and marketing departments. It proposed that the effectiveness of production departments would be associated with internal and, but to a lesser extent, interdependency factors; while the effectiveness of marketing departments would be related to environmental and interdependency factors; and for R& D, only interdependencies would be critical.

These ideas were tested by asking marketing, production, and R&D managers in 24 large industrial firms to judge the influence of sundry factors on departmental performance. The managers were also asked to evaluate the effectiveness of the other two departments in their organization. The controller in each company also judged the effectiveness of the respective departments. The controllers would not only have sufficient knowledge of the respective departments, but also would be objective and independent judges. The study then compared the effectiveness factors with the judgements of departmental performance.

The results generally supported the predictions. Internal contingency factors proved to be the major explanators of effectiveness for production departments. Importantly, the production managers felt positive about the appropriateness of financial performance data for measuring departmental effort. In fact, they rated it much more highly than did managers of other departments. Interdependencies, especially with marketing departments, were of secondary importance while environmental variables were of little importance. Organizations, it seems, successfully buffer production departments from fluctuations in the environment with long lead times, machinery maintenance programs, and inventories. In this way uncertainty and instability, anathema to efficient and effective production operations, are minimized. In production departments, management accounting information systems are highly suitable for the performance assessment role.

For R&D departments, by contrast, an intricate pattern of relationships emerged between financial performance data and the major contingency factors. R&D managers felt strongly that financial measures of performance were inappropriate. This is not surprising as the real output of R&D is nearly impossible to predict and becomes evident, if at all, in future accounting periods. Yet one or two breakthroughs may lead to a major new product line which lasts for years. Nevertheless, current spending budgets have little or nothing to say about these outputs. So financial performance data, as the R&D managers sense, is not a good source of information for measuring the effectiveness of R&D. Paradoxically, however, the controllers and non-R& D managers perceived internal financial performance data as highly appropriate for measuring R&D output. These managers, Hayes explains, may have little or no experience with non-financial measures and, having no other way to evaluate R&D, turn to financial data as a last resort. In any event, non-R&D managers believe R&D can and should be subjected to financial performance criteria.

Neither external nor interdependency measures proved to be appropriate for assessing R&D effectiveness. R&D departments, it seems, are remote, almost aloof, from the rest of the corporate environment. The most important link scientists and technicians have is with other scientists in their own discipline around the world, and ultimately the best performance evaluation comes from these colleagues. Such evaluations, called 'social tests', are discussed at length in the next chapter.

Generally, then, interdependency and external variables are not associated with R&D effectiveness. There are, however, two puzzling exceptions. First, co-operation on joint tasks with marketing (an interdependence variable) and the importance of improving product quality (an environmental variable) were negatively associated with effectiveness! Apparently the demands placed on R&D by marketing and other managers to come up with profitable products is seen as detrimental to the long-run continuing search for basic universal truths. Pressure for applied projects is seen by R&D managers as hindering pure or basic projects. The important implication, however, is that controllers and management accountants should look beyond their standard repertoire of budgets and cost accounting standards if they wish to develop effective performance assessment instruments for R&D departments. Traditional accounting measures are less than satisfactory and, more, they are seen to be detrimental.

For marketing departments, environmental variables, including the importance of maintaining product quality levels of meeting future product requirements, had by far the greatest association with departmental effectiveness. This is an unanticipated finding. Interdependency variables also proved to be important, but to a lesser extent. The association of 'concern with customer's future requirements' with both the marketing managers' 'own judgement of performance' and the 'felt pressure to perform highly on joint tasks with production', suggests that the marketing department plays the critical boundary-spanning role of linking the organization to important outside factors. Obviously, traditional management accounting techniques are not well suited to measuring how well the department performs this job. The data also indicate that marketing and production departments do not get along very well on co-operative efforts. This comes as no surprise; the natural conflicts and rifts between these departments are well documented.

These are valuable and interesting findings. Yet the real interest of this study is that it did not include any accounting and information systems variables. Rather, it deliberately went beyond the standard research approach of exploring the effect of various factors on the management accounting systems to look at more fundamental issues. This proved to be a clever strategy, permitting identification of the relative importance of various internal, interdependency, and environmental factors for effective performance as well as assessment of the adequacy of accounting techniques to measure these factors. The important finding is that traditional managerial accounting tools, which focus on internal departmental factors, are relatively poor assessment tools for R&D and marketing. Budgets, essentially surrogates for an entire set of factors which influence performance, do not perform the surrogation function very well for these departments.

Yet the point goes even deeper. It suggests a major reorientation away from the traditional accounting and information systems approach to one which gives special attention to measuring environmental and interdependency factors. A preoccupation with internal factors will no longer do.

The wider perspective offered by this study makes it abundantly clear that, in whatever discomfort, accountants must acknowledge, if not publicly at least amongst themselves, that in some circumstances their management accounting tools and techniques fall short of the mark. We are in urgent need of better ways of monitoring performance on critical external and interdependency factors. Perhaps an obsession with objectivity, conservatism, consistency, and codes of accounts keeps us from breaking away from traditional budget reporting and variance analysis techniques. There is, of course, the danger that venturing into the subjective realm of non-accounting performance measures would impair the integrity of other management accounting information. Yet not to do so leaves the door open to others, including computer-based MIS and systems departments, who are all too eager to get in on the business of providing assessment information to the organization; and assessment, after all, is the main business of accountants.

This, of course, is in no way a denial of the importance of conventional managerial accounting practices and information systems. They are without question an integral aspect of the management of organizations. Rather, it is an earnest proposal that management accountants expand the scope of their scorekeeping, attention-directing, and problem-solving systems to include information about interdependency and environmental factors. If management accountants do not provide such scorekeeping information, the managers themselves will develop their own systems, or rely on other information experts, to gather and record information to track departmental performance. Careful research indicates that, in many organizations, such information systems have already supplanted formal accounting systems (Hopwood, 1978).

The overarching message of the research, then, is that the traditional managerial accounting approach remains excessively narrow. Perhaps this is not so surprising; after all, most of our current management accounting techniques were invented many years ago.

Differentiation, integration and accounting systems for transfer pricing

Another important contribution to the growing literature on organizational theory and accounting and information systems is the theoretical work of Watson and Baumler (1975) who related the concepts of differentiation and integration to management accounting. One of the central problems facing organizations, they argue, is coping with uncertainty stemming from environment and technology. Organizations respond to this in different ways. Some create special subunits to deal with the uncertainty, thus permitting other subunits to operate in stable and certain environments. This, along with the natural tendency of organizations to set up highly specialized subunits, leads to segmentation of the organization into specialized parts, each of which develop different working styles, mental processes, and perceptions of reality. This differentiation, as it is called, is an essential requirement for organizational success.

Accounting systems, they propose, enhance differentiation by treating subunits as separate units responsible for costs, profits, investments, or even revenues. Differentiation, however, contributes substantially to the problems of insuring that the efforts of the various differentiated subunits converge on global organizational goals. This integration, as it is labeled, becomes more difficult as the organization becomes more differentiated; and the greater the differentiation, the greater the number of conflicts which arise during integration.

The necessary integration is achieved through a wide variety of mechanisms—rules, standardization, hierarchy, plans, liaison roles, task forces, designated integrators, and matrix organizational design. Importantly, research has shown that those organizations that achieve the required degree of both differentiation and integration are more successful than those that do not strike the correct balance (Lawrence and Lorsch, 1967). So achieving the precise balance of differentiation and integration is critical to organizational performance.

Another common way of coping with the problems posed by uncertainty, differentiation, and integration is to divide up the organization into quasi-autonomous subunits which trade with each other as if they were separate independent companies. Such arrangements call for an accounting-based transfer pricing system which designates the prices to be used for internal trade and the mechanism for establishing them. Under this organizational design, the transfer price system, usually the responsibility of the controller and management accounting department, enhances differentiation and plays a key role in integration. So designing and managing a fair and equitable transfer price system emerges as an important part of the management accounting role. This is no easy task.

The most effective way of determining proper internal prices, it is generally accepted, is to use current market prices or prices charged outsiders. Often, however, these are either unavailable or inappropriate and the accountant must find other means for establishing prices. The optimal way, Watson and Baumler argue, is to have a system of negotiated transfer prices. The reason for this is that negotiation requires confrontation, and confrontation is regarded as the best means of conflict resolution; better than, say, forcing, smoothing, compromise, or avoidance (Lawrence and Lorsch, 1967). So settling transfer price disputes through negotiation by the parties involved should be better than arbitrarily setting prices from above and forcing them on the managers. The quasi-autonomous organizational subunits, then, treat each other as if they are arms-length parties competing in the market-place. When negotiations break down the controller and management accounting staff office are brought in to act as arbitrator. The effective resolution of transfer price disputes is crucial to the effective functioning of the entire organization.

In sum, transfer price systems, which serve to enhance differentiation and facilitate integration, emerge as another key aspect of management accounting. In most circumstances the best transfer price system, in the absence of firm market prices, will be one featuring negotiated prices with arbitration by the management accounting staff when negotiations falter. The management accounting function, then, is expanded beyond merely providing information for scorekeeping, attention-directing, and problem-solving to include responsibility for the transfer price system—a critical integration mechanism in most large complex organizations.

Organizational structure and budget-related behavior

Another important study investigating macro-organizational properties was conducted by Bruns and Waterhouse (1975), who looked at the relationships between two major controls—budgets and organization structure. The research domain included several organizational structure factors, numerous budget behavior characteristics, and measures of the breadth and complexity of accounting control systems. The study also collected data on the influence of managers at various levels in the organization. Budget-related behavior was defined as the activities, actions, and interactions of managers with each other and their tasks that relate to budget systems either directly or indirectly.

The data on organizational structure were gathered in twenty-six firms through questionnaire interviews with the chief executive. The data on the managers' budget-related behavior were collected from managers who were directly involved in preparing, using, or performing against a budget. Complexity of control was computed by combining three measures: (1) whether the manager's responsibility center was treated as an investment, profit, discretionary cost, revenue, or standard cost center; (2) the level in the organization where performance standards were established; and (3) the chief executive's estimate of the number of employees involved in either planning or evaluation aspects of budgeting. The three measures were combined into a scale of control systems complexity.

The results proved fascinating. Perhaps the most important discovery was that organizations seem to choose between two general control strategies—administrative and interpersonal. The administrative control strategy was associated with larger and more technologically sophisticated companies. These firms are decentralized but at the same time employ formalized and standard operating procedures and rules to govern work relation-ships. Managers in these companies participate a great deal in setting budget targets, spend a lot of time on budgeting activities, and see the budget as limiting innovation and flexibility. Paradoxically, however, they perceive themselves and other managers as having a great deal of control over what goes on in the organization. Participatory approaches to budgeting emerged as an important part of the administrative control strategy.

The interpersonal control strategy predominated in firms that are either small, highly dependent on other organizations, or centralized. In these firms financial control systems tended to be based on simple and narrowly defined measures such as standard cost variances. Budget-related matters, including explanations of budget variances and discussions of specific methods for reaching budget targets, were used extensively in superior–subordinate inter-actions. Financial controls also were utilized, not only as a vehicle to specify and direct subordinates as to what to do, but, more importantly, as a means for superiors to induce pressure by requiring explanations of variances and to challenge the methods used to reach budget targets. Lack of autonomy was related to a reduction in superior–subordinate interactions during budget preparation periods and during discussions of the means necessary to achieve budget targets. Managers, however, were not disgruntled with these interac-tions, nor were they dissatisfied with their overall relationships with superiors. In fact, they readily accepted the need for a centralized organization with close personal interaction with superiors on budget-related matters. The interpersonal control strategy appears to be a key element for firms that require centralization of important decisions.

Several other interesting findings and insights emerged. For one thing, when managers participated actively in budget planning they felt they had more overall influence on what goes on in their organization than when budget participation was low, even under conditions of specialization, stan-dardization, and formalization. When structuring of activities is high, managers spend more time on budget activities. What seems to be happening is that when organizational arrangements are more structured, budget-related behavior increases. This finding is a valuable contribution to the long-standing debate on participation and budgeting, since it demonstrates a concrete benefit for participative budgeting.

Another interesting result is the finding that control system complexity is associated with centralization–decentralization issues. Centralized organ-izations, where the managers' autonomy is restricted, used more detailed financial control systems and had more employees per capita involved in financial control systems than did the decentralized organizations. Here financial control systems were based on broad, general, and more aggregate measurements and the managers were permitted to use a great deal of discretion in selecting the actions necessary to achieve financial results.

This study, then, is important and insightful. It is built on concepts and questionnaires used in previous studies; and, since it sampled organizations from a wide range of different industries, markets, and production methods, the results can be extended across a wide swathe of organizational life. A key contribution is the identification of two distinct control strategies. Large, decentralized organizations rely on formalized operating procedures and rules and general, but complex, financial controls. By contrast, smaller, dependent, and centralized organizations rely on simple financial accounting information to induce pressure for budget attainment and to give specific instructions as to methods necessary for meeting budget goals. An equally important contribution is the finding that organizational structural properties have a substantial influence on behavior related to financial control systems. So any universal prescriptions about the design and use of financial controls must be treated with suspicion; budget properties and related behavior seem to vary systematically with different patterns of organizational structure.

Administratively-oriented control strategy

Merchant (1981) followed up these leads and investigated the role of budgeting systems in the broader administrative control strategy. The study collected data on three contextual factors (size, diversification, and decentralization); six budget-related behavior variables (required explanations, influence on budget plans, interactions with subordinates, budget overrun reactions, interactions with superiors, and personal involvement in budgeting); four budget characteristics (frequency of budget updates and reporting time blocks, budget sophistication, motivation, and satisfaction); and perceived departmental efficiency.

The theoretical framework for the study held that as organizations grow and become more diverse, they decentralize decision-making power while at the same time increasing the use of formalized communications, structuring of activities, and standardized information to evaluate performance. This control strategy allows them to cope with the difficult co-ordination problems caused by the diversity of the autonomous, differentiated subunits; and budgeting systems, an important part of the overall control strategy, should feature: greater participation by middle- and lower-line managers, greater importance placed on achieving budget plans, more formal patterns of communication, and greater budgeting systems sophistication. These ideas were tested by interviewing 170 manufacturing managers in nineteen electronics firms.

The results generally supported these ideas. Budgets in the larger firms were not as detailed as in the smaller firms, suggesting that general performance indicators are more suitable for decentralized structures. The motivational impact and the usefulness of the budgeting process proved to be high for all firms and, surprisingly, was not influenced by size, diversity, or decentralization.

Then, in an innovative move, Merchant split the sample into small and large firms and investigated the relationship of budgeting variables to performance for both groups. Managers in the larger, decentralized, and more diverse firms participated more, and had greater personal involvement in budgeting, than did those in small firms, had fewer formal communications with superiors and subordinates, and saw budget performance as an important part of the corporate reward system. The larger firms also showed a significantly higher association of performance and budget variables. Performance was associated with participation in the budgeting process, the importance placed on meeting budget targets, formality of communications with subunits, and the sophistication of computer support. For the smaller firms budgets were more detailed. None of the small firms used zero-based budgeting, while for the larger firms that did it was negatively associated with performance. Perhaps organizations only resort to measures like zero-based budgeting when performance is unsatisfactory.

The study, then, proved to be an important link in the growing chain of knowledge of how financial control systems fit into the fabric of organizational design. It built on previous investigations and replicated previous efforts; and, importantly, it provided support for the thesis that larger, decentralized firms employ an administrative control strategy of which the budget is an integral, if not the most important, part.

COMPREHENSIVE THEORIES OF MANAGEMENT ACCOUNTING INFORMATION SYSTEMS

The above studies have contributed significantly to the growing body of literature and knowledge about the role of management accounting and information systems in large, complex organizations. They demonstrate clearly that these systems are, as Waterhouse and Tiessen (1978) state, interwoven with other organizational systems to form an integral part of the organizational fabric and play a critical role in the overall web of control processes. They also establish the relevance of specific organizational variables to the design of management accounting systems.

In addition, however, they reveal an urgent need to go beyond merely establishing associations of various impersonal and personal organizational factors with management accounting systems. They spotlight the need for theories incorporating sets of relationships amongst macro-organizational properties. As it turns out, a few researchers have already taken on this difficult task with rewarding results.

Control styles and predictability of environment

Waterhouse and Tiessen (1978), for example, developed just such a theory using environment and technology as the causal forces. Firms operating routine technologies in a predictable environment, they postulate, prefer to centralize decision-making. In order to gain compliance with the central decisions, procedures are specified by formalizing, standardizing, and developing rules for role performance. Middle- and lower-level managers, therefore, have little discretion and power. Planning and control information is straightforward, with management accounting systems focusing on efficiency measures such as standard cost and variance reports. These relationships can be summarized as shown in Figure 8.1. By contrast, firms operating in unpredictable environments with non-routine technologies decentralize decision-making and authority, thus giving middle- and lower-level managers a great deal of discretion and power. Rules, standardization, and formalization are absent. In this context management accounting systems featuring general performance information and stressing output measurements are the major means of control, and become the key mechanism for planning and co-ordination.

Management accounting information is also used for internal resource allocation and, as a result, becomes politically charged as the management accounting department becomes involved in bargaining with line managers. Information, of course, is a source of power and so the management accounting department, as the organization's information center, becomes powerful. The line managers, knowing that budget performance is critical to their careers, create slack budgets by drawing on their superior knowledge of the options available for operating methods.

Decentralized organizations, of course, do not rely exclusively on financial controls. They also socialize their managers through organizational myths and fables. Management accounting information systems, however, are the major formal means of keeping the decentralized units in line with global objectives. These relationships can be depicted as shown in Figure 8.2.

Waterhouse and Tiessen, then, outline a neat but rich framework that links management accounting systems to environment, technology, decision-making, and power. Although the framework bears a close resemblance to the schemes by Burns and Stalker, and by Arrow, which were discussed earlier, it focuses more directly on the management accounting, information, and control systems.

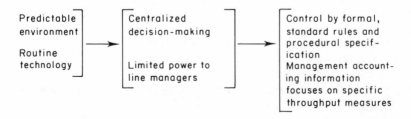

Figure 8.1 Control for stable contexts by centralization, formalization, and accounting throughput measures.

156

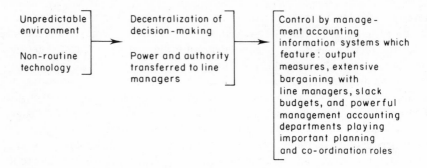

Figure 8.2 Control for unpredictable contexts by decentralization, powerful accounting departments and accounting output measures.

Accounting systems in adaptive, running-blind, and stagnant bureaucracies

Another comprehensive framework was developed by Gordon and Miller (1976). Their theoretical scheme includes environment, decentralization, differentiation, integration, bureaucratization, resource availability, and decision-making styles as major variables. The central thesis runs as follows.

Any accounting information system should be designed in light of the contextual variables surrounding the specific organization. Environmental, organizational, and decision-style traits are not distributed randomly amongst organizations; rather they come in three commonly occurring configurations—adaptive, running-blind, and stagnant bureaucracies.

Adaptive firms are abundant in managerial, technical, and financial resources and operate in dynamic environments. They decentralize into organizational units which are low in differentiation but which are adequately integrated. The managers in these firms pay close attention to key environmental trends and develop explicit competitive strategies which help them to be innovative and proactive in focusing on environmental opportunities. Needless to say such firms perform well. Accounting, information, and intelligence systems, a key factor in their success, feature:

(a) information about the external environment;
(b) information about inflationary trends, new technology, product ideas, and consumer trends;
(c) uniform and centralized accounting systems applied consistently across the decentralized units;
(d) unimpeded internal flows of information, both laterally and vertically; and
(e) a broad array of general-level information for managers.

These information systems are well suited to dynamic environments and flexible innovative decision-making styles.

Running-blind firms are not so fortunate. They operate in heterogeneous environments characterized by rapidly changing markets. Power and decision-making is centralized in the hands of a few top executives. Organizational subunits are highly differentiated with separate and conflicting goals making integration difficult. Decision styles are intuitive, inflexible, and insensitive to environmental conditions. Top management are entrepreneurial, take many risks, and seem prone to acquire new subsidiaries carelessly, regardless of the industry they compete in. Consequently, new product lines and different technologies are introduced into the corporate family at random; and, importantly, information systems are inadequate for timely scanning of the environment, controls are lacking, top management are ill-informed about activities in the subsidiaries, and communications flows are top-down. Not surprisingly, performance for such firms is low.

Nevertheless, accounting and information systems designers can help reduce the magnitude of these problems by:

(a) gathering timely facts for top management about out-of-control situations;
(b) providing information on competitors' new products and technological innovations;
(c) avoiding overloading top management with large quantities of detailed information;
(d) gathering data on environmental trends and changing economic conditions;
(e) setting up profit objectives and resource allocation plans on a company-wide basis;
(f) developing information on divisional cost, profit, and physical output performance; and
(g) setting up well-designed cost accounting and control systems.

These initiatives should help foster effective decision-making styles, highlight key environmental events, facilitate discussions between top and divisional managers, and go a long way to eliminating the effects of sub-optimization at the divisional level.

The third archetype, the stagnant bureaucracy, operates in what was historically an extremely stable and homogeneous environment, but one which is becoming more and more dynamic. Traditional structural and decision styles are still utilized but are now out of step. Differentiation is low, integration is achieved by rigid rules and predetermined programs, and power is centralized. Decision styles are inflexible, conservative, and lacking in analysis; and, to make matters even worse, both managerial and technocratic expertise is absent. Information and intelligence systems do not highlight important trends, provide only minimal amounts of top-down communications, and rarely scan the environment. Stagnant bureaucracies, of course, perform poorly.

Nevertheless, better accounting and information systems can help make such firms more responsive to their changing environment by:

(a) gathering information on external conditions;
(b) providing timely information on problematic trends;
(c) establishing profit planning systems to pressure complacent managers at all levels;
(d) providing inflation accounting statements to highlight the stagnant state of the firm; and
(e) developing forecasted statements.

Such initiatives, Gordon and Miller predict, would help to focus management on shifting conditions, thus shaking them out of their lethargic and complacent ways.

These ideas, of course, are not without limitations. In fact, when we try to evaluate them they seem to rest on an illusive theory which artificially delineates the types of firms. The types, of course, are offered only as archetypes and are based on case studies. Nevertheless, they are innovative and imaginative caricatures. Undoubtedly many management accounting and information systems designers will recognize them, particularly the running-blind and stagnant bureaucracy; and the prescriptions for designers who find themselves in similar situations seem particularly well conceived. Perhaps the major message is that accounting and information systems need only focus on a few select variables to be effective.

CONCLUSION

This chapter argued that organizational theory can enrich our understanding of the workings of management accounting and information systems in complex organizations. Although progress along these lines has been slow, the research and theory-building achievements are impressive. We now have an organized way of relating the scorekeeping, attention-directing, and problem-solving, to different organizational structures. We also better understand the links between budget-related behavior and various upper management climates. We know more about how elements in the competitive environment require differing degrees of management control sophistication. We have a better idea about the way financial controls fit into the overall pattern of control in organizations. We have become aware that while traditional management accounting systems are highly satisfactory for measuring performance in production departments, they fall short of the mark for marketing departments, and are counterproductive for R&D units. We also recognize that new and innovative concepts of accounting and information systems, those which collect data about environments and interdependencies, are desperately needed. And we have a systematic way of thinking about the design and management of transfer price systems and their role in managing integration in complex organizations.

The idea of linking organizational theory to accounting and information systems has also given us a good start at developing rich theories that include several contextual variables and their association with financial control systems. We have, for example, a neat theory about how successful, large, and diverse firms utilize an administrative control strategy while successful, small, and vertically integrated firms employ an interpersonal one. We also know that firms operating a routine technology in a stable environment should focus their management accounting systems on specific measures of the efficiency and effectiveness of throughputs; while firms with non-routine technologies in unpredictable environments require management accounting systems which feature general output measures, powerful accounting departments, and hard bargaining on budget levels. And we have some helpful prescriptions for effective accounting and information systems in adaptive, running-blind, and stagnant bureaucracies. The beginnings of a well-rounded and rich body of knowledge to explain the otherwise puzzling differences among organizations in the design and use of their management accounting and information systems are beginning to surface.

It is also encouraging to realize that this approach is slowly gaining recognition as part of the conventional body of knowledge of accounting (Dermer, 1975). And outstanding management accounting textbooks, such as Horngren's (1982), which traditionally stressed cost accumulation systems and quantitative analytical techniques, are beginning to emphasize that management accounting system design must be seen as interdependent and inseparable from organizational structure and behavior.

This emerging body of knowledge, of course, is not without its problems and limitations, which have been soundly documented by critics such as Otley (1980). To begin with, accounting researchers have tended to accept concepts from organizational theory at face value and ignore documented weaknesses, particularly problems encountered in measuring them. Neither is there any consensus on which specific contingencies should lead to specific management accounting configurations. Some studies, for example, focus on environmental variables. Others stress competition; some emphasize the critical nature of autonomy, centralization, and structuring; while still others pinpoint technology and task as the key determinant. A confusingly wide array of accounting and information systems characteristics have been linked to such properties. The net result, Otley concludes, is a great deal of confusion and non-convergence of the findings, conclusions, and design recommendations.

Most of the studies did not assess the effectiveness of the particular management accounting system being investigated (Sathe, 1975). Nor did they research the impact of accounting information on organizational performance; and, as several authors point out, they did not include critical organizational aspects of goal formation, conflict patterns, and power balances (Hopwood, 1978; Hopper, 1980).

We still, it seems, have a long way to go. New accounting methodologies, for example, must be discovered to cope with turbulent environments and complex organizational designs (Amigoni, 1978). We also need new theories which connect up accounting and information systems with the entire organizational control package (Dermer, 1975; Young, 1979; Otley and Berry, 1980); and we need comprehensive theories which tell us how these systems work within the wider context of environment, power, strategy, and organizational structure. Although it seems clear that accounting and information systems are influenced by these forces, we are becoming aware that these systems are also important determinants in their own right of other key organizational structures and processes (Hopwood, 1978; Burchell et al., 1980; Dent and Ezzamel, 1982).

Either way, it seems clear that organizational design pivots on control and information needs (Banbury and Nahapiet, 1979). So better methodologies, perhaps building on cybernetics and general systems theory, must be invented to cope with the complex, two-way train of influence (Otley, 1982). We may even have to retreat to a research strategy involving long case studies which track a multitude of variables over a long period of time (Caplan and Champoux, 1978).

The problem, it seems, is to develop conceptual methodologies which will permit us to work with a multitude of abstract variables which are influencing each other simultaneously. I do not worry so much that we have not as yet invented such apparatus. At least we have come to recognize the issues. We should remember that physics used classical Newtonian ideas, which treated the behavior of elementary particles like the determination of a clock, as the springboard for erecting the new relativistic quantum field of physics which conceives of the behavior of these particles more like the contingencies of a pinball machine. It may be comforting for us to know that even this new physics lacks a general unifying theory of the physical world. The challenge for accounting and information researchers, then, is to use our present findings, based upon an organizational theory approach to the problems, as a springboard for inventing new conceptual apparatus which will enable us to handle the pinball machine like behavior of organizational structures and processes including accounting and information systems.

A way into this problem is to look for more fundamental properties which subsume the multitude of various factors at work into higher-order concepts. One such concept is uncertainty, a property of organizations which has, in fact, been the cornerstone of a good deal of organizational theory efforts. We turn next, then, to a discussion of some outstanding contributions which use the cutting edge of uncertainty as their central concept to explain assessment scorekeeping, and control in organizations.

References

Amigoni, F., 'Management planning and control systems', *Journal of Business Finance and Accounting*, 1978, pp. 279–291.

Banbury, J., and J. E. Nahapiet, 'Towards a framework for the study of the antecedents and consequences of information systems in organizations', *Accounting, Organizations and Society*, Vol. 4, No. 1, 1979, pp. 163–177.

Bruns, J. C., and J. H. Waterhouse, 'Budgeting control and organization structure', *Journal of Accounting Research*, Autumn 1975, pp. 177–203.

Burchell, S., C. Clubb, A. G. Hopwood, T. Hughes, and J. Nahapiet, 'The roles of accounting in organizations and society', *Accounting, Organizations and Society*, Vol. 5, No. 1, 1980, pp. 5–27.

Caplan, E. H., and J. E. Champoux, *Cases in Management Accounting: Context and Behavior*, National Association of Accountants, New York, 1978.

Dent, J. F., and M. A. Ezzamel, 'Organizational control and management accounting', paper presented at the American Accounting Association Annual Meeting San Diego, California, August 1982.

Dermer, J. D., 'Human information processing and problem solving: implications for behavioral accounting research', in Livingstone, J. L. (ed.), *Managerial Accounting: The Behavioral Foundations*, Grid Inc., Columbus, Ohio, 1975.

Golembiewski, R. T., 'Accountancy as a function of organization theory', *The Accounting Review*, April 1964, pp. 333–341.

Gordon, L. A., and D. Miller, 'A contingency framework for the design of accounting information systems', *Accounting, Organizations and Society*, Vol. 1, No. 1, 1976, pp. 59–69.

Hayes, D. C., 'The contingency theory of management accounting', *The Accounting Review*, January 1977, pp. 22–39.

Hofstede, G. H., *The Game of Budget Control*, Konmklijke Van Grocum & Comp. NV, Assen, Netherlands, 1967.

Hopper, T. M., 'Role conflicts of management accountants and their positions within organization structure', *Accounting, Organizations and Society*, Vol. 5, No. 4, 1980, pp. 401–411.

Hopwood, A. G., 'Towards an organizational perspective for the study of accounting and information systems', *Accounting, Organizations and Society*, Vol. 3, No. 1, 1978, pp. 3–14.

Horngren, C. T., *Cost Accounting: A Managerial Emphasis*, Prentice-Hall Inc., Englewood Cliffs, NJ, 1982.

Khandwalla, P. N., 'The effect of different types of competition on the use of management controls', *Journal of Accounting Research*, Autumn 1972, pp. 275–285.

Khandwalla, P. N., 'Mass output orientation of operations technology and organizational structure', *Administrative Science Quarterly*, March 1974, pp. 74–97.

Khandwalla, P. N., *The Design of Organizations*, Harcourt, Brace Jovanovich, Inc., 1977.

Lawrence, R. P., and J. W. Lorsch, *Organizations and Environment: Managing Differentiation and Integration*, Division of Research, Harvard University Graduate Business School, 1967.

Merchant, K. A., 'The design of the corporate budgeting system: influences on managerial behavior and performance', *The Accounting Review*, October 1981, pp. 813–829.

Otley, D. T., 'Budget use and managerial behavior', *Journal of Accounting Research*, Spring 1978, pp. 122–149.

162

Otley, D. T., 'The contingency theory of management accounting: Achievement and prognosis', *Accounting, Organizations and Society*, Vol. 5, No. 2, 1980, pp. 413–428.

Otley, D. T., 'Concepts of control: the contribution of cybernetics and systems theory to management control'. Presented at the American Accounting Association Annual Meeting, San Diego, August 1982.

Otley, D. T., and A. J. Berry, 'Control, organization and accounting', *Accounting, Organizations and Society*, Vol. 2, No. 5, 1980, pp. 231–244.

Perrow, C., *Complex Organizations: A Critical Analysis*, Scott, Foresman and Company, Glenview, Ill., 1972.

Sathe, V., 'Contingency theories of organizational structure', in Livingstone, J. L. (ed.), *Managerial Accounting: The Behavioral Foundations*, Grid Inc., Columbus, Ohio, 1975.

Sloan, A. D. Jr., *My Years with General Motors*, Doubleday & Company, Inc., New York, 1963.

Waterhouse, J. H., and P. A. Tiessen, 'A contingency framework for management accounting systems research', *Accounting, Organizations and Society*, Vol. 3, No. 1, 1978, pp. 65–76.

Watson, D. J. H., and J. V. Baumler, 'Transfer pricing: a behavioral context', *The Accounting Review*, July 1975, pp. 466–474.

Young, D. W., 'Administrative theory and administrative systems: a synthesis among diverging fields of inquiry', *Accounting, Organizations and Society*, Vol. 4, No. 3, 1979, pp. 235–244.

CHAPTER 9

Uncertainty and Accounting and Information Systems

The last chapter provided impressive evidence that particular variables, or configurations of these variables, tend to have a significant influence over the characteristics of an organization's management accounting and information systems. Yet when we try to generalize from these findings we soon run into difficulties.

One way into this problem is to find generalizations that are neither too specific that they epitomize triviality nor too general that they harbor ambiguities and suppress more fundamental premises. Such a middle ground proved to be the territory of Thompson's (1967) widely acclaimed theory of organizational action, a theory which included a rich and elegant set of propositions about how organizations measure and keep score of their performance as well as that of their various subcomponents.

To grasp Thompson's ideas about organizational assessment fully, it will be helpful to explore his general train of thought about why organizations act as they do. Patterned variations in the problems posed by technology and environment, he argued, result in systematic differences in the way organizations run themselves. Organizations with similar technological and environmental programs are likely to organize themselves in similar ways. For a closed, deterministic system we can predict accurately the state it will be in at any specific time. In these circumstances a rational-model approach is highly suitable. We understand how all the variables work, as well as their interactions; thus, the outcomes of the system are predictable.

But when a system contains more variables than we can comprehend at one time, or when some variables are subject to uncontrollable influences, the rational perspective will no longer do. We must turn to a different type of thinking known as a natural-systems logic. From this viewpoint the organization is interdependent with its environment. Its relationship is the result of an evolutionary process. Survival is the goal. The relationships among the various parts of the organization and their activities are spontaneously kept in equilibrium, and thus viable, in the face of environmental disturbances. Thus, the system is seen as open to environmental uncertainty.

From Thompson's perspective, if we are to fully understand why organizations act as they do, we must employ both rationalistic and the natural-systems logic. Under stable conditions a rational (or closed) model is appropriate; whereas when uncertainty enters the picture we must revert to a natural (or open) systems type of thinking. And it is the patterned variations in the impersonal forces of technology and market which lead to systematic differences in organizational actions (i.e. design, structure, and management systems) including the way they go about keeping score and assessing themselves.

For Thompson it was the cutting edge of uncertainty that presented the fundamental problem for complex organizations; and coping with uncertainty is the essence of the administrative process.

Under conditions of certainty, goals are known, resources available, tasks are well-understood, and output is absorbed automatically. The stable environments do not present large problems for the selection of organizational management systems. Operations proceed smoothly according to the rules of rationality. This is the case, above all, in the technical core of large industrial enterprises which are buffered from environmental shocks by inventory reserves, production scheduling, and idle capacity. Predictable environments are congenial to organizational effort, specialized units with repetitive tasks are established and operated according to plans and predetermined yardsticks. Management accounting systems, backed up by inducement schemes geared to ensure conformity to plans, provide accurate and timely information for performance assessment. They play a critical role in the relentless drive for efficiency.

If we pause to think about it, we are surrounded by such organizations. Routinely they deliver newspapers, carry conversations over long distances, transport people back and forth to work, stock supermarkets, keep track of money, educate children, and even entertain us on picture tubes. These daily miracles are achieved through marvelously efficient action systems which are buffered from environmental disturbances that might upset their routines. They perform with such precision that we are outraged if the morning paper is late or if the supermarket runs out of our favorite brand of catsup.

Simultaneously, however, organizations must deal with aspects of their environment which are neither stable nor certain. In fact, these are more often the rule than the exception. They stem from a number of sources, including environment, goals, technologies, and interdependencies. So organizations, in addition to operating the routine and stable technical core, must be able to absorb and accommodate environmental uncertainties.

Uncertain environments, however, pose major challenges to rational forms of organizational design. Those organizational designs and management systems, so well suited to stable circumstances, will no longer do; and while it may appear at first glance that the development of suitable designs and systems is a random trial-and-error process, evidence is mounting that organizations with similar sources of uncertainty respond in similar ways. Systematic variations in uncertainty tend to lead to patterned, and therefore predictable, variations in organizational structures and management systems.

UNCERTAINTY AND ASSESSMENT

Part of Thompson's work dealt with the crucial problem of organizational scorekeeping and assessment. Under relatively certain conditions, for, say, a mass-production factory, scorekeeping is straightforward and focuses on whether or not optimal results have been accomplished. This type of scorekeeping becomes problematic, however, when uncertainty enters the scene. A marketing department, for example, has no way of knowing whether or not it has optimized operations. The same applies to accounting and computing departments; and for R&D units optimizing resources consumed is not even the goal. Assessment must shift from measures of historical efficiency to criteria of fitness for future action.

Thompson derived an ingenious scheme for analysing the assessment problem under various patterns of uncertainty. Scorekeeping, he proposed, is rooted firmly in two factors—the nature of standards of desirability and the familiarity with the necessary steps to be taken to accomplish a task. At one end of a continuum, standards are one-dimensional and preferences are clear-cut. Health is always preferred to illness, wealth is fancied over poverty; efficiency is deemed better than inefficiency; and world peace is clearly preferable to global holocaust. Also, the direction for improvement is obvious—from illness to health; from inefficiency to efficiency, and from hostilities to peace. Standards are unequivocal, unambiguous, and crystalized.

But standards of desirability are not always represented by a single unambiguous dimension. Sometimes they involve a choice between two or more dimensions. It is not merely a matter of health over illness, but rather a choice of health or wealth. Further, there can be shades of health and shades of wealth involved in the choice. Also, much of the time we are dealing simultaneously with some degree of health and some amount of wealth; and to further complicate the issue, the choice may be ambivalent since it lies between two roughly acceptable alternatives, such as long-run profits and short-run cash flows, or even between two equally repulsive choices such as illness today versus poverty next year. Finally, preferences change with time; one day we prefer wealth but the next we favor health. When standards are ambiguous, the choices are agonizing and we are hard-pressed to decide.

Standards, of course, are familiar territory for management accounting and information systems designers. In fact, they are an essential aspect of almost any financial control system. Standard cost and variance reports, profit planning and budgeting systems, expense budgets, and the like are an integral part of the management accountant's repertoire; and we assume rightly or wrongly that the standards incorporated into these systems represent yardsticks against which actual outcomes are compared to yield clear-cut messages. If the standard is met, the results are good. If they are missed, the results are unsatisfactory.

166

The other critical factor involves the degree of knowledge about the task conversion process. When knowledge is complete the effect of instrumental action can be traced to known results. In the machining department of a tractor parts factory, for example, the correct sequencing of work through machines is known, the precise technical tolerances are predetermined, and the exact quantities of raw materials, direct labor, and supervision are known with a high degree of precision. Highly predictable results stem from well-understood actions.

But sometimes the effects of actions cannot be predicted with any degree of certainty. Outcomes are the result, not only of actions taken inside the department, but also of events and actions taken outside. In our marketing department example, sales results cannot be related to specific instrumental action within the department. The effect of pricing decisions, choice of distribution channels, selection of advertising media and message, and bonus schemes for salesmen cannot be traced directly to specific sales transactions. The actions of competitors, governments, and credit companies also have an important influence over the outcome. At this end of the continuum, then, some consequences of actions are known, others are generally agreed upon but unproven, some are suspected, some occur in far-distant future periods, and still others go unnoticed.

Thompson combined the two continuums and used their extreme values to derive four assessment situations, as depicted in Figure 9.1. In cell 1, uncertainty is low. Predetermined actions have known effects and desirable economic standards are crystal-clear. The optimum economic relationship between inputs and outputs can be derived and efficiency is the appropriate test. Efficiency is achieved when the maximum amount of output results from a given level of input resources. The scorekeeping question is—Was the result produced with the least cost? Or conversely, for a given level of output, efficiency is the minimum amount of input resources necessary. The scorekeeping question asks—Was the given amount of input used in a way

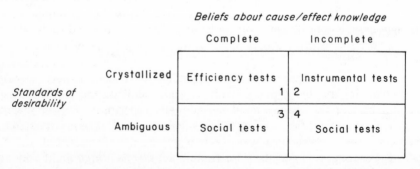

Figure 9.1 Assessment situations and appropriate tests. (Source: Thompson, 1967, p. 86. Reproduced by permission of McGraw-Hill, Inc.)

to achieve the greatest result? Either way, a known scientific relationship exists between resources consumed and outputs produced. Perfection is the goal and the efficiency test measures relative perfection.

But when uncertainty enters the scene, efficiency scorekeeping quickly loses its robustness. One source of uncertainty is incomplete cause–effect knowledge, as shown in cell 2. Here the net effects of causal action can no longer be assessed. As the optimum ratio of inputs to outputs cannot be known with any degree of certainty, it is not possible to determine whether the desired state of affairs has been achieved efficiently. There is no way of knowing if the best instrumental action was taken because the possibility always remains that a better course of action exists. We do know, however, whether or not the instrumental action achieved the desired state. The scorekeeping question centers on effectiveness—did the action result in the desired goal? The robust efficiency test gives way to the less satisfactory, but more appropriate, instrumental one.

Instrumental tests, of course, are widely used. In professional sports, for example, won–loss columns, and which teams reach the playoffs, are a common way of judging performance. Managers and coaches are well aware that their continued employment hinges on these simple instrumental tests. In the public domain, even though standards of desirability for outputs (such as levels of employment, inflation, and interest rates) are less clear, voters and political commentators alike set arbitrary levels of satisfactory attainment. Most large industrial and commercial organizations carve themselves into smaller components, each of which is relatively self-contained in terms of resources, products, and markets. Performance is deemed satisfactory if predetermined desired profit targets are met. *Optimum* profit levels, however, are indeterminate since the possibility always remains that some other combination of resources, products, and markets would yield more profit. We do know, however, whether or not the *desired* level of profit has been achieved.

In cell 4 uncertainty reaches its maximum and assessment takes on a new dimension. Knowledge of instrumental action is uncertain and standards of desirability are ambiguous. Both efficiency and instrumental tests are unsatisfactory and organizations retreat to a less satisfactory but more appropriate means of assessment—the social test.

The idea of a social test may be foreign, even repugnant, to many accounting and information systems managers. The basic idea is that accomplishment and fitness are judged by the collective opinions and beliefs of one or more relevant groups. A personnel department, for example, provides services (hiring, firing, pay and promotion schemes, safety programs, union negotiations, etc.) to the sundry departments in an organization. The collective opinions and beliefs of these client departments are good indicators of the personnel department's fitness for future action. Another good source of assessment comes from the various personnel associations that periodically award prizes for outstanding achievement in personnel work. In these examples assessment leaves the realm of economic fact and enters the domain of social opinion, beliefs, and values.

Finally, in cell 3, uncertainty stems from ambiguous standards of desirability. The efficiency of cause–effect relations can be computed but uncertainty exists about what output is desirable. Again, social tests must be brought to bear.

If we pause and think about it, social tests are not so uncommon. In fact many of them are a regular and official part of organizational life. Scientists in R&D departments present papers at conferences where their research undergoes close scrutiny and criticism by colleagues from other organizations. Students elect the 'teacher of the year'. Panels of journalists decide best article awards. Small groups of critics make artists, playwrights, and writers famous, or even infamous. A panel of expert accountants from industry, government, and universities judge the annual reports of corporations. Research funds are granted by a group of distinguished academics who judge the fitness of the applicants to conduct the research work. Deans and department heads use the number of research grants received for promotion decisions; and for many, the ultimate social test is the Nobel Prize, which is awarded for outstanding contributions to various scientific and social fields. Examples abound and in each case the social tests are anchored not in organizational rationality, but in the collective opinions and beliefs of relevant social groups.

Such tests, of course, are not without problems. It is well to recall that when Giuseppi Verdi applied to the Academy of Music in Rome, he was turned away for 'lack of ability'; the French impressionist painters were shunned by the Academy of Art; and several universities rejected Albert Einstein's application for enrolment due to 'weakness of background and lack of promise'. Still, in the absence of efficiency and instrumental tests, social ones, even though capricious and precarious, provide at least some information about fitness for future action.

Social tests, in fact, play a critical role in organizations. More often than not an organizational component, even if deemed to be a separate and autonomous subunit, is in reality highly dependent on several other components. A typical example is a parts and assembly plant which is treated as an autonomous profit center within an integrated consumer durable goods organization competing in a wide range of home appliances. Transfer price systems and methods for allocation of joint costs are used to develop efficiency and instrumental tests for the plant. These tests, however, lose some of their bite and credibility since output is highly dependent on the performance of other interdependent components, such as engineering, marketing, and sales. Consequently, social tests, although informal and even invisible, come to the fore. The expectations, beliefs, and opinions of the other managers in the network are the crucial test of performance and fitness for future action. Does the component fill its quotas? Does it deliver as promised? Does it follow the rules? Are its members good team players?

The confidence expressed in a component by the other co-ordinate interdependent units is an important and relevant assessment test.

In addition to scorekeeping for individual departments, organizations also attempt to assess the overall performance of the entire organization. In stable environments historical improvement, particularly growth, is taken as evidence of both current fitness and past performance. In dynamic environments, however, historical improvement is of little consequence and organizations turn to comparisons with similar organizations. Business firms, for example, try to convince investors, bankers, shareholders, suppliers, customers, and employees that they compare favorably with competitors. To do this they point to increasing share of market, amounts spent on R&D, and the number of new products brought on the market. Universities publicize the more rapid than average improvement in the quality of their students and the quantity of research done by their faculty. Historical improvement and favorable comparison with similar organizations are the vehicles for convincing relevant social groups of organizational fitness.

Assessment and scorekeeping, however, become even more difficult when there are several important external groups to satisfy. Organizations, realizing they cannot compare favorably on all criteria, try to hold some constant, and show improvement in crucial areas. A business firm needing a bank loan will attempt to score well on the balance sheet, especially working capital and liquidity ratios, by investing in inventories and paying suppliers in a timely fashion, whereas firms seeking new equity capital will attempt to score well on the income statement, particularly in the earnings per share category. Universities try to convince government funding agencies that their operating budgets are kept at a minimum consistent with some quality standard, all the while demonstrating to alumni and prospective students that the quality of teaching, already very high, is improving. They also try to convince accrediting agencies and research funding committees that faculty scholarly output is better than ever.

Often, then, organizations appear to be speaking out of both sides of their faces at the same time when in reality they are merely trying to hold some aspects of performance constant and show improvement in those areas important to critical external assessment. Coping with the need to satisfy simultaneously many different elements is no easy matter.

The problem becomes all the more difficult when dependency on various groups fluctuates. Here the organization must adjust the relative weightings of the multiple and varying criteria. The US automobile industry is a case in point. For many years shareholders' requirements for growth in earnings per share, customers' wants for bigger and more powerful cars, and managers' needs for large annual profit-based bonus and stock option schemes motivated the Big Three US automobile companies to concentrate on the larger, accessory-loaded automobiles which, of course, produced the highest profits. In the interim, however, important environmental elements shifted away from shareholders, managers, and large-car customers. Safety, pollution, quality of working life, energy conservation, and eventually jobs for auto workers emerged as dominant criteria. The Big Three, spurred on by declining profits, the success of Japanese competitors, and government regulations, slowly but surely shifted its assessment criteria to stress factors such as safety tests, fuel consumption, improvement in working conditions, and the number of jobs at stake. Although the scorekeeping task is difficult when critical elements change and weightings shift, the search for clues about the shifting weights enhances flexibility and helps organizations shift to a different but more viable equilibrium with changing demands.

Thompson, then, brilliantly utilized two uncertainty-creating factors and three general types of assessment tests to derive a rich general theory of how organizations deal with the critical problem of scorekeeping, both for components and for the entire organization. Some of the terrain is familiar to accounting and information systems managers, while other parts of the territory are new—particularly the idea that scorekeeping, under some conditions, must leave the economic realm and enter the domain of social opinions and beliefs.

When environments are stable and technologies perfect, organizations assess their components according to past efficiency. If these conditions are met only reasonably well, organizations continue to use efficiency scorekeeping and assess interdependence through evaluations by other components. If, however, technologies are imperfect, assessment must be based on instrumental tests as dictated by internal goals and strategies. But if components are internally autonomous, assessment must shift to extrinsic measures; and when standards of desirability are ambiguous, organizations must turn to the opinion of relevant social groups. Finally, under conditions of multiple criteria, organizations must be sensitive to, and quick to change the relative weightings of, the various criteria as the importance of relevant social groups also shifts with the fluctuating environment.

That accountants should gather, store, and report information about social opinions and beliefs, however, is a new and perhaps uncomfortable idea. There are, to be sure, many difficulties and challenges involved in this type of information processing, most of which are not found in our current stock of knowledge. Accounting textbooks and manuals, as yet, are not much help.

The idea is nevertheless slowly finding its way into our accounting and information systems knowledge base. We can no longer afford to ignore it; and when we do get into it, as we are doing in public sector organizations, we find it fascinating; after all, it may be a lot more fun and intriguing to design an information system around the collective opinions and beliefs of relevant social groups than to set up a standard cost accounting system.

UNCERTAINTY AND BEHAVIORAL AND OUTPUT CONTROLS

Thompson's ideas proved to be the springboard for Ouchi's (1977) theory about organizational control and scorekeeping. He recognized that formal financial control systems were only one aspect, admittedly an important one, of the various control mechanisms organizations apply; and he went on to identify the different circumstances which give rise to the utilization of the different controls.

Ouchi started his analysis by considering the problem of goal congruence. The central problem for organizations, he insisted, is to find suitable means for directing the efforts of a large number of different persons and diverse components towards global purpose. Consequently, organizations design systems to monitor, evaluate, and reward individuals in a manner which encourages them to work towards the organization's overall goals. The controls provide the glue which prevents the efforts of the individuals from flying off in many directions at the same time.

Controls, Ouchi argued, come in one of two fundamental forms. The first, labeled behavioral control, involves observing the actions of individuals as they go about their work. The second, called output control, consists of monitoring individual outputs. Behavioral controls are perhaps the most common. They entail direct personal observation of individuals as they work. They also involve issuing appropriate commands when corrective action is judged to be in order.

Foremen, for example, watch the workers on an assembly line closely, knowing that, if the work is done exactly as prescribed, the expected quantity and quality of product will automatically ensue. Department managers in a retail store keep a watchful eye on the way sales personnel dress, approach customers, ring up sales, and wrap parcels. Apprenticeships for trades, internships for medical students, and training camps for aspiring athletes involve intensive training periods where neophytes work under the close surveillance of certified experts. Behavioral control assumes knowledge of cause and effect relationships; if the correct means are followed, the desired ends will follow. Under these conditions effective control can be achieved by having superiors watch and guide the actions of subordinates.

Behavioral controls, it is important to note, are not necessarily hard-hearted. In fact, they are often exercised within a flexible, considerate, and warm relationship. Either way an essential ingredient is the acceptance by subordinates of the authority invested in the superior to watch, command, and guide their actions. The basic ingredients of successful behavioral controls, then, are an understanding of the cause and effect relationships of instrumental action, a knowledgeable superior, and an acceptance by the subordinates of the established authority hierarchy.

Output controls are of a different nature. They involve collecting and reporting information about the outcomes of work effort. Accounting systems are an example. They collect, filter, store, aggregate, and disseminate information about sales volumes, unit costs, spoilage, and resource utilization. Organizations, of course, make full use of output controls. Cost accounting systems, variance analysis reports, operating budgets, and profit–cost–volume charts abound.

Output controls, it should be recognized, have one great advantage. Upper management do not have to be involved in direct observation of the actions and behavior of subordinates. Nor do they have to be knowledgeable about the means used to achieve the results. They merely rely on output reports to know whether or not results conformed to expectations.

Consider some practical examples. For a chemical refinery, the actual yield of chemicals and the consumption of feedstock is measured and compared with predetermined standard quantities. Direct surveillance and issuance of instructions is not necessary to achieve control. Upper management can afford to ignore the behavior of employees as long as outputs meet required levels. For a television show, network officials can rely on the 'ratings' without knowing how the producer went about putting together a successful production. Teachers can use examination results to control students without knowing anything about the students' study habits. The point is that formal impersonal information can be used instead of direct observation of the instrumental action.

Output controls, however, must be used judiciously. In some circumstances they are a mixed blessing. At higher levels, for example, output controls are far from ideal. High levels of interdependencies obscure individual contributions; complexity is high, specific technical expertise about top-level jobs is thin; and role ambiguity is common. Yet ambitious upper-level managers often go overboard to provide evidence of their contributions. They seek out and develop output measures. A budget, for example, is welcomed since it reduces role ambiguity and provides managers with a sense of knowing where they are going and how they are doing. The temptation, however, is to treat output controls as unambiguous evidence of performance, when in reality they contain only vague information.

Organizations, then, have a choice of two powerful mechanisms —behavioral and output controls—for directing managers and employees towards global objectives. There are, however, a few important practical issues to resolve. Are the two controls independent? Under what conditions should each be employed? Are they substitutes for each other? Can they be used in tandem? In order to answer these questions Ouchi derived a simple but powerful analytical scheme, depicted in Figure 9.2, based on two antecedent conditions—knowledge of transformation processes and availability of output measures. These conditions are almost synonymous with Thompson's basic assessment variables. The appropriate control mode, Ouchi observed, is dictated by these antecedent conditions. When knowledge of the transformation process is perfect, behavioral controls are sufficient. Superiors simply issue the appropriate orders. And when output measures are available, formal reports are satisfactory. Superiors have no need to observe the actions of their subordinates.

In cell 1, task knowledge is high and output measures available. So both kinds of controls are suitable. In a tin-can plant, for example, foremen watch the actions of employees on the line and plant management keep records

Knowledge of the transformation process

		Perfect	Imperfect
	High	Behavioral and/or output measurement (Apollo program)	Output measurement (Women's boutique)
Ability to measure output		1	2
	Low	3 Behavioral measurement (tin can plant)	4 Ritual and ceremony "clan" control (research laboratory)

Figure 9.2 Uncertainty situations and control measurements. (Source: Ouchi, 1979, p. 843. Reproduced by permission of the Institute of Management Sciences.)

and receive reports about production quantities, spoilage, efficiency, and overtime. And in a Zen monastery each monk is assigned an irrational riddle, called a mondo, and told precisely how, where, and when to sit while puzzling over its meaning. Periodically, each monk comes before the Master and is questioned closely, whereupon the Master ascertains whether or not the monk has penetrated the meaning of the mondo and thus attained a measure of enlightenment—the desired output. If so, the monk is given the next level of mondo to puzzle through. The monks accept both the Master's position as unquestionable head of the monastery and his judgement as an enlightened person. Both behavioral and output controls are suitable for tin-can plants and Zen monasteries.

In cell 2, knowledge of the transformation process is imperfect and so observation and surveillance of subordinate behavior is not fruitful. Output measures, however, are available. So formal reports and information about results is the preferred means of control. In the case of a life insurance agency the correct way of selling customers life insurance is not known. But the results of sales efforts—dollars of life insurance coverage and premiums—can be easily measured. Although the life insurance agency has only the option of output controls, they are highly satisfactory.

Moving to cell 3, knowledge of the transformation process is complete but output measures for individual efforts are not available. This situation is illustrated by the 'double-play' in baseball. Knowing how an effective infielder must behave in conjunction with the other infielders to make a double-play, but being unable to count or measure each player's contribution to the number of double-plays, the coach has no alternative but to observe how the individual executes the play and, if called for, make specific suggestions for improvement of technique. Such behavioral controls are not only appropriate but, in the absence of output measures, essential.

In cell 4 we encounter the most difficult and problematic control setting. Not only are output measures unavailable, but also knowledge of the task transformation process is imperfect. So neither behavioral nor output controls work very well. The organization must seek other mechanisms. Usually these are imperfect, indirect, and unsatisfactory.

The US foreign service corps is a case in point. The corps is charged with the goal of improving the foreign relations of the United States throughout the world. The outputs of the individual officers and the country offices cannot be usefully measured; and knowledge does not exist of how to transform the actions of the foreign officers into good foreign relations. For the corps, therefore, the prime control turns out to be the hiring process. Prospective candidates are put through an extensive series of examinations, interviews, and scrutiny of background to guarantee that those eventually hired exceed generally accepted standards of training and ability. Those selected then undergo intensive training and indoctrination with ceremony, protocol, and ritual receiving great emphasis. It is assumed that 'good people' will deliver 'good' foreign relations even though neither the precise way of producing nor measuring good relations is available. The control mechanism in this case is a form of social control, a subject which will be discussed at length later in this chapter.

In order to test these ideas a survey of managers and employees in 78 full line department stores was conducted. The results, in addition to supporting most of the ideas, proved to be the source of even more insights into the control process. Task knowledge was associated with both types of control. Output controls were used more, and behavioral controls less, as the knowledge of the task becomes less well-understood. Employees in receiving, shipping, stock, and other clerical jobs, as well as department managers and sales supervisors, were subjected to more behavioral and less output control than were salespeople and buyers. Also, when subunits were highly specialized, and therefore dissimilar, the use of output measures increased. Output controls, of course, feature 'hard' numbers and give the impression of allowing comparability and uniformity of meaning across subunits engaged in quite different tasks. Not surprisingly, then, they are favored over other controls for specialized units. By contrast, when tasks are similar across subunits, the organizational structure is relatively less complex and the need for measures of output is reduced.

Another fascinating finding was that the levels of client income were positively associated with both the completeness and the use of output measures. In stores catering to high-income clients, for example, sales records proved to be the major control. What seems to happen is that department stores have three major objectives—sales, store maintenance, and customer service. Maintenance encompasses attendance, punctuality, proper dress, reports and paperwork, cash drawer control, sales suggestions, helping new sales clerks, and general attention to keeping the department neat and orderly. Service involves matters such as co-ordinating delivery, facilitating credit, gift wrapping, and handling returns and exchanges. High-income clientele will not put up with shoddy maintenance and poor service. Rather, they demand competence, using a variety of devices, including berating the sales clerks, speaking to the manager, and writing to the president. Upper management are well aware of this and so can place a great deal of emphasis on sales volume with impunity. It is not necessary to bother with output measures for maintenance and service. When employees come under the close scrutiny of clients it is unnecessary for management to monitor performance in these areas.

In stores patronized by low-income clientele, by contrast, mistreated customers do not fight. They simply flee, never to return. Management are aware of this and are loathe to use sales reports for fear of producing a 'hard-sell' atmosphere at the expense of customer service and maintenance. Consequently, output measures are not stressed.

Larger firms invest more in employee training than do smaller ones. They place a great deal of emphasis on orientation sessions for new employees, careful training on new methods, extensive demonstration of new products, and technical back-up for departmental managers during employee performance reviews. These activities are, of course, an indirect form of behavioral controls. They 'mold' correct behavior and so dampen the natural tendency of sales personnel to focus on sales, while neglecting service and maintenance. Large organizations, then, invest in training in order to reduce their reliance on output controls.

So the control problem is more complex than originally thought. The view of control as merely a monitoring, evaluating, and rewarding process is clearly inadequate. Output measures can never fully capture all the sought-after performance; and in many cases they capture only a small fraction of the performance domain. As we saw, department stores have multiple goals and rely on client reactions, training, and direct surveillance to complement output measures. Importantly, then, the control process requires a judicious balance of several mechanisms.

Encouraged by these findings, Ouchi and Maguire (1975) used them as the take-off place for further investigation into the control process. This time data were collected from over 2000 employees and 300 managers in five department store chains. The results supported the conclusions of the initial study. The level of hierarchy, for example, influenced the type of control utilized. Behavioral controls increased at lower levels, while output controls decreased with one important exception. At the very bottom level output control increased sharply; and combined controls increased substantially at each subsequent lower level.

Several reasons were offered for this. For one thing, upper levels in organizations feature imperfect task knowledge, task complexity, and high interdependencies with other parts of the organization. Obviously surveillance, close monitoring, and issuing instructions would be inappropriate. So control falls back on overall output measures such as sales, sales returns, inventory turnover, stock-outs, and mark-downs.

At lower levels, by contrast, tasks are simple, interdependencies are low, and superiors have more expertise with the details of the work. Here behavior controls can be used to advantage. Curiously, the use of output controls declines at each lower level in the hierarchy until the lowest level is reached, when their use suddenly increases sharply. One explanation is that if output is to be measured at all levels in a department store the data must be collected at the lowest level and then aggregated for each subsequent higher level. This leads to an over-emphasis on output measures for sales personnel, the denizens of the lowest level. Further, it is here that tasks are simple and behavioral controls easy to apply. Consequently, salespersons are subject to intense amounts of both behavioral and output controls. This creates a dilemma since salespersons are paid on the basis of sales volume, but are supervised closely and forced to spend time on maintenance and service, which compete with their selling efforts.

A different, but not conflicting, interpretation would be as follows. By far the greatest numbers of employees are clustered in relatively homogeneous departments at the lowest level in department stores. These wage costs are second only to the cost of merchandise. The departments are buffered from environmental shocks and interdependencies with the rest of the organization by service departments such as credit, delivery, buying, and warehousing. Consequently, they operate under relatively stable conditions. So, in the interests of both efficiency and effectiveness they can be, and indeed are, subjected to intense amounts of both output and behavioral controls. Either way, the lower levels are subjected to massive doses of controls.

To summarize, control is essentially a process of monitoring, evaluating, and rewarding individual actions either by observation and surveillance or by using records of output. Two antecedent conditions—the availability of output measures and the degree of perfection in the knowledge of the task transformation process—dictate the appropriate type of control. Under some conditions, unfortunately, neither type is suitable and organizations are left to resort to other, but less satisfactory, mechanisms.

These ideas have very practical considerations. We know that organizational control systems often go awry or even backfire. A major reason for this is inattention to the central demands of the two antecedent conditions. Designers may have an obsession with accounting measures. The political goals of powerful people may take priority in selecting controls. The careerism of ambitious middle and lower managers may intervene so that the correct control response is not followed. The unhappy result is the utilization of inappropriate means of control and, eventually, a great deal of grief for the accounting and information systems managers.

Market, bureaucratic, and clan control

Ouchi followed this investigation with a brilliant analysis of the organizational control problem at a higher level of abstraction (Ouchi, 1979, 1980). From this vantage point three basic controls—market, bureaucratic, and clan—were identified and a powerful framework derived identifying the appropriate conditions for each. Bureaucratic controls, as discussed above, consist of both behavioral and output measures.

Accounting and information systems designers, however, will be less familiar with the concept of market controls. Successful markets have two conditions—self-interest and honesty. Self-interest provides the necessary motivation for the market. Honesty provides the necessary reliability to assure that the expectations of individuals are delivered as promised. When both self-interest and honesty are present, market prices subsume the information about all the individuals trading in the market. Consequently, individuals do not need to collect, store, and process mounds of information about everyone's needs and spending preferences. The invisible organization of the market captures and condenses this information into market prices.

Thus the information capacity of the market is a marvelously efficient vehicle for mediating amongst individuals. This is particularly so for spot markets where commitments and obligations are short-term. Market prices, then, enable individuals to pursue their goals in a wonderfully efficient manner. The invisible organization of the market-place provides the required control. There is no need for more complicated arrangements.

The idea that organizations might use markets for control may come as a surprise; obviously this is not the main business of markets. Yet if circumstances are favorable it is possible to use them to advantage. Ouchi quotes a practical example from one of his research sites, the Parts Division of a major company where a sharp contrast in organizational control style existed between the warehouse and the purchasing department. In the former, bureaucratic controls prevailed, while the latter relied on market controls.

In the warehouse 150 foremen and supervisors oversaw the work of nearly 1400 pickers and packers. The foremen gathered information about the workflow from two sources: first, by watching the workers to ascertain who was doing a good job and who was not; second, they queried workers about the way in which they performed their tasks and, if appropriate, gave orders to follow proper procedures. The other source of information was records of daily output for each worker. The foremen used these reports to confirm personal observations. The foremen, of course, worked within the limits of formal rank and organizational authority, along with the informal limits bestowed on them by the workers. Surveillance, output records, and the organizational hierarchy ensured an effective and efficient flow of work.

In the purchasing department, by contrast, only a few supervisors and a dozen or so clerks purchased hundreds of thousands of items each year from thousands of suppliers. The purchasing agents received bids for each order from a handful of suppliers and accepted the lowest bid quoted on the condition that the supplier had a reputation for reliability and honesty. Instead of undertaking costly surveillance and monitoring of the efficiency, quality control mechanisms, and delivery systems of each potential supplier, the company utilized market prices and competition to promote efficiency and quality on the part of the suppliers.

Within the purchasing department itself, market controls also were at work. As long as the purchasing agents were getting competitive bids for each order and sampling delivered products for quality, there was little need for either surveillance or output records. The manager needed only to spot-check that the purchasing agents were accepting the lowest bids. Market control, then, proved both effective and efficient for controlling both suppliers and purchasing agents.

Unfortunately, however, markets are not always efficient. There are several causes of this. Sometimes all facets of the transaction do not take place on the spot. Commitments may feature future obligations, as in the case of a new-car warranty, or payments may be promised over several years, as for a mortgage contract. Sometimes a sale is unique, such as when a market price is not available for a corporate acquisition. Such market imperfections lead to what are known as transaction costs.

Transaction costs occur when each party to an exchange must be satisfied that the value received accords with expectations. Lawyers, appraisors, auditors, and accountants must be brought in to assure that the parties carry out their side of the contract. These services add a costly, but necessary, layer of administration on top of the market organization. Now at a certain point, market imperfections drive transaction costs so high that the market fails. When this happens the bureaucratic form replaces market organization and is now the preferred mode of control.

A bureaucracy, of course, is a means of mediating amongst a large number of individuals who have agreed to exchange their talents for organizational rewards. Once they join, however, the individuals must be directed in their actions towards organizational purpose. Organizations accomplish this by establishing a hierarchy of supervisory positions and endowing incumbents with the authority to oversee the work of others. The individuals, it is important to note, willingly give up their autonomy and submit to the hierarchy. In addition to the hierarchy, organizations establish reporting systems for measuring outputs of both individuals and departments.

Hierarchies and output measures, then, are the key elements of bureaucratic control. They are not, however, cost-free. Staffs of accountants, information system specialists, analysts, personnel people, lawyers, and a host of other support staff are paid to design and administer the bureaucracy. These are, in effect, the transaction costs of bureaucratic arrangements.

Organizations, in spite of these costs, can be effective if they can measure the outputs and contributions of each individual, or if they have a clear understanding of the task-transformation process. This, of course, is not always the case. Sometimes standards of desirability do not contain reasonable performance information. Further, standards are, at best, only approximate representations of desired behavior and output levels, and soon lose their effectiveness when they do not contain reasonable performance information. Also, standards are prone to idiosyncratic interpretation by managers and employees alike. They become even more problematic when tasks are unique, when the task conversion process is not perfectly understood, or when job interdependencies are high, making it impossible to determine the value added by each individual. When standards no long provide either the necessary motivational force or the direction necessary for goal congruence, the bureaucracy fails.

Clan controls

When market controls lose their information content and bureaucratic controls fail, organizations have little recourse but to turn to a more subtle and less tangible means of control which Ouchi labels 'clan controls'. These are a special form of social control. They have several distinctive and intangible qualities. Clan controls are an extreme form of belief, held by the individuals in the organization, that their interests are best served by the complete immersion of every member in the interests of the whole. A strong sense of solidarity prevails and commitment towards organizational goals runs high.

Clan controls are subtle, illusive, but powerful. Members share a profound common agreement about what constitutes proper behavior; it may take a long time to learn and new members are not able to function effectively until they are absorbed. In the US Senate, for example, it takes newly elected senators several years to discover and assimilate its traditions. Performance evaluation is a continuous process of subtle signals from old-time members. In the final analysis clan controls are more powerful than either market or bureaucratic ones.

A striking example of clan control comes from the exploits of the Japanese Kamikaze pilots who shocked and stunned the world with their certain-death attacks on US warships during World War II. The name Kamikaze was taken from the legendary 'divine wind' which miraculously destroyed Kublai Khan's huge invasion fleet and saved Japan from certain defeat and repressive colonization.

The force consisted of a special squadron formed spontaneously in the autumn of 1944 from pilots and officers of the Japanese First Air Fleet in a last-ditch, desperate attempt to slow down the American invasion forces. Its mission was to destroy as many enemy aircraft carriers and other warships as possible. Each pilot attempted to crash his plane, loaded with a 250 kilogram bomb, into a warship. It is important to understand, however, that the resources of the First Air Fleet were severely depleted and that the chances of scoring a hit by a Kamikaze attack were very high compared with conventional bombing.

Each pilot fervently believed his individual interests were served best by complete personal immersion in the needs of Japan and the Emperor. It was understood that each flier would sacrifice himself and his plane by crashing into an enemy warship. National ruin without resistance was eternal ignominy. These beliefs were shared intensely by each pilot.

Rituals, ceremonies, and slogans played an important role in sustaining the organic solidarity of the force. Talks and memos from officers included slogans such as: 'to the divine glory of his majesty', 'win the Holy war', 'save the divine nation', and 'we are the imperial forces of heaven'. On the evening before their fatal mission, chosen pilots meditated and then wrote a philosophical and cheerful letter to loved ones at home. Fellow-pilots, not lucky enough to be chosen for that particular mission, sang the Kamikaze song; and before take-off the pilots performed the Hachimaki ceremony of wrapping the traditional white cloth, with a red circle on front symbolizing the rising sun, around each other's helmets, all the while chanting patriotic slogans.

The history of Kamikaze force is a rich example of the awesome potential of clan control. All the necessary ingredients were present—tradition, ritual, agreement on correct behavior, dedication to global purpose, and exclusive membership. Surveillance and output measures were out of the question. Not only were they unnecessary, they would have been seen as disgusting. The clan controls were more powerful than even the human desire to live.

Another interesting, if less dramatic, example of clan controls comes from the accounting profession. With no two clients being the same, a wide variety of complex problems with deep yet comprehensible structures are encountered. The accountant responds to these problems by skillful application of a well-stocked kit of cleverly designed, but intricate tools (Simon, 1977). The technical core of the accounting firm is dominated by skilled professionals armed with a repertoire of standard programs for predetermined situations (Weick, 1976). Their work consists of diagnosing client problems and skillfully applying the appropriate program. For most accountants it is highly pleasurable work. Just as the surgeon uses a scalpel, the accountant uses a pencil; both must be sharp and applied independently to exceedingly complex functions (Mintzberg, 1979).

Another important aspect of the professional accounting job is a personal and close relationship with the client. This requires autonomy, since clients are spread around a geographic territory. Thus, at any one time the complement of professional accountants is widely dispersed. Clearly, therefore, close surveillance and monitoring is impossible and, in any event, would be anathema to the professional; and, as the long-run output of the professional is quality service, satisfactory output controls are nearly impossible to get hold of.

Not surprisingly, then, professional accounting firms rely heavily on clan controls. The accountant, as mentioned earlier, must master a number of complex tools, learn how to diagnose problems, and become skillful at applying the tools to the problems. These skills are acquired only after a long period of education at universities, training by professional associations, and on-the-job experience. They must pass rigorous examinations, while absorbing the profession's generally accepted principles and formal codes of ethics. Graduation ceremonies and certification rituals further reinforce the high level of solidarity and commitment to the goals of the accounting profession and its service to the wider society. These external controls, as Montagna's (1968) research demonstrated, are much more important than internal ones.

Nevertheless, accounting firms employ bureaucratic and market controls to the extent feasible. The time spent on each client is reported in great detail; it is compared with that of previous years, and used for billing purposes. Each audit file is reviewed closely by a senior member of the firm before finalization of the financial statements, tax returns, and management letters. Close monitoring of billable hours also provides a sort of a market test. Yet in the final analysis these controls are less satisfactory than social controls as the major mechanism.

The Kamikaze force and the accounting firms, of course, are extreme examples. Yet if we stop to think about it, clan controls are widespread. They are used to some extent in nearly all our institutions—families, schools, universities, fraternities, clubs, athletic teams, corporations, public accounting firms, professional associations, and governments. They are obviously a powerful means of motivating individuals towards global goals. Although they come to the fore when the efficacy of market and bureaucratic controls fade, they are also used frequently along with the other two types.

Having identified and defined in detail three very different types of control, we are ready to move on and address the issue of when, and under what conditions, each of them, or combinations thereof, should be employed. As a way into these issues Ouchi again utilized the two antecedent control conditions—the ability to measure outputs and the degree of perfection of means–ends relationship knowledge—to derive the matrix containing four control situations as in Figure 9.2.

In the first cell the control mechanism for the Apollo moon shot program is considered. An unambiguous output measure is available—Did or did not the capsule get there and back successfully? For the president of the United States, and the directors of the space program, this is unquestionably the key measure. In addition, however, behavioral controls can be used since each step for the operation can be specified in advance; and since the cost of failure is prohibitive, an elaborate behavioral control system, involving hundreds of ground controllers using powerful computers to monitor every step, is preferable and, in fact, was used as the control mechanism for the moon shot.

In the next cell we have only imperfect knowledge of how to operate a women's boutique successfully. Behavioral controls are thus ruled out; but precise measures of output, such as sales, profit margins, average markdowns, and inventory turnover rates are readily computable. Some of these, such as sales and gross margins, are almost market controls. In this case market and bureaucratic output controls are appropriate.

As for the tin-can plant in the next cell, it is impossible to measure the output of any individual working on the line; output controls cannot be used. The technology, however, is well understood. Supervisors can watch both the actions of each employee and the workings of the machine to see if they accord with proper action. If they do, they can know without counting or inspecting that the right quantity and quality of tin-cans are coming off the line. Behavioral controls are highly appropriate here.

In the case of the research laboratory in the final cell, however, behavioral controls are ruled out because the precise rules of action defining the process of scientific discovery are not clear. Nor are output measures appropriate since it may take years to determine the ultimate success of R&D efforts. As neither bureaucratic nor market forms of control are effective the organization must turn to clan mechanisms, including: highly selective recruitment of well-schooled professionals, seminars for 'hazing' ideas and papers, professional society meetings, encouragement of the writing of articles for learned journals, and awards for breakthroughs. These and other social tests are used to reward researchers who display the underlying attitudes and values that lead to organizational success; and the researchers are mindful of what should be achieved, even though it is almost impossible to determine what is being accomplished.

In sum, market controls are preferred, where possible, because they require only prices and honesty. When transaction costs become excessive, markets fail and must be replaced by bureaucratic mechanisms. These require information about appropriate behavior and output, as well as the acceptance of the authority hierarchy. In turn, however, bureaucratic controls fail when standards of desirable performance are not available. They give way to clan controls based on shared values, beliefs, and goals. Three distinctive types of controls, then, are identified; and importantly, the conditions that determine their appropriateness are defined.

These are rich and elegant ideas about control in organizations. Some of them will be new, even uncomfortable, for accounting and information systems managers who are technical experts on output controls but unfamiliar with the idea of social controls. What is valuable about Ouchi's work, then, is that it places accounting and information systems within a broader framework of other organizational control systems and it defines the conditions of where and when to use them. The framework is a powerful way of analyzing the informational and social requirements of control system design. We now have a perspective of control system that is quite different from our previous view.

PRACTICAL IMPLICATIONS

These ideas are not wholly theoretical. In fact they have very important practical implications for guiding accounting and information systems managers. Their power can be demonstrated with a practical illustration of the management control system in a new health center.

The center was established under the auspices of a leading hospital as an autonomous unit in a separate location (see 'Hyatt Hill Health Center', in Anthony and Dearden, 1981, p. 720). Its purpose was to provide a full range of preventative as well as therapeutic health care to the residents of a nearby slum district. The mission departments included Pediatrics, Internal Medicine, Community Mental Health, Nursing, Dental Health, Social Service, and Nutrition. Each department was staffed by high-caliber physicians and practitioners who held joint appointments at the parent hospital. These professionals incurred a substantial loss in earnings by working at the center. The quality of their work was controlled by careful screening and selection of physicians, a continuing peer review by department heads, and random reviews of medical records by a review committee. The primary objective of the center was to be a prevention-oriented family centered source of health care, available to all community residents. The administrators also hoped that in the long run the center would become financially self-sufficient.

The center had a good financial accounting system, as well as line-item budget controls. Feelings that costs were above average for this kind of an establishment, however, led the administrative director to have a consultant install a new management control system. The source data for the new system came from detailed forms which reported the actual time spent with a patient, the total minutes available, and the salary rates for each practitioner. These data were used to calculate the cost per minute for each physician, and to create a series of reports including: total costs for each department, average cost for each practitioner per visit and by type of visit, and average cost per encounter for each department. The reports included standard and average cost data and highlighted whether or not each physician had spent more or less time than average for each encounter, and whether or not direct patient care time had changed from the previous period.

The new control system was used to assess the monthly performance of each physician. The data were distributed to the department heads and discussed at executive and departmental meetings. Also the director met individually with each physician, and used the new control system as a focal point for reviewing their allocation of time.

Reactions to the new system were mixed. The administrators were pleased with it and believed it had greatly increased cost-consciousness behavior on the part of the staff. Evidence of this was the hiring of low-salary people to relieve the physicians from routine tasks. The department heads allowed that the new system made them more aware of time constraints and costs, but believed that it ignored important long-term effects of spending time out in the community. They also complained that the new system had brought about a philosophical change by the administration to increase the volume of direct patient care and a decreased emphasis on the quality of care and on preventative medicine.

Let us use some of the ideas in this chapter to analyze and highlight some critical problems with the new control system. For one thing, there are two quite different tasks involved—direct therapeutic medical care (TMC) and preventative-oriented, family-centered health care (PFC). In the case of TMC, objectives are unambiguous—to effect a successful cure; and cause–effect knowledge is complete for some patients (a broken leg) but incomplete for others (cancer). The new control system does a good job of measuring the efficiency of TMC activity. It is likely, however, that effectiveness is more important than efficiency; yet the new control system paid it no heed. There were, however, traditional indirect controls on effectiveness—careful selection of practitioners, peer reviews, and test checks of medical records. The motivation of the new control system is strong; and its message is efficient TMC.

The case of PFC, however, is quite a different matter. Objectives are obviously ambiguous and the ability to measure outputs is low. Also the knowledge of the transformation process is incomplete. Clearly, then, the new management control system, with its efficiency orientation, is not only unsuitable but also counterproductive to PFC activities. Routine, programmable tasks have a natural tendency to drive out non-routine, non-programmable ones (Simon, 1977). When this tendency is strongly reinforced by the control system, with the physicians consequently spending more time on TMC than previously, the results could prove highly detrimental for PFC activities.

The ideas in this chapter also provide clues about the design of a more appropriate management and control system. When efficiency and instrumental tests are of only limited usefulness, we turn to social ones. There are three relevant social groups involved in the center—the slum community, the funding body, and the physicians themselves. Periodic surveys should be taken of the families in the community regarding the center as a key aspect of PFC is acceptance of the center by this social group. Information should also be collected about increases in the number of families registered, the number of vaccinations, dental check-ups, fluoride treatments, and the like, to demonstrate to funding agencies that historical improvement has taken place. The fostering of a 'clan' atmosphere for the physicians could be undertaken to advantage. The physicians have willingly given up a higher income to dedicate themselves, at least for a time, to solving the health problems of the slum. Clan control, in fact, is remarkably well-suited to the type of work necessary to achieve the major aim of the center.

To summarize, we have a classical case of the skillful design of a technically sound control system which is quite unsuitable to the prevailing circumstances. The detailed cost accounting system was thoughtlessly designed and used without regard for the purposes of the organization or the nature of its work. Efficiency of TMC became the focal point for performance measurement. As a result the new management control system had a profound effect.

The practitioners shifted their efforts to TMC to the neglect of the center's fundamental purpose.

Clearly, then, the ideas outlined in this chapter have very practical implications for analysis of real-life situations. They offer a means for determining a fitting assessment and control requirements for varying circumstances, as defined by the particular context of uncertainty. The arguments are compelling; and they have an appealing sense of endurement.

CONCLUSIONS

It is time to review our discussion of the concepts and frameworks outlined above, and hazard some conclusions about a few major issues which surface. First it seems abundantly clear that these ideas provide a solid framework for a new approach to the problems of designing appropriate assessment and control systems. The new approach is based on two principles—the need to go beyond, although not to exclude, rational systems, and the need to work in a middle ground between universal laws and profound understanding of unique systems.

The rational approach attempts to optimize the use of resources in a given objective function, and is highly satisfactory for stable and predictable parts of the organization such as the technical core. Efficiency tests are an integral part of the drive to optimize; but efficiency loses its power in the face of changing and uncertain environments. So the rational approach, so well suited to a predictable closed system, must give way to an open or natural systems perspective which focuses on the mechanisms whereby organizations react, adapt, and survive in the face of an incessantly changing environment. Historical efficiency tests must give way first to the criteria of instrumental effectiveness and ultimately to the opinions and beliefs of relevant social groups. A natural systems approach replaces a rational one.

The other basic element of this new perspective is that it rejects either the quest for universal truths or the preoccupation with exhaustive analysis of the uniqueness of the scorekeeping and control systems in one organization. Instead, a middle ground is advocated where the patterned variations in the uncertainty are linked with systematic differences in organizational action, including the assessment of performance and control of the activities of individual managers and of the entire organization. Different kinds of uncertainty lead to different patterns of assessment and control.

By following a natural systems perspective and looking for patterned variations, Thompson and Ouchi were able to capture the full range of assessment and controls mechanisms used in organizations (efficiency, instrumental, social, bureaucratic, output, behavioral, market, and clan controls). These ideas put accounting and information systems for control into the wider and more realistic organizational context, thus providing accounting and information systems managers with a richer understanding of how to make their systems effective.

Yet, somehow, we are left with the feeling that the picture is incomplete and that something important is missing. The ideas are neat, tidy, and obviously powerful. Yet they seem almost at odds with the realities of the motion, or more accurately the commotion, we readily experience and observe when we work in any specific organization or study it up close.

The problem, I think, lies at least partly with the idea of a one-way direction of influence among the major forces. The rationale followed by Thompson and Ouchi is that environment and technology dictate the nature of the uncertainty, which in turn has a compelling effect on the appropriate control and assessment systems. Yet it may be that these contingency notions are naive—a one-way causal train of events may be too simplistic (Otley, 1980).

We see, for example, in the health center illustration, that the new management control system, with its focus on efficiency, caused a shift in effort on the part of the physicians and other professionals, from PFC efforts to TMC; and, because the nature of TMC work contains a different type of uncertainty than does PFC, it is apparent that the new system influenced the type of work undertaken by the professionals. This, in turn, determined the nature of the organizational uncertainty. So instead of causation flowing from environment and objectives to technology and in turn to management control system, the train of influence went in exactly the opposite direction! This, of course, is not an isolated instance. What, then, are we to conclude? Do we need to tamper with these models and ideas of assessment and control? Do we need to alter them in significant ways? Or must we abandon them and start afresh?

I think not. The problem lies in the fact that we have not paid enough attention to differences between longer-term macro-movements in the dynamics of organizational action and shorter-term micro-fluctuations. When the macro- and the micro-elements are seen as two separate yet coexisting systems, any picture of the complex dynamics of organizational action, including assessment and control, is more complete.

The micro-movements, then, seem to be the missing link in Thompson's and Ouchi's theories. The nature of environment, technology, and uncertainties give the long-run macro-movements the shape and use of assessment and control systems. Efficiency tests meet the long-run needs in predictable stable conditions; while social assessment is required for highly uncertain contexts. Yet in the short run, accounting and information systems may veer in what may appear to be an anarchistic random pattern which does not follow our neat models. The macro-movements are like a deep river, flowing surely and steadily downstream while the micro-movements form whirlpools, and even detour for a while from the inevitable trip to the ocean.

These micro-movements, of course, arise from the exigencies of the moment. Consider the following examples. A new president of an electrical consumer-good company reacts to Japanese competition by stressing product quality; the focus of the financial control system in the plant shifts from efficiency to effectiveness. A large foreign exchange loss, due to devaluation in the currency of a country where a large subsidiary is located, brings a shift to centralized management of capital and investment and an information system which spotlights currency expense and potential foreign exchange losses. The new controller of a sophisticated machine tool company hit with financial losses due to a slump in demand redesigns the financial control systems to stress efficiency and cost-cutting. Organizations, must, of necessity, react to these unpredictable shocks and disturbances. Along with this, of course, are short-run changes in the focus and intensity of assessment and control systems.

An analogy may be useful in getting this idea across. Each year we experience the four seasons. Our physical climate is shifted from hot to temperate, from temperate to cold, from cold to temperate, and from temperate to hot again. Yet sometimes in winter we have very warm spells. And sometimes in the summer we experience 'unseasonal' cold snaps. The daily movements ebb and flow over the more general heating or cooling movement of the season. It is the same with accounting and information systems. The micro-movements swirl and dart, first this way and then that way, over the surface of the macro-movements. Together the short-run micro-fluctuations and the long-run macro-movements create the texture and shape of the fabric of organizational assessment and control systems. Thus, we reach the laws of motion of the total system.

Thompson's and Ouchi's models provide the clues about the long-run macro-directions for our scorekeeping and control systems, but they are silent on the short-run macro-movements necessary because of the exigencies of the moment. It remained for others to build on this foundation and penetrate the dynamism of micro-flows of information.

In the next chapter our focus switches from the structuralism of macro-forces to some marvelous and insightful ways of capturing the rich and vibrant process of daily information flows in organizations.

References

Anthony, R. N., and J. Dearden, *Management Control Systems: Text and Cases*, rev. edn., Richard D. Irwin, Inc., Homewood, Ill., 1981.

Mintzberg, H., *The Structuring of Organizations*, Prentice-Hall, Inc., Englewood Cliffs, NJ, 1979.

Montagna, P. D., 'Professionalism and bureaucratization of large professional organizations', *The American Journal of Sociology*, 1968, pp. 138–145.

Otley, D., 'The contingency theory of management accounting: achievement and prognosis', *Accounting Organizations and Society*, Vol. 5, No. 4, 1980, pp. 413–428.

Ouchi, W. G., 'The relationship between organizational structure and organizational control', *Administrative Science Quarterly*, March 1977, pp. 25–113.

Ouchi, W. G., 'A conceptual framework for the design of organization control mechanisms', *Management Science*, September 1979, pp. 833–848.

Ouchi, W. G., 'Markets, bureaucracies and clans', *Administrative Science Quarterly*, March 1980, pp. 129–141.

188

Ouchi, W. G., and M. A. Maguire, 'Organizational control: two functions', *Administrative Science Quarterly*, December 1975, pp. 559–569.

Simon, H. A., *The New Science of Management Decision*, rev. edn, Prentice-Hall, Inc., Englewood Cliffs, NJ, 1977.

Thompson, J. D., *Organizations in Action*, McGraw-Hill Book Company, New York, 1967.

Weick, K. E., 'Educational organizations as loosely coupled systems', *Administrative Science Quarterly*, March 1976, pp. 1–19.

THREE. Future Directions for Accounting and Information Systems

CHAPTER 10

New Perspectives for Accounting and Information Systems

Thompson's ideas proved to be a watershed for a flood of behavioral accounting studies. By ingeniously invoking a natural systems approach, one which subsumed the formal and the rational perspectives, he saw scorekeeping and reporting in a much richer and more realistic vein than did previous researchers. The realization dawned that the flow of information in organizations, both formal and informal, is not merely a technical subject with a flimsy relationship to other organizational systems; rather it is a sturdy part of the organizational infrastructure influencing in its own right other systems and processes in important ways (Earl and Hopwood, 1980). As is often the case it took the eye of a stranger to see the issues clearly.

It is remarkable that accountants and information systems designers did not twig to this sooner. Perhaps we have been too close for too long to the trees of debits and credits, cost allocation schemes, and computerized reporting systems to see the forest of information and communication flows. Yet as we rush pellmell into the era of the information society, a narrow and technical view will no longer do.

Armed with these new insights, behavioral accounting efforts soon scaled the walls of the rational approach and spread over a wider and richer territory. We learned, for example, that information management is the key role of a manager. We came to realize that informal and non-routine information systems have more impact than formal and routine ones. We saw that managers and computers could be merged into a powerful decision support system. We recognized that the frame of references used to process information flows is often more important than the information processed; and we came to understand why organizations overinvest in information gathering.

Collectively, these ideas now form the base for a new body of knowledge dealing with the entire landscape of information gathering and processing in organizations. This chapter reviews some of the major works in this new tradition. Along the way it unearths a rich set of insights for accounting and information systems managers.

MANAGERS AS NERVE CENTERS

Our conventional textbooks portray the work of managers as neatly working out a blueprint for the organization, making sure it is properly staffed, and then using budgets and reports as feedback on progress to clearly defined ends. From this perspective, managerial work consists of planning, organizing, staffing, directing, co-ordinating, and reporting. In his famous research study, Mintzberg (1972, 1975) and his staff set out to confirm this view. Their method was simple. They merely followed five different top executives around for a week observing and recording what each did. They found that the reality of managerial work differed greatly from the conventional tableau.

Instead of methodically planning organizational objectives, the managers appeared to be immersed in an unrelenting stream of unconnected activities. They encountered about 250 separate incidents per week, which on average lasted less than ten minutes. They also kept dozens of longer-term projects orbiting simultaneously, periodically checking progress, juggling them a little, and then relaunching them; and, importantly, they seemed to abhor reflective tasks such as planning. Disorder, brevity and discontinuity—not orderly progress towards predetermined goals—was the order of the day. Yet the managers seemed to thrive on it.

Managerial roles

In order to make some sense out of this apparent chaos the researchers pigeonholed each incident into one of three major managerial roles—decisional, interpersonal, and informational. This proved to be an insightful step. Before long a clearer but newer picture of managerial work emerged.

Decision roles took considerably less time than either of the other two. This may come as a surprise to those of us who teach accounting and computing where we stress the decision-making role. This is not to say that decisional roles (entrepreneurial, disturbance handler, resource allocation, and negotiation) are not important. They are critical; and the managers have the authority and responsibility to make decisions; indeed they are required to make them. Yet, surprisingly, managers in the sample spent only a fraction of their time on them.

Interpersonal roles took more time. In fact, figurehead chores such as greeting visitors, taking important customers to lunch, attending weddings, and presenting gold watches to retiring employees consumed about 12 percent of the working day. The formal authority vested in them called for the managers to spend a great deal of time in personal contact with other people, including: clients, suppliers, peers, media, government officials, union representatives, professional association contacts, and trade association officers. Managers also spent a lot of time with subordinates—hiring, coaching, encouraging, reprimanding, and even firing them. Even though they do not involve decision-making, these interpersonal roles are important; and they can be performed only by the manager.

Informational roles, surprisingly, took more time than either decision-making or interpersonal roles. Rather than behaving like wise owls in a tree, they acted more like trout in a mountain stream—poking briefly here, flitting there, investigating this, nibbling that, turning suddenly and darting into a new pool to repeat the process. Information seemed to be their basic source of energy.

Managers as organizational nerve centers

Managers, it seems, spend the majority of their time processing information; and the manner in which they gather, store, move, and share it should be of vital interest to accounting and information systems managers. Managers receive information from external and internal sources, and they give it out in their disseminator, spokesman, and strategy-maker roles, as in Figure 10.1. Three aspects of this information processing activity stand out.

For one thing, each day managers collect information from a wide variety of sources. They receive mounds of mail. They are flooded with reports. They get briefings from their superiors and subordinates. They go on observational tours. They scan professional journals. They talk on the telephone. They grill peers and subordinates. They even plant private sources in strategic

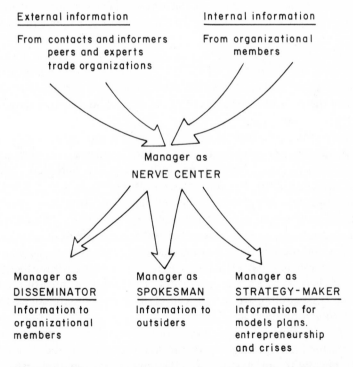

Figure 10.1 The manager as organizational nerve center. (Source: Mintberg, 1972, p. 93. © 1972 by the Regents of the University of California. Reprinted from *California Management Review*, Vol. XV, No. 1, pp. 93)

places. In fact, they spend most of their time planting, cultivating, and harvesting information from private networks.

There are good reasons for this. To be effective, managers must be the nerve centers of their organizational units. In order to perform this role they must know, not necessarily everything, but at least more than their subordinates. This is true in formal organizations as well as informal ones such as street-corner gangs. The leader is the person at the center of the information flow—not necessarily the best technical expert or the toughest street fighter. The leader is the one who perpetually monitors the environment for information and disseminates it within the organization. Subordinates must be informed, peers must be appraised, and bosses must be briefed. Managers also act as spokesman for the unit by passing information along, as required, to outsiders.

For leaders, then, information is their most valuable asset. It is a precious commodity; and managing their private information network is their most important skill. It must be carefully husbanded, skillfully exchanged, and judiciously passed around. Information is the manager's major lever to power.

Another outstanding feature of the way managers process information is their predilection for soft, verbal, detailed, and current information. They reach out eagerly for every scrap, including speculation, hearsay, rumor, and gossip. They also show a strong preference for verbal communication and seem to thrive on telephones, meetings, encounters in the hall or washroom, and coffee-break chats. In fact, the managers in the survey spent nearly 80 percent of their working time in verbal activities; and they like their information fresh, hot, and spicy.

The final striking feature of managerial information processing is the way they use information to make decisions. Managers are constantly gathering odds and ends of data from their network. These bits and pieces are tucked away in the brain until one new piece suddenly acts as a trigger for all of it to come together, like a bolt from the blue, and form into an important message. This is not to say that managers are unthinking bundles of nerves reacting synoptically to each piece of information. Instead, it seems as if they have plans and models tucked away inside their heads to be updated as new information appears. Nevertheless, when this 'ah-hah' strikes, the managers react as if charged by an electric current. They think nothing of interrupting meetings, rescheduling workdays, cancelling long-standing engagements, in order to follow the new insights.

A manager's work, then, is information processing, not aloofly orchestrating a master plan. Managers are the nerve centers of their organization. They frantically monitor, store, and disseminate information, especially the soft and current variety, and then use it to make intuitive, off-the-cuff decisions. This style, it should be underlined, suits the nature of managerial work. It also matches managers' thinking processes. Just as war is too important to leave to the generals, information processing, from the manager's perspective, is too important to leave to accounting and MIS departments.

Implications for designers

The implications in Mintzberg's findings are far-reaching. If information processing is the essential ingredient of managerial work, then designers, who are the technical experts in this field, should be an invaluable source of expertise for the manager. Yet this all too often is not the case.

The real surprise, one which should set us back on our heels, is that formal accounting and information systems appear to be blatantly ill-suited to the process of managerial work. The very strengths of formal systems—providing information that is hard, accurate, aggregated, and historically factual—are the antithesis of that which managers crave—soft, live, detailed, and current information. They also prefer to store it in their brains, not in filing cabinets or computer disks. Accounting and information systems, by contrast, arrive like billiard balls—cold, hard, polished, and perfectly formed. Paradoxically, their very strengths are anathema to managers.

Further, there is an odd, almost hidden, element in their relationships with information system designers. Managers do not seem to be very concerned about this obvious misfit. In fact, they seem almost to fancy it this way. It may be that information is so essential to their success that they prefer to run their own information network rather than having to rely on a staff officer not under their direct jurisdiction. This way they have a monopoly on the important information that drives the organization. This allows them the opportunity to exploit the information and even to hoard, obstruct, divert or distort some of it.

It is highly plausible that managers do not wish to have anyone other than themselves in charge of their information networks. The accounting and information systems managers, of course, do not have access to this type of information. At the same time, the information collected by the formal system is stored in the computer and so is only indirectly accessible through formal reports and channels to the managers. Managers and designers, it turns out, are competitors in the information business.

These are arresting ideas on a number of counts and they have very practical implications. They unequivocally establish the view of managers as informational nerve centers and not, as we previously thought, reflective decision-makers. They also suggest that there is a great need for an 'in-between' information system, one which will systematically process the information that managers need to perform their three major roles effectively. This could be done by information specialists who systematically seek out, document, and report the soft information managers find so valuable. This would not only break the critical information monopoly of the managers but also improve upon the crude information systems which managers themselves design. Accounting and information systems designers, then, must learn how to collect, store, and distribute the soft but important information which managers so desperately need.

This may not be as far-fetched as we might at first think. Recent developments in information technology, as we shall see later, put this well within the realm of possibility. A real-time data base accessible to all managers is one of the highly touted advantages of the new information technology. It is conceivable, then, that managers and designers can combine their needs and skills to get the best of both worlds.

Mintzberg's research and its ensuing ideas are, of course, not without limitations. To begin with the sample size used was exceedingly small; so extrapolation of the findings across a wide spectrum of managerial work is dangerous. Further, the view that managers merely react to information stimulus, while involved in a hectic round of brief, discontinuous activities, may be superficial. It is plausible as an alternative explanation that managers have already thought through what they intend to do and where they are going. Their daily routine, then, is merely going through the motions until the opportune time arises to start doing it. Further, while managers do not seem reflective during the work day, anyone who has observed them in airplanes or on commuter vehicles cannot help but notice the careful attention they give to formal reports and documents. Night after night they take home briefcases brimming with formal reports which they meticulously read in a comfortable chair in the den. Thorough processing of formal information and reflective activity are an important aspect of managerial life; but they are not undertaken during the hectic work day.

Nevertheless, Mintzberg's research has made a huge contribution to our understanding of managerial work. Managers sense a good deal of truth in this description of their lives. It squares much better than the textbook picture with what they intuitively know about their jobs. For accounting and information systems managers these ideas are important; and they provide wonderful insights into both the content and media appropriate for better systems designs.

INFORMATION AND COMMUNICATION FLOWS

Another study recently investigated the entire spectrum of information and communications flows in organizations. While previous research had failed to establish a link between *formal* accounting and information systems and performance, a few studies had shown that *informal* information networks can have a substantial impact on performance. Previous research had been too narrow (Grinyer and Norburn, 1975). This insight provided the inspiration for Earl and Hopwood (1980) to develop two simple but powerful frameworks which include both formal and informal types, thus capturing the full range of information flows in organizations.

Accounting and information systems managers are already well acquainted with the information systems in cell 1 of Figure 10.2. Standard cost reports, operating budgets, financial statements, sales analysis, inventory reports, and transaction summaries are examples. Many of these are woven directly into operational systems as is the case for chemical plants, numerically controlled machine tools, and bank transaction processing machines. The utility of the official routine information system is indisputable. They are essential; and they serve the organization well.

The information systems in cell 2 will also be familiar. These are formal systems which are not produced on a regular basis. Capital budgeting controls, break-even charts, product profitability analysis, and valuation studies are examples. Broad-based computer data banks, which can be accessed by managers throughout the organization, also fit here. Also, a great deal of non-routine but official information is processed by official liaison departments, integration offices, regular executive meetings, and special task forces. They play a critical role in moving information across departmental boundaries, as well as up and down the organizational hierarchy. They also represent an important opportunity for managers to keep in touch with, impress, and influence other managers in the organization. They are an essential means of moving official but non-routine information around the organization.

In cell 3 we find unofficial but routine information systems. These are usually maintained to compensate for the inadequacies of official routine systems. Many of these consist of 'black books' and 'just-in-case files' which managers carefully maintain to keep track of what they, not the accountants, believe to be the critical factors of departmental performance. They are used to fend off attacks, by superiors, peers and others, on department achievement. Such systems are reported to be widely used (Simon et al., 1954; Hopwood, 1974; Macintosh and Daft, 1982).

Most of these information systems are remarkably well designed. Let me quote from my own experience during a recent research project investigating the association of organizational contextual variables with official and routine budgeting and operational statistical reporting systems. After completing the formal questionnaire about the official systems, many of the managers would lean forward, ask if I would like to see the 'real' control system, reach into a bottom desk drawer and bring out a small book, usually hand-written, which contained pertinent statistics about departmental performance and current status. The Sales Vice-President of one company, for example, kept a black book which contained information for the current month and the year to date, about: salesmen's mileage, expenses, number and duration of sales calls, as well as order book levels, product maintenance calls, and customer complaints. The manager used this information system during his regular Monday morning briefing with the president.

This proved to be a typical case. Managers maintained these systems of keeping tabs on departmental performance as an informal means of reporting to superiors. In nearly every case they were richer and more realistic than the normal line-item operating budget. As Argyris (1977) reports, they often provide more concrete and accurate representations of each manager's unique situation than do official information systems. They can also be utilized to create and defend employee groups which question the status quo and challenge stability and conservatism (Hedberg and Jonsson, 1978). For progressive accounting and information systems designers these information systems could be the springboard for making formal–routine systems more concrete, realistic, and relevant.

Yet, surprisingly, it is the unofficial–non-routine information systems in cell 4 which are the main vehicle of managerial information processing. They include grape-vines, business lunches, coffee-break chats, encounters in the halls and washrooms, and unofficial plant tours. There are several common-sense reasons why managers rely on them so much. They carry news and information quickly. They process qualitative information. They convey nuances in meaning which are beyond the capacity of formal systems. They make it possible for urgent and complex problems to be shared with other managers in timely fashion. They are also a major vehicle for influencing other managers. These information systems are paramount for managers and they rely heavily on them.

The framework in Figure 10.2, then, shifts our focus from a narrow and technical view towards the wider, richer, and more vibrant reality of information flows and processing in organizations. Designers are well advised to keep these ideas in a safe place and bring them out when perspective and understanding are needed. Large investments in routine and official information systems should not be undertaken before understanding the organization's non-routine and unofficial systems.

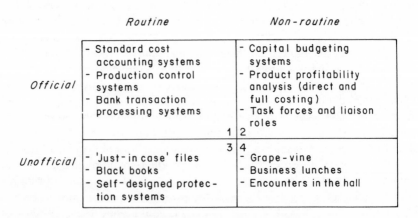

Figure 10.2 The information processing mix. (Source: adapted from Earl and Hopwood, 1981. Reproduced by permission of North-Holland % Elsevier Science Publishers BV)

Uncertainty, information, and decision

These ideas proved to be the springboard for Earl and Hopwood, and later by Burchell *et al.* (1980), to derive a rich set of notions about the relationship of information systems and decision making. The framework, shown in Figure 10.3, is based on two familiar dimensions of decisions—cause and effect relations and the degree of certainty in objectives—and stems from earlier work by Thompson and Tuden (1959).

Uncertainty is low in cell 1 where cause and effect relations are known and objectives are certain. The intelligence, design, and choice phases of decision-making are programmable. Predetermined rules, formulae, and algorithms can be applied to problems which arise. Decisions can be made by computation; so information systems to assist these decisions should be 'answer machines' that provide solutions on the spot. Standard cost systems for direct costs, economic order quantity inventory systems, credit inquiry systems, and linear programming models for transportation problems are examples. For these situations, information systems provide accurate, timely, and unequivocal answers.

In cell 2 uncertainty arises from objectives. Disagreement may exist over which objective is primary; or managers may be ambivalent about the major choices amongst multiple objectives; or objectives may simply be unstated. Whatever the reason, uncertainty over objectives, spurred on by individual self-interest and rapidly changing environments, brings with it conflict over principles and perspectives.

In these circumstances decision-making should be oriented towards opening up and maintaining channels of communications. Opinions and different perspectives need to be identified and debated in an open and lively fashion. Information systems can facilitate this by helping managers develop and argue points of view which are conflicting but consistent with the underlying facts, data, and context (Boland, 1979). As Mason (1969 and 1971) argues, information processing for strategic planning should promote a

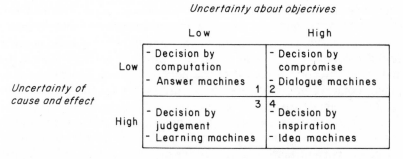

Figure 10.3 Uncertainty, decision-making, and ideal information systems (Source: adapted from Earl and Hopwood, 1981. Reproduced by permission of North-Holland/Elsevier Science Publishers BV)

debate whereby two quite different but equally feasible strategic alternatives are articulated from the same data base. Dialogue machines, and it is important to seize this point, act as a catalyst for debate, unlike an answer machine which provides the best solution. Dialogues, not answers, are needed.

Dialogue information systems, of course, are not uncommon. Think-tanks and retreats are examples. Informal consultative and participative processes are also dialogue machines. They bring conflict, power plays, and bargaining over objectives out into the open where dialogue and compromise lead to better decisions.

Moving to cell 3, where objectives are clear but causation is uncertain, formal information systems are not capable of yielding a final optimal answer. Yet they can be of considerable support during the decision-making process. The need here is for exploration of problems, investigation of the analyzable parts of the decision, and the application of judgement and intuition as learning takes place. In these situations information systems can, at best, only suggest a set of feasible solutions, provide data along the way, and help managers assess alternatives thoroughly. Examples of learning machines include: inquiry systems for probing data bases, computerized models with sensitivity analysis capabilities, and simulations with 'what-if' facilities. Such information systems help managers learn more about the possible alternatives and their consequences before they make the final judgement call.

So-called 'decision support systems' (DSS) are excellent examples of learning machines. They utilize the computer to assist and support managers with relatively non-structured and non-programmable tasks (Huff, 1981). The manager uses a CRT to interact with computer data bases and statistical models to analyze problems, formulate alternative solutions, and assess the possible consequences of the major action options.

Keen and Scott-Morton (1978) provide several practical DSS illustrations. For example, a portfolio management system (PMS) designed for a large bank allows its investment managers to interact on a graphic capability CRT with several large data bases and several mathematical models in order to manage investment portfolios for clients. The system allows the manager to display all kinds of information, including: a directory of all accounts for which the manager has responsibility; the holdings of a particular security across all accounts; a histogram of the distribution of holdings in an account by industrial category; a review of the holdings of any particular account, including financial information such as current market price and earnings data; a histogram of any available data item such as the current yield or the price–earnings ratio for all holdings within an account; scattergrams and regression lines of any two data items for securities held in an account; a graph of the current performance and historical data concerning securities or market indices; a summary of the basic data for any specific account; and a display of the standard information about any specific security.

PMS provided the portfolio managers with a repertoire of capabilities which could be integrated easily into their total daily activities. It proved to be a major success. Other similar DSS examples include: multifaceted corporate financial planning systems; sophisticated annual product planning systems for marketing managers; a geographical data analysis and display system used by urban planners, police administrators, and school boards; and a complex product planning and parts management system for a truck manufacturing company.

In these examples the manager interacts in a dynamic fashion with computer-based data banks and software models while working through semi-structured tasks. The computer, models, and data base support managers during the decision process, helping them learn new ways to structure their problems and evaluate alternative solutions, all the while acting as a catalyst for inspiration. The data base, models, computer hardware, software, screens, printouts, and, of course, the manager, combine into a marvelous learning machine.

Finally, in cell 4 uncertainty stems from lack of understanding of cause and effect relationships, as well as from unclear objectives or disagreement about which ones are paramount. Decisions call for inspiration; thus accounting and information systems should help to trigger creativity. Brainstorming sessions, during which any idea, no matter how ridiculous it appears at first glance, is given serious consideration, is another example. The Delphi technique, whereby possible critical events are listed and scenarios developed about the consequences of two or more occurring at the same time, is an excellent example of an idea machine. In the extreme situations, semi-confusing information systems can be designed deliberately to shake organizations out of rigid behavior patterns in times of changing environmental conditions (Hedberg and Jonsson, 1979).

Organic organizational arrangements, boundary crossing, interactions with outsiders, and exposure to creative thinkers are valuable cohorts for idea machines. While inspiration cannot be programmed, it can be given a boost with information systems which provide multiple streams of thought to trigger creativity.

In sum, decision requirements vary with the nature of the underlying uncertainty. Information system requirements, it follows, should also vary according to decision needs. Decision-making by computation is well served by answer machines. Uncertain objectives call for compromise and supporting information systems should promote dialogue, but when cause and effect are unclear, sound judgement calls for learning machines. Finally, when uncertainty stems from both sources, decisions require inspiration, and information systems should be designed to provide ideas.

Yet, as Earl and Hopwood observe, the realities of organizational information systems and decision-making do not always mirror these ideas. In fact, as depicted in Figure 10.4, they often differ markedly from these prescriptions.

There are no problems in cell 1, but in cell 2 we find ammunition instead of dialogue machines. Information systems are designed not for debate,

202

Uncertainty about objectives

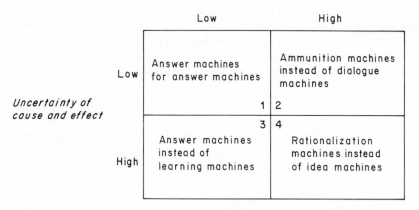

Figure 10.4 Actual and required accounting and information systems. (Source: adapted from Earl and Hopwood, 1981. Reproduced by permission of North-Holland/Elsevier Science Publishers BV)

dialogue, and compromise, but rather to support the vested interests and values of specific groups. They emerge from political processes where one side attempts to prejudice the criterion for selection of a solution and then proceeds to influence the other parties on the basis of that criterion. Traditional management accounting systems, of course, are often used as ammunition machines. Reports containing only financial information, for example, are used to reduce multiple objectives to a single financial goal when, in reality, organizational needs also include marketing, engineering, and human relations aspects. By focusing on only one objective, information systems can be exploited to further the political ambitions of particular vested-interest groups (Dirsmith and Jablonski, 1979).

The classic example comes from politics, where various political parties try to influence law-making in legislative assemblies. Using the same data base, provided by the Bureau of Statistics, one party develops an information system which supports a reduction in government meddling in the economy while another party, using the very same data base, develops information which indicates the need for an increase in government planning. Ammunition machines are dangerous because they override the need for constructive dialogue and compromise.

In cell 3, where learning machines are required, we often find answer machines instead. Perhaps this is not surprising; after all, accounting and information systems designers are good at developing systems for decisions by computation. Because successful answer machines are widespread, designers are prone to camouflage or ignore uncertainty when cause and effect are unknown. A tidy-minded answer machine in the wrong settings results in the legitimate boundaries of computation being pushed aside and opportunities to exploit uncertainty, lost.

In cell 4, instead of the necessary idea machine we often find information systems designed to act as 'rationalization' machines to justify and legitimize actions already decided upon. Capital budgeting proposals, for example, are put together after the managers have decided that a particular long-term project should be pursued (Bower, 1970). Task forces are struck to investigate issues which have already been decided upon by top management.

Rationalization machines, of course, can have legitimate uses. Sometimes it is necessary to create a rationale to justify decisions to others. Problems arise, however, when they overwhelm the creativity and inspiration necessary for uncovering new and unique decisions. So instead of interactive information systems which promote learning and growth, rationalization machines are used to rubber-stamp the status quo. When objectives and cause–effect are unclear, accounting and information systems should be used to facilitate learning; not to rationalize pre-determined decisions.

The above ideas provide a framework which captures the entire mix of vibrant and varied information systems used in organizations. Accounting and information systems need to play different roles, such as dialogue, learning, and idea creation, depending upon the type of uncertainty involved in the particular decision. Otherwise they will be misused and exploited as ammunition and rationalization machines.

These ideas go far beyond conventional accounting topics. They make it clear, despite any discomfort this may bring, that an overemphasis on formal systems and technical problems is at variance with the realities of organizational information flows. Unless accounting and information systems managers abandon the traditional narrow and technical perspective they will continue to be isolated from substantive organizational processes. As Earl and Hopwood aptly conclude, information management, not management information, is the name of the game.

USING ACCOUNTING SYSTEMS FOR SELF-INTEREST

The intricate workings of ammunition and rationalization machines are captured vividly by Culbert and McDonough (1980) in their award-winning book about the pursuit of self-interest in the workplace. We must look, they say, below the surface behavior of people at work to see the realities of organizational life where rivals, subordinates, and bosses wage an invisible war. Accomplishments and contributions to global organizational purpose, even when the level of performance is extremely high in quality, and individual competence is beyond question, are not automatically recognized. On the contrary, others are primarily concerned with pushing for self-serving rules and practices while parading themselves as the guardians of the corporate welfare. What is advocated under the guise of 'objective accountability' appears totally different when self-interests are exposed.

The major weapons in this invisible war, Culbert and McDonough argue, are formal accounting and information systems. Organizations need managers who can get the product out of the door at a good profit. So they try to specify in advance the type of commitment and responsibilities needed in order to strike an agreement with the various managers who then will stand accountable for what has been agreed upon. In order to enforce the agreements and make accountability objective, standards are struck for inputs, outputs, and impacts. These 'objectives' are contained in formal accounting and information systems.

Sometimes objective accountability for inputs is selected by evaluators as the turf for the self-interest battle. Inputs are the materials, wages, capital, and the actions necessary to convert the inputs into outputs. Objective standards are struck for input levels so they can be compared to actual levels. Evaluators (superiors, rivals, peers, and subordinates), on the one hand, are then quick to point out that input standards were not met, or that essential operations were neglected, or that procedures were not followed, regardless of either the level of output achieved or the overall impact on global objectives.

This self-convenient logic can be used, for example, by a divisional manager to explain why he fired the marketing manager despite the fact that the marketing manager has consistently met sales objectives. Managers, on the other hand, make much of the fact that they met the standards for inputs and meticulously followed all procedures and rules, and thus are not to blame for unsatisfactory outputs and undesirable impacts. Engineers, for example, fall back on the standards of inputs rationale when they are on the carpet because the bridge they designed collapsed.

When the problems of input accountability are recognized the objective accountability war is shifted to the level of outputs. Outputs are the tangible accomplishments, such as finished product, services provided, and sales volumes, of the effort exerted on inputs. They are the 'hard results' and the 'bottom line' of accomplishment. The rationale for output accountability is simple—hold people accountable for achieving agreed-upon output objectives and do not interfere with how they do it; either they make it or a new crew is brought in. This, of course, is the essence of what is known as MBO (management by objectives).

There are, however, several major flaws in this way of managing. The abuses have been well documented over the years. Agreed-upon profit levels, for example, can be accomplished in the short run by: neglecting machinery maintenance programs, reducing institutional advertising, cutting back on customer services, and ignoring the need for training programs for middle managers. When outputs are emphasized, managers can meet them but at the expense of the long-run impact on future profits and accomplishments.

The difficulties with objective accountability for both inputs and outputs lead evaluators to shift the territory of evaluation to impact. Impact is the effect of effort on the higher-order, over-arching institutional objectives such as the 'long-run health' of the organization or the 'contribution to society and mankind'. The television sponsor wants commitment to good taste, and not merely high Nielson ratings. Parents want schools to provide for the social adjustment of their children, not merely high scores on national mathematics or reading contests. The roughest and toughest objective accountability battles take place over impact.

Evaluators try to find out in advance whether or not accountable managers stand for given organizational imperatives. They want to know whether or not the manager will stand 'open-endedly' ready to do whatever may be called upon as specific situations evolve in order to serve over-arching purpose. These missions then are treated as 'absolutes' even though in reality they are 'relatives' as they must be selected on the basis of values and morals which, unlike input and output standards, can never be objective. Objective accountability for impact is, in reality, a subjective value-laden territory.

So the objective accountability game can be played at three levels—inputs, outputs, and impact; and wily evaluators, including rivals, know how to switch from level to level in order to further their own self-interests at the expense of the evaluee. A manager, for example, may be contributing mightily to agreed-upon long-run missions but the evaluator merely points out that the input standards, as shown clearly by the formal management accounting and information reports, were not met. But if input standards were achieved, the evaluator points out that bottom-line outputs, once again clearly shown by the formal accounting and information reports, have not been met. When both input and output standards have been achieved, evaluators shift to the lack of commitment by the manager to over-arching mission. So it is the ground on which the war of self-interest is fought, and the orientation that best fits the self-interests of specific parties, that decides the winner. As Culbert and McDonough conclude, the key to winning is to keep the opposition debating within a structure that supports your own position, but be quick to switch the territory when your opponent begins to score well. Formal accounting and information systems usually provide plenty of ammunition for attacking opponents on either inputs, outputs, or impact.

PROCESSING INFORMATION THROUGH FRAMES OF REFERENCE

Let us agree that the form and utilization of the information system must be appropriate to the nature of the uncertainty embedded in the decision. This is an attractive suggestion; yet it does not go far enough. The appropriate form and utilization of the information is only half of the equation.

Information must be passed through a mental frame of reference before it has meaning; that is to say, before it gives a relevant message. Consequently, the selection of a framework is paramount to the meaning given or message received.

An illustration may be helpful. During much of the 1970s, accounting data in the form of account balances were passed through the historical cost accounting model. For many large companies the resulting income statement indicated that a healthy profit had been earned. In a period of prolonged inflation, however, if the same accounts are processed through a current replacement cost accounting model, the income statement now indicates a loss. The selection of an appropriate accounting framework is absolutely crucial to the message carried by the information system. The prevailing historical cost framework was inadequate. As a result, many organizations failed to recognize early on that a critical development had taken place, and so were slow to adapt to their changed circumstances. This problem was addressed by McCall (1977) in a highly innovative and insightful piece of work.

We make sense of events, McCall argues, on the basis of our personal frames of reference. These frameworks are, of course, based on prior beliefs and theories. If, however, our beliefs and theories do not square with the altered facts we are prone to ignore them, classify them as random errors, or redefine them in ways that fit the old framework. In fact, we routinely protect old frames from contradictory evidence rather than adjust them. Yet detecting incongruities and reacting appropriately is essential for organizational adaptation.

McCall identifies four major types of incongruities between events and frames of reference. These are shown in Figure 10.5.

Intertemporal incongruities

The first inappropriate reaction occurs when the prevailing framework is applied, but does not fit. This is called an intertemporal incongruity. A

Prevailing frame of reference is

		Believed to explain the incongruity	Believed not to explain the incongruity
Environmental incongruity is	Recognized	Intertemporal incongruity (bombing in World War II and Vietnam) ___1	Congruous incongruity (Saturn's mischievous moon) 2
	Unrecognized	3___ Falsely false incongruity (the boy who cried wolf)	4 Artificial sense (that's the way we do it around here)

Figure 10.5 Types of incongruities resulting from interactions between events and frames. (Source: based on McCall, 1977)

striking example occurred during US bombing raids on enemy factories in World War II and also in Vietnam. Evidence from intelligence units unexpectedly indicated that the bombings helped make enemy production better. Although they leveled factories, the bombings also wiped out the cumbersome traditional bureaucratic procedures used by the factories. So when machines, equipment, and production schedules were pieced together again, they were rearranged in a much more efficient manner. High-ranking officers were aware that the bombings were not as effective as was originally thought; yet they discounted this important incongruity in favor of the positive short-run effects of leveling the factories.

History, of course, is brimming with important intertemporal incongruities. When Copernicus and Galileo demonstrated scientifically that the earth rotated about the sun, rather than the reverse, as the prevailing belief held, they were made to recant. Old frameworks die hard.

The famous Hawthorne Studies of Roethlisberger and Dickson (1939) illustrate the importance of not ignoring intertemporal incongruities. When the productivity and behavior of the workers did not conform to their preconceived themes, they kept experimenting and working out new frameworks that might explain these events until eventually they gave birth to the 'small group behavior and human relations school of organizational behavior'. In a similar way, Copernicus and Galileo changed our ideas of the solar system and Watson discovered the double-helix and unraveled the structure of DNA. Detecting and reacting appropriately to incongruities is exceedingly difficult; yet it is essential for organizational adaptation.

Congruous incongruities

The second inappropriate response occurs in cell 2 of Figure 10.5 when the incongruity is recognized but set aside because the prevailing frame will not explain it. This is called a congruous incongruity. A long-standing example is Saturn's mischievous moon. When discovered it was spinning the wrong way; yet it was treated for years as an event explainable by existing theory when, in fact, it made no sense in the conventional frame.

A more typical example is the hard-headed businessman who, protesting that governmental actions such as environmental protection policies make no sense and have no comprehensible patterns, dismisses them as unpredictable events which cannot be comprehended. Instead of attempting to understand the policies from the government's frame of reference and thereby discerning sensible patterns with adaptable implications, the businessman continues to see them from within his comfortable, traditional anti-government framework, treating them as unpredictable events. The unfortunate aspect of this is that opportunities to develop new ways of thinking are missed. A broken, but successful, play in football can be seen either as a breakdown or as a chance to add it to the playbook. Congruous incongruities can be the springboard for the development of wider and more comprehensive frameworks.

Falsely false incongruities

The next inappropriate response occurs, as in cell 3, when people expect false incongruities but experience real incongruities. After arriving at a firebox which is notorious for false alarms, firemen may find no-one waiting and drive off, when in fact there really is a fire. The townspeople who ignored the boy-who-cried-wolf lost all their sheep when finally he told the truth. Experiences are discounted as being falsely incongruous. Falsely false incongruities are particularly insidious because they go unnoticed; so the possibilities of finding new meanings are lost.

Artificial sense

Intertemporal, congruous, and falsely false incongruities all involve the application of frameworks which are accurate for explaining some events but are not accurate for explaining others. But in cell 4 the prevailing frame accumulates over time, eventually taking the form of myths and traditions. Changing environments slowly but inevitably outstrip the prevailing framework. Even when it is recognized that the prevailing frameworks do not do the job, they often continue to be applied to current situations as if events had not changed.

This is particularly treacherous. When obsolete frameworks combine with outdated beliefs a false sense of security is created. Frameworks, locked into procedure manuals or preserved in organizational folklore, are the ones first applied to current events. People who question their appropriateness are told: 'That's the way we do it around here; just do your job and carry out orders.'

Sometimes more than one incongruity crop up at the same time. The result is an illusion of chaos. When things become chaotic, McCall proposes, we should sit back and examine the reasons. Once we see that new frameworks are needed we can update them and make sense out of a chaotic non-sense.

Incongruities, of course, occur frequently. The problem is that they create unstructured situations for managers who then get rid of them by treating them as abnormal, or by thoughtlessly cramming them into familiar frameworks instead of looking for more appropriate ones. It is precisely here that accounting and information systems can play an important role. They can do this by including accurate descriptions of normality that are based on extended observations and are free of interpretation. This type of information will help managers recognize incongruities for what they are, not as exceptions to the rule. Managers who study exceptions, rather than dismiss them as anomalous cases, can more easily expose the inadequacies of prevailing frameworks.

These ideas are intriguing and important. They give us a new twist to the design problem by stressing a critical aspect of information processing which is often overlooked by designers. No matter how perfect the information system, if the framework used to interpret the information is past its time the message from the system will be wrong. This critical aspect of information processing should never be ignored. Inappropriate frameworks must and can be challenged with appropriate accounting and information systems.

INFORMATION PROCESSING AS SYMBOL

The final work examined in this chapter is an analysis of the motivations of managers to gather information in quantities far greater than they can possibly use. The ideas we will look at stem largely from the creative work of Feldman and March (1981), who went beyond conventional information engineering and economics to investigate and understand human encounters with information. Their analysis looks at information processing behavior by managers in an entirely new perspective. As a result, several brilliant insights ensue for accounting and information system managers.

The conventional view, of course, is that information processing is an integral part of the decision process. Information is collected, stored, and processed as long as its marginal cost is less than the incremental value of its effect on decisions and actions. Organizations, or more accurately the individual managers within them, will secure, analyze, and retrieve information in a timely and intelligent fashion to improve decision-making. Consequently the reliability, precision, and relevance of information are carefully weighed.

Excess information processing

Yet, surprisingly, this activity represents only a small portion of the total information processed within organizations. Closer observation reveals that organizations collect far more information than they could ever reasonably use for decision-making. Even more remarkably, most of the information collected is totally unconnected to decisions. At first glance it seems that organizations, even the best ones, overinvest in a glut of redundant information.

Common explanations

There are two common explanations for this. One is that much of the information gathered turns out to be unsuitable for the specific decision under consideration. Thus, the process continues until suitable information is found. The other is that individuals frequently find themselves with too much data and suddenly stop processing information of any kind. Although they are, in fact, overloaded with information, they experience this glut as a shortage.

Both explanations still cling to the idea that information gathering is inevitably connected to decision-making; and while the idea that individuals are able to weigh the cost and benefits of information systems, and then optimize information collection and utilization is enticing, it must be set aside if the realities are to be grasped. The fact of the matter is that organizations provide several powerful motivations, unrelated to decision-making, for managers to overinvest in information gathering.

Overlooked and subtle explanations

One obvious, but often overlooked, motivation is the fact that the costs and benefits of information collection often are not located in the same part of the organization. The accounting office, the computer bureau, the MIS department, and the marketing research unit incur the costs of collecting information, assuming that the managers of user departments are using the material. For the managers, then, information is almost a free good. Rather than having to pay for it on the spot as the benefits accrue, the costs are absorbed elsewhere in the organization. The motivation is clearly in the direction of collecting more than can be used.

A more subtle, but just as important, reason for the systematic overcollection of information is related to the widespread practice in organizations of criticizing decisions after the fact. A common version of this is known as 'Monday-morning quarterbacking'. On Monday morning, ardent and home town fans second-guess the decisions made on Sunday by the quarterback in the heat of the battle. Major blunders harmful to the home team are readily apparent. What seems so clear in retrospect, of course, was not at all obvious at the time.

Similarly, managers make decisions in the face of uncertainty, knowing only too well that individuals at all levels in the organization will be quick to make *post-hoc* criticisms. The inevitable judgements come in two extremes. One asserts that events occurred which were underestimated, and that the manager should have collected more information. The other concludes that events which did not occur were overestimated and the manager probably overcollected, and therefore wasted, information. Managers recognize that either way criticisms will be forthcoming, but that the majority will be of the first type. The wiser choice, then, is to have more information than is needed.

Yet another fundamental reason for gathering non-decision related information is that organizations are constantly involved in a type of exploratory data analysis that resembles gossip. They need to monitor their environment constantly for potential surprises in order to be reassured that there are none. Managers recognize that many decisions come up in a hurry, and that information gathering requires a long lead time. Rather than be caught short, they gather information of any sort, including gossip, news, and hearsay, that might contain something relevant. Usually, of course, such information is only of passing interest, although news and gossip can enliven what might otherwise be a mundane existence.

Strategic and symbolic information processing

There are, however, even more powerful motivations provided by organizations for managers to collect and process what would otherwise seem to be redundant information. Feldman and March label this 'strategic' information. The dynamics of this sort of information processing are subtle and elaborate. Managers recognize that information is an important instrument of persuasion, that it can be a source of influence and power. They are therefore into a process whereby contending liars, competing in the persuasion game, send and receive mostly unreliable information.

This is a complicated game and is played under conditions of conflicting interests. Wily players do not treat information as if it were neutral and innocent. They must make inferences and discount a great deal of the perverse information they receive, recognizing full well that strategic misrepresentation is a harsh reality of organizational life. Not surprisingly, they counter with strategic information systems of their own. This subtle game of distorting and misrepresentating information to one's own advantage stimulates an oversupply of strategic information.

But the most pervasive reason organizations collect more information than they can possibly process, Feldman and March argue, is deeply rooted in a central ideological norm of western civilization—the belief in intelligent choice. Organizations, of course, are the central arena for displaying and honoring this paramount social value. So managers find value in information that has little or no relation to decision-making. Information gathering is ritualistic assurance that one does indeed respect this central value. It is a means of reaffirming the value of rational decision-making. It is a representation to others of one's competence. It is a symbol for all to see that one believes in intelligent choice.

Part of this myth holds that more information leads to better decisions. So the more information a manager holds, the better he must be in the eyes of others. Managers establish their legitimacy by their use of information. The visible and observable aspects of gathering and storing information are not unlike the ritualistic gray suit, white shirt, and dark blue tie of the committed IBM executive of a decade ago. Information is not merely a basis for action, it symbolizes and reaffirms a core value of society. Seeking and collecting information, and this is the striking point, has important symbolic value for the manager far beyond its worth in decision-making.

Managers, especially prudent ones, posture accordingly. They diligently ask for and carefully store information. They carry it home after work in visibly bulging brief cases; and they assiduously orchestrate decisions to ensure that all believe they take action only on the basis of reasonable and intelligent choice. The command of information, the access to information sources, and the apparent application of information to decisions all work to enhance the manager's reputation for competency and inspire the confidence of others. Information, then, takes on value as symbol far beyond its worth as a basis for actions. It symbolizes one's broad commitment to reason and to rational decisions.

But matters do not rest here. With remarkable insight, Feldman and March delved further into the phenomenon of excessive information processing. Such behavior, they argue, can be neither neutral nor static. The very act of asking for, collecting, storing, and using information for defensive, strategic, and symbolic purposes is almost certain to be of instrumental importance.

An instance may serve to bring home this important insight. The person who learns a foreign language because it is fashionable symbolizes a commitment to cultured life. Yet having learned the language, the individual finds it valuable. It helps him understand his own language better. It opens up a treasure trove of literature; and, by traveling in countries where that language is native, it provides not only great pleasure, but also access to a rich history and culture. The fascinating result is that the individual does, in fact, becomes more cultured. What was done symbolically has become instrumental.

It is the same with symbolic information processing. At the outset a manager may treat information gathering as a manifestation of his or her devotion to the belief in the systematic application of information to decisions. But by posturing as a believer the manager actually becomes good at using information intelligently. Symbolic processing leads to an unexpected bonus. The quality of individual decisions and actions, in fact, does become better. Information processing unexpectedly fuels organizational evolution and adaptation.

At this stage the process becomes even more dynamic. Individuals suppose that information is indispensable to decision-making and act to make it important. In the process, happily, they discover new ways of making it indispensable to decision and action. The symbolic use of information is transformed into functional necessity. The circle is complete.

Accounting and information departments play a hand in this. Having formal information processing responsibilities, they naturally are biased towards the use of accounting and information systems for rational decision-making. Further, those managers who are adept at using information also believe that information gathering is invaluable. These managers, along with their emulators, become a powerful coterie. They try to enhance their own importance by convincing others of their beliefs. They become good allies for accounting and information systems executives in attempting to persuade other managers to read reports and use formal information systems; and, like the person who wanted to learn a foreign language, many of those who try, find it serves their purposes. They, in turn, become believers in the general value of information. As the process snowballs it works to the advantage of accounting and information systems departments.

These ideas provide remarkable insight into the well-recognized, but hitherto poorly understood, phenomenon of redundant information processing by organizations. Conventional explanations, such as information overload and filtering of irrelevant decision information, fall short of the mark.

More fundamentally, organizations provide several powerful motivations for managers to gather and process more information than they can use in decision-making. Although they normally do not pay the cost of information gathering, they reap the benefits. Post-decision criticizing results in defensive information gathering. Power and influence accrue to those with the largest information network. Strategic misrepresentation requires superfluous information processing. Most importantly, information processing symbolizes to others that the manager believes in the social value of intelligent choice. Yet in the final analysis this is all to the good. Ritualistic posturing and symbolic information processing ultimately leads to better decision-making; and, as the managers become more facile at processing information intelligently, they promote the idea throughout the organization and become valuable allies of accounting and information systems departments. Redundant processing converts to positive instrumental action.

CONCLUSION

The arrival of the natural systems approach to understanding the actions of organizations cleared the decks for several ideas which go well beyond the bounds of the rational decision perspective. Accounting and information flows in organizations came to be seen as a separate and substantive organizational phenomenon. Previously the manager, as a user of the system, had been the focal point of behavioral accounting efforts. But now the interest has shifted to a more general level—the management of information and communications flows in organizations.

As a result several important insights have emerged to create the foundations of a new perspective. We have come to realize, for example, that our previous picture of managers as thoughtful reflective planners, carefully organizing, co-ordinating, and controlling their organizations, or their piece of it, was well off the mark. More realistically, managerial work involves a never-ending stream of brief, varied, and discontinuous incidents carried out at an unrelenting pace. A key aspect of this activity involves the manager in an informational role. He is the nerve center of a cultivated information network, continually collecting, storing, and judiciously disseminating bits and pieces of information. Formal, hard, accurate, and aggregated accounting and information systems, predicated on the old view of managerial work, are ill-suited to the realities of managerial work. It is not surprising, then, that managers have become their own director of central intelligence.

We have also come to recognize that informal and non-routine information systems are only a small part of the rich and varied mix of information processing in organizations. Formal accounting and information systems, so well suited to routine decisions, must change their stripes under various conditions of uncertainty. They no longer serve only to provide answers; rather they must also facilitate dialogue, learning, and the generation of ideas. Often, however, we find ammunition, answer, and rationalization machines in their place. Accounting and information systems, suitably tailored to the nature of uncertainty of the particular decision under consideration, can act as a powerful catalyst for better decisions and constructive change.

We now appreciate the possibilities of rolling the managers and computer-based information systems into a larger decision system with awesome potential for resolving ill-structured problems. Computer-based information systems need no longer be separated from the management process. Both can be intertwined into a decision support system vastly more powerful than either one on its own. Embedding the computer in the bits and pieces of the decision-making process represents a radical development in the management of organizational information flows.

We have also been reminded that information inevitably is processed through a personal frame of reference; and even if the information system is impeccable, organizations will fail to recognize and adapt to critical environmental events if their prevailing frame of reference is obsolete. This aspect of the information processing equation is often overlooked or ignored. Frameworks based on prior beliefs and theories can lead to intertemporal incongruity, congruous incongruity, falsely false incongruity, or false sense that all is well. The way to avoid these incongruities is to incorporate accurate descriptions of normality into information systems so that an incongruous event is studied, not as an exception, but as a new reality, requiring a new framework. Over the long haul, however, inappropriate frameworks will likely prove to be the major hurdle to realizing the full potential of accounting and information systems.

Finally, we have come to realize that managers collect and process far more information than they can possibly use in making decisions. Perversely, organizations provide several powerful motivations for this. Since the costs are absorbed by accounting and MIS departments, information is a free good for the manager; *post-hoc* decision criticism is such a common practice that the able manager harvests information simply to counter charges that not enough information was collected; and managers collect information just in case sudden changes occur which otherwise would catch them unprepared. Even more fundamentally, managers recognize that information is power, and can be an important instrument of persuasion. They understand well that they are involved, along with other managers, in a game of strategic information processing.

Further, the adroit manager uses information processing to symbolize that he subscribes to the societal belief in rational and intelligent choice. Ritualistic information processing provides assurance to others that he holds the proper attitude towards careful decision-making. Yet, paradoxically, information-related behavior that may seem to be purely symbolic and unrelated to decision-making is likely to convert to instrumental importance as managers become better at processing information and using it intelligently. Those who are good at using information persuade others to follow suit. Soon they too believe in the value of information gathering; and when everyone is processing information the organization is bound to evolve, adapt, and survive. In the final analysis, then, what appears at first glance to be a vast overinvestment in information processing turns out to yield a high return.

These insights have greatly enriched our understanding of the complex realities of information and communication flows in organizations. We now have at our fingertips a handful of simple but powerful frameworks for analyzing these flows. The stepping stones to a broader and richer understanding of effective information management are in place. Accounting and information systems need no longer be confined to rational decision-making and control processes. This is, of course, at once both a difficulty and an opportunity for designers. Providing information systems to stimulate ideas is different territory than providing answers for inventory order points. Still, information flows in organizations are too important to be left to the managers. Managing them effectively represents a great opportunity for accounting and informational systems executives to become a powerful force in the process of developing effective organizations.

References

Argyris, C., 'Organizational learning and management information systems', *Accounting, Organizations and Society*, 1977, Vol. 2, No. 2, pp. 113–123.

Boland, R. S., 'Control, causality and information systems requirements', *Accounting, Organizations and Society*, Vol. 4, No. 4, 1979, pp. 259–272.

Bower, J., *Managing the Resource Allocation Process*, Division of Research, Graduate School of Business Administration, Harvard University, Boston, Mass., 1970.

Burchell, S., C. Clubb, A. Hopwood, J. Hughes, and J. Nahapiet, 'The role of accounting in organizations and society', *Accounting, Organizations and Society*, Vol. 5, No. 1, 1980, pp. 5–27.

Culbert, S. A., and J. J. McDonough, *The Invisible War: Pursuing Self Interests at Work*, John Wiley & Sons, Inc., New York, 1980.

Dirsmith, M. W., and S. F. Jablonski, 'MBO, political rationality and information inductance', *Accounting, Organizations and Society*, Vol. 4, No. 1, 1979.

Earl, M. J., and A. G. Hopwood, 'From management information to information management', in Lucas, H. C. Jr, *et al.* (eds), *The Information Systems Environment*, North Holland, Amsterdam, 1980.

Feldman, M. S., and J. G. March, 'Information in organizations as signal and symbol', *Administrative Science Quarterly*, June 1981, pp. 171–186.

Grinyer, P., and D. Norburn, 'Planning for existing markets: perceptions of executive and financial performance', *Journal of the Royal Statistical Society* (Series A, 1975), pp. 70–97.

Hedberg, B., and S. Jonsson, 'Designing semi-confusing information systems for organizations in changing environments', *Accounting, Organizations and Society*, Vol. 3, No. 1, 1978, pp. 47–64.

Hopwood, A. G., *Accounting and Human Behaviour*, Haymarket Publishing, London, 1974.

Huff, S. L., 'Decision support systems: an emerging view', Symposium on Accounting and Information Systems, Queen's University, Kingston, Canada, May 1981.

Keen, P., and M. S. Scott-Morton, *Decision Support Systems: An Organizational Perspective*, Addison-Wesley Publishing Inc., Reading, Mass., 1978.

Macintosh, N. B., and R. L. Daft, 'A technology model of management control systems'. Paper presented at the American Accounting Association annual meeting, San Diego, August 1982.

Mason, R. O., 'Basic concepts for designing management information systems', AIS Research Paper No. 8, Graduate School of Business Administration, University of California, Los Angeles, October 1969.

Mason, R. O., 'The prospects for corporate long range planning', AIS Research Paper No. 70-10, Graduate School of Business Administration, University of California, Los Angeles, January 1971.

McCall, M. W. Jr, 'Making sense of nonsense: helping frames of reference clash', *TIMS Studies in Management Sciences*, Vol. 5, North-Holland, Amsterdam, 1977, pp. 111–123.

Mintzberg, H., 'The myths of MIS', *California Management Review*, Fall 1972, pp. 92–97.

Mintzberg, H., 'The manager's job: folklore and fact', *The Harvard Business Review*, July–August 1975, pp. 49–61.

Roethlisberger, F. J., and W. J. Dickson, *Management and the Worker*, Harvard University Press, Cambridge, Mass., 1939.

Simon, H. A., H. Guetzkow, G. Kozonetsky, and G. Tyndall, *Centralization vs. Decentralization in Organizing the Controller's Department*, Controllership Foundation, New York, 1954.

Thompson, J. D., and A. Tuden, 'Strategies, structures and processes of organizational decision', in Thompson, J. D. *et al.* (eds), *Comparative Studies in Administration*, University of Pittsburgh Press, 1959.

CHAPTER 11

A Contextual Model of Accounting and Information Systems

It is obvious from the preceding chapters that designing an effective accounting and information system is an exceedingly complex endeavor. It requires taking into consideration a large number of factors including: (1) generally accepted management accounting and information systems techniques; (2) personal factors such as cognitive style, leadership style in using the system, and participation in both the target level setting and the total design of the system; and (3) impersonal forces such as environment, technology, interdependencies, and organizational structural characteristics. If we stop to think about it, the number of factors involved seems overwhelming. We can easily become lost in thought. Most will agree with experts such as Mason and Mitroff (1973), Livingstone (1975), and Lawler and Rhode (1976), who call for conceptual apparatus that includes the psychological type, the kind of task, and the characteristics of the organizational context, accounting and information systems. Putting this advice into practice, however, is no easy matter.

This chapter addresses this problem by putting forth a new theory of accounting and information systems; one which follows the guidelines of these experts.[1] The model employs a macro-organizational concept—technology—and a human information processing construct—personal decision style. So it embraces both impersonal forces and personal factors. These variables are encapsulated into a contextual theory of accounting and information systems. A key advantage of the concept of technology employed, and this point should be underscored, is that it subsumes many of the impersonal forces discussed in earlier chapters. First, we will describe the decision style variables.

Decision style variables

Decision style theory is based upon the idea that personal traits can have an important influence on how people use information systems. While several theories of personality and human information processing are available, Driver and Mock (1975) offer an approach that is well suited for inclusion in a comprehensive information systems theory.[2] Driver and Mock observed that people differ distinctly in the way they use information and make decisions. Some individuals tend to use small amounts of information while

217

218

making decisions and processing their work; others seem to utilize large, even massive, amounts of data and information. Some individuals use information in a quick and decisive manner; others massage it slowly, deliberately, and creatively—even lovingly. Some use information to anticipate the future by developing tightly controlled short-run plans; others seem content to wait until they get feedback from the environment before reacting to events as they unfold. Some individuals prefer brief, summarized, and to-the-point communications and reports; yet others exhibit an affinity for thorough, long, involved, and fluid discussions and reports. Finally, some individuals prefer clear-cut, bureaucratic, formal organizational arrangements; whilst others prefer to get work done within more democratic, matrix-type structures.

In sum, marked differences exist in the way in which individuals prefer to use information, make decisions, and get work done. Driver and Mock sketched out a theoretical explanation to account for these differences. They postulated that two basic individual cognitive characteristics influence how an individual uses information and makes decisions. These are: (1) an individual's preference for processing either a small or large amount of information, and (2) an individual's tendency to see either single or multiple meaning in the information processed. These two dimensions were used by Driver and Mock to derive four distinctive decision styles, as in Figure 11.1.

The 'decisive' individual, they theorize, uses a minimal amount of information and likes to see the information generate one firm solution. When using information these individuals value efficiency, speed, and consistency. They prefer brief communications and summary reports which focus on one solution, results, and action. As for planning, decisives use a minimal data base to develop tightly controlled, short-range plans. They prefer to work under organizational arrangements which feature well-understood rules, clear reporting lines, and short spans of control.

The 'flexible' style person also uses minimal data but sees information as having different meanings at different times. These persons prefer to operate by reacting intuitively to events as they occur, rather than developing and operating to a plan. They prefer loose and fluid organizational patterns; and

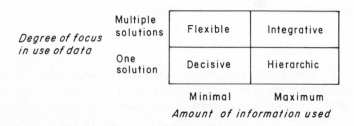

Figure 11.1 Decision style model. (Source: Driver and Mock, 1975, p. 497. Reproduced by permission of the American Accounting Association)

although leaning towards short and to-the-point communication, they like to consider a variety of solution alternatives.

The 'hierarchic', by contrast, uses masses of data to generate one best solution. These persons use information with great thoroughness, precision, and perfection. They prefer long, thorough, and formal communication and favor large data bases when developing long-range plans. They also lean towards reports featuring orderly problem statement, method exposition, and generation of one best solution; and they favor the classic organization with broad spans of control and elaborate procedures.

Finally, the 'integrative' style person uses large amounts of data; but generates a multitude of equally viable solutions from this base. These persons have an affinity for information which they use in a creative way, often for simulation and gaming. They also use a lot of data to develop plans, but plans are altered constantly. Preferred communication patterns are complex and fluid, featuring long involved discussion. These persons work best in non-autocratic, non-hierarchic organizations of the matrix type.

The general line of reasoning employed by Driver and Mock is similar to other human information processing systems models which treat personality as both a mediator and an instigator of the information processing needs of individuals. It follows that designers can identify personal characteristics about the information processing propensity of users. Since these tendencies are predictable and stable over time and situations, designers can tailor information systems towards them. The end result could be more effective information systems. The other variable selected for the contextual model was Perrow's (1967, 1970) concept of technology, an important attribute of the work itself.

Technology variables

This concept of technology is valuable because it is a simple yet rich way of absorbing the uncertainty stemming from a myriad of contextual factors. It will be recalled from earlier chapters that a growing body of research has established levels between accounting and information systems and several contextual variables (such as environmental uncertainty, product competition, rate of technological and scientific change, interdependencies, managerial climate, differentiation and integration, production methods, autonomy, and structuring of activities).

The valuable point in all this is that these contextual factors have a great deal more influence on the design and use of accounting information systems than previously thought. The problem, however, is that a great number of contextual variables seem to be at work. What is needed, then, is an analytical framework that is capable of both absorbing these factors and capturing them in a simple way. Perrow (1967) offers a clever but simple way into this problem by defining technology in terms of contextual factors.

Perrow built his concept of technology on the two polar types of decisions

identified by Simon (1977). According to Simon some tasks are well structured, repetitive, and routine; so definite procedures can be worked out for
handling them. Simon called these programmed tasks. Other tasks, by
contrast, are ill-structured. Cut-and-dried methods for handling them are not
available. They must be handled on the basis of a general problem-solving
capacity which relies on intelligent, adaptive, problem-oriented action. These
are non-programmed tasks. Appropriate design of organizational structure,
Simon argued, must facilitate both programmed and non-programmed decisions and tasks.

Perrow unfolded the structured/ill-structured continuum into a two-dimen-
sional scheme. The degree of structuring of tasks, Perrow suggested, is
influenced by two factors. The first is the nature of the response to the task
stimuli. The second is the variety or number of exceptions that arise in the
task conversion process. Following this lead, he defined technology as the
combined effect of both factors. The sundry environmental factors identified
in the studies cited above can be thought of as filtering through these two
dimensions. This is depicted in Figure 11.2.

In this way organizational contextual factors are linked to task characteristics. Perrow's scheme, then, offers a neat but powerful way of collapsing the
myriad variables of organizational environment into two dimensions. This
definition of technology is especially promising for research in information
system design because, as demonstrated later, the two technology dimensions
appear to have a substantial influence on the work-unit information system.

The first dimension of technology, task variety, is a function of the frequency of unexpected and novel events that occur in the conversion process.
When individuals encounter a large number of unexpected situations, with
frequent problems, then variety can be considered high. When there are

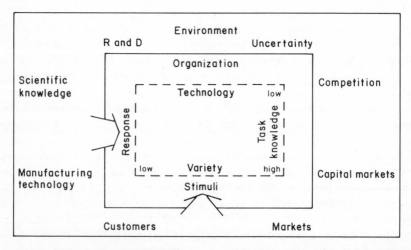

Figure 11.2 Environment, organization and technology. (Source: Macintosh,
1981, p. 44. Reproduced by permission of Pergamon Press Ltd)

few exceptions, and when the day-to-day job requirements are considered repetitious, then the task contains little variety. Variety in a work-unit can range from the simple repetition of a single act, such as on an assembly line, to work that is a series of unrelated problems or projects.

The other dimension of technology concerns how individuals respond to problems that arise in the course of their work. When a problem arises in a conversion process that is well understood participants engage in analyzable search. Analyzable search is an objective, computational process that uses stored knowledge and procedures such as instructions, manuals, programs and standards, or conventional technical knowledge such as in a textbook or handbook. Cause–effect relationships are understood, so the knowledge base represents correct ways of responding to problems that arise.

Yet some work is not well understood. The cause–effect relationships characterizing the conversion process are unclear, so when problems arise it is difficult to find the one correct solution. Readily available stores of knowledge, information, and prescribed solutions do not exist. Thus a different set of search procedures is called for, one called unanalyzable search. The individual may have to spend time thinking about what to do; or he may actively search beyond the available store of procedures; or he may act without much reflection, relying instead on accumulated experience, intuition, and judgement. Personal experience is a source of knowledge which we have a difficult time articulating to others but, nevertheless, a source in which we have confidence and trust. The final answer to a problem is not the result of a computational procedure, nor is there certainty that the final answer is the correct one.

These two dimensions of work-unit technology, variety and search behavior, can also be conceptualized as the type of uncertainty involved in the work situation. Variety, on the one hand, reflects the heterogeneity and novelty of stimuli that arise in the conversion process. When variety is low, individuals experience little uncertainty about stimuli that will arise in the course of their activities. As variety increases there is greater uncertainty about what will happen next; unexpected problems occur often. The search procedure, on the other hand, reflects the amount of uncertainty associated with identifying the correct response when an exception arises. When an individual has procedures and routines available which provide a prescribed response, uncertainty is low. But in the case of unanalyzable search there is considerable uncertainty about the identification of the correct response. Uncertainty, then, stems from both dimensions.

When the two dimensions of technology are combined they form the basis of four major categories of technology; routine, technical–professional, craft, and research. These categories are shown in Figure 11.3.

Routine technologies are characterized by little task variety and the use of rational search procedures when contingencies do arise. Examples are the repetitive work on a assembly line, continuous chemical processing, the

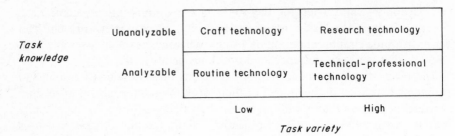

Figure 11.3 Categories of technology. (Source: Macintosh, 1981, p. 44. Reproduced by permission of Pergamon Press Ltd)

audit verification function in the professional accounting firm, and the filing activity in government departments that handle birth and death certificates.

Technical–professional technologies tend to be fairly complex because there is substantial variety in the tasks performed; but the various problems can usually be handled by referring to a store of established knowledge and decision-making techniques. Engineers, for example, can refer to books and technical manuals to discover the correct formulae to use in calculating tolerances and stress loads. Tax accountants search through statutes, interpretation bulletins, and judicial rulings to complete tax returns. Professional accountants look to generally accepted accounting principles, accounting board pronouncements, and SEC requirements when preparing financial statements for clients. In these examples the response is complex, but professionals are trained to understand it. So there is little uncertainty regarding the response; but it is hard to anticipate the exact kinds of problems which may arise.

Craft technologies are characterized by a fairly predictable stream of activities, but the conversion process is not well understood. There is no store of rational knowledge and techniques to apply to the conversion process. Tasks require extensive training and experience on the job before they are mastered. For craft-type tasks a decision-maker responds more on the basis of wisdom, intuition, and experience than by reference to an established body of rules and procedures. Examples include master chefs, professional athletes, manufacturers of fine glassware and other artistic products, money market managers, and professional accountants performing the quality control task of reviewing audit working papers. In craft activities individuals work with a limited set of problems, but choosing correct responses involves a great deal of personal judgement and experience.

Finally, when task variety is great and when the correct solution to a problem is not identifiable through an established store of knowledge and procedures, we encounter research-type technologies. Here uncertainty stems from two sources: the wide variety of inputs and the inability to predict the best way to reach the desired output. A great deal of effort is devoted to analysis. Typically it is difficult to identify a single correct solution because several acceptable options can be found. This type of technology is frequently found in research organizations because unexpected problems are dealt with and a great deal of energy is devoted to finding the most acceptable solution. Other examples include one-of-a-kind machine tool manufacturing, government policy analysis groups, long-range planning units, and financial statement qualifications by professional accountants.

Having identified four distinct types of technology—routine, technical-professional, craft, and research—Perrow theorized that each type of technology is served best by distinctive organizational arrangements designed to suit the special needs of the task. The general premise is that, one way or another, organizations attempt to maximize the congruence between their technology and their organizational structure. From this perspective technology is the defining characteristic of organizations. It is an independent variable. Structure, the arrangements among people for getting work done, is the dependent variable.

Perrow singled out two groups of people within an organization: those concerned with the technical administration of the conversion process and those concerned with the supervision of the people directly involved in the raw material conversion process. Perrow uses 'technical' administration as middle management and others who are concerned with the administration of production and 'supervision' as lower management concerned with the supervision of production. So readers should interpret the technical administration as the upper and middle line managers and technical staff and supervision as the lower line organization.

Perrow then identified four key characteristics of organization structure that describe these two groups and their interrelationships: (1) the discretion each group possesses in carrying out its tasks; (2) the power of each group to mobilize scarce resources and to control definitions of situations; (3) the basis of co-ordination of activities within each group, either through planning and programming or by relying on intricate feedback processes including negotiated adjustments in task sequencing; and (4) the degree of interdependence between the two groups. Using these four characteristics Perrow suggested appropriate organizational structures for each of the four technologies (see Figure 11.4).

Routine technologies contain little ambiguity and events can be foreseen. So discretion is low for both technical and supervision groups. The technical groups have the power. They program work for the line organization and so control the line supervisory groups. Co-ordination for both groups comes through planning. Interdependence between technical and supervision is limited; they have little need to interact. These organizational arrangements closely approximate the classical bureaucratic model.[3]

Organization structure for research technologies provides a sharp contrast with that of routine ones. In research technologies ambiguity is high and events are difficult to foresee. So discretion is high, for both technical and supervision groups, over the processes selected to carry out tasks. Both

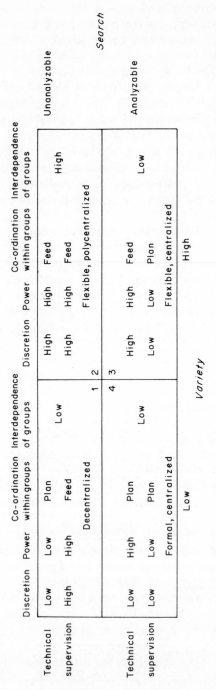

Figure 11.4 Perrow's technology-based model of organization structure. (Source: Macintosh, 1981, p. 45. Reproduced by permission of Pergamon Press Ltd)

groups have a lot of power to mobilize resources and define situations. Co ordination in both groups is on the basis of feedback and negotiated alterations in task arrangements. Interdependence between technical and supervision groups is high, they work closely together and may, at times, be almost indistinguishable. This model resembles the organic bureaucratic structure.

In technical–professional technologies the technical group has great discretion in choosing programs, and considerable power to mobilize resources and define production situations. Co-ordination within the technical groups is achieved through feedback of information for problem-solving. The situation is quite different for line supervisory groups and people on the shop floor. Discretion and power are minimal. Co-ordination is accomplished through planning; and since the technical group sends down designs for execution, there is little interdependence between the technical and supervisory groups. Machine tool manufacturers and automobile assembly plants are prime examples.

For craft technologies the situation is almost reversed. Here it is the supervisory group which has discretion and power and co-ordinates through feedback. The technical level is weak and responds to the needs of the line production units; it co-ordinates its work through planning. Interdependence of the supervision and technical groups tend to be low. Decentralized organizational arrangements dominate.

Larger firms, of course, incorporate all four technologies. They tend to factor their tasks into organizational subunits along the lines of the four types of technology. Public accounting firms are a good example. Routine audit assignments are handled by audit staffs. Auditing work is much the same from client to client. It is programmable and is guided by detailed and specific audit manuals. Exceptions to this routine work, such as complex corporation tax problems, are routed to the tax department where highly specialized technical–professional tax accountants complete the work on the basis of tax laws, interpretation bulletins, and court cases. Audit review work comes the closest to a craft task. It is carried out by supervisors and managers who perform the quality control review of the audit working papers by relying on intuition and experience. For some problems, however, such as pension accounting, well-established procedures do not exist. These are channeled to the research department which investigates the problem at length until a reasonably workable solution emerges which is formalized into a policy and practice document for distribution to the operating units. Public accounting firms, then, can route clients and problems encountered to the appropriate operating unit and so absorb, in an effective and efficient way, the sundry environmental factors which impinge upon them. Most large organizations seem to organize around types of tasks in this manner.

Perrow's work had a profound influence on the field. It was the inspiration for a great deal of research. It received early acceptance and continues to be a key causal variable in studies of organizational design.[4]

Perrow, then, outlines a rich theory of organizational structure derived from two factors: the amount of variety in the tasks and the degree of analyzability of the task conversion process. Perrow, however, did not include the appropriate characteristics of management information in his theory. Yet some clues are provided when a few of the ideas about personal decision styles are applied to Perrow's technology-based theory of organization design. Each of the four decision styles, as will be seen, seems remarkably well suited to a particular technology. Before piecing together such a comprehensive model of information systems, it is necessary to define the task-related information system variables.

TECHNOLOGY AND INFORMATION SYSTEMS

Two dimensions of task-related information systems are considered important: amount and ambiguity. These dimensions are chosen since they parallel the dimensions used in the decision style theory. Amount pertains to the quantity of information provided and processed by the personnel of a department. Ambiguity refers to the precision of the information thus provided. At one end of a continuum, information is unambiguous. An example would be the information contained in an on-line terminal used by a bank teller. When a customer presents a slip to withdraw cash the teller interrogates the system to determine the balance of the account. Either enough funds are available in the customer's account to cover the withdrawal or the balance is insufficient. The information received provides a clear and unambiguous message. Another example would be the material usage variance in a cost accounting report for a production department. The information provides a relatively unambiguous signal about the actual amount used compared to the standard amount. In these examples the information conveys a clear message, and is subject to only one interpretation. It is unambiguous and leads to one clear-cut solution.

At the other end of the continuum, information is ambiguous. It does not necessarily convey one clear message and may, in fact, convey several different and even conflicting messages. An example would be the information contained in a budget report for a legal department of an industrial firm. Actual and budgeted spending levels are reported, as well as differences. The message conveyed by this information, however, is tentative. Any conclusions are tenuous. Variances such as underspending do not necessarily indicate either effective or efficient performance. At best it can only be concluded that spending was less than planned. Similarly, strategic planning econometric models based on various scenarios of likely configurations of exogenous variables do not yield one optimal solution for goal-seeking organizations. At best they produce several acceptable solutions. The information in these examples does not convey a clear, concise message. The information has more than one focus. It is ambiguous and does not yield one clear-cut solution.

A third dimension of information systems is the way information is used.

Sometimes it is processed in a quick decisive manner and at other times it is given careful thought and deliberation. This third dimension is not, of course, an attribute of the information itself, but of the participants using the information in different settings. These relationships fall out into four distinct patterns of information:

(a) The concise information system. Small to moderate amounts of information that is precise and unambiguous, and is used in a quick and decisive way.
(b) The elaborate information system. Large amounts of information, frequently in the form of data bases or simulation models, which tend to be detailed and precise; recipients normally use such information in a slow and deliberate manner.
(c) The cursory information system. Small amounts of information, neither precise nor detailed and frequently superficial, that is used in a casual yet decisive way.
(d) The diffuse information system. Moderate to large amounts of information, covering a wide range of material, frequently ill-defined and imprecise, that typically is used in a slow, deliberate manner.

TECHNOLOGY, DECISION STYLE, AND TASK INFORMATION SYSTEM

Information systems, then, can be categorized, according to amount, ambiguity, and use, into four distinct styles. This is a point worth underscoring. System designers can develop information systems which will vary in style. All systems need not be the same; but what is more important is that each of the four information system styles seems to match one of the four technologies described earlier. Technology might also dictate the appropriate decision style. This matching of information system and decision style with technology is outlined in Table 11.1.

In the case of routine technologies (Row 1 in Table 11.1) work can be programmed for the line by the technical groups, and organizational arrangements approximate the classical bureaucratic model. These conditions seem ideal for decisive individuals who prefer clear-cut lines of authority, short spans of control, and well-defined rules. These individuals prefer to use small quantities of information and to make decisions quickly. It follows that information systems should provide minimal amounts of information which focus on one solution. The information system can be directed towards a limited set of well-understood applications. Information can be brief, clear, and concise; and normally will point to an unambiguous action or decision. A concise information system, then, is suited to routine technologies and decisive individuals.

An example of a concise information system is an airline reservation

Table 11.1 A comprehensive contextual model of information systems

Organizational situation					Information system			
Search procedures available for task completion	Perceived nature of tasks	Technology type	Organizational structure	Personal decision style	Amount	Ambiguity	Use	Style
Analyzable search	Uniform and stable	Routine	Classical bureaucratic	Decisive	Minimal	Single focus	Quick and decisive	Concise
Analyzable search	Non-uniform and unstable	Technical–professional	Functional bureaucratic	Hierarchic	Large	Single focus	Careful and deliberate	Elaborate
Unanalyzable search	Uniform and stable	Craft	Decentralized autonomous	Flexible	Minimal	Multiple focus	Intuitive reaction	Cursory
Unanalyzable search	Non-uniform and unstable	Research	Organic matrix	Integrative	Large	Multiple focus	Slow and creative	Diffuse

Source: Macintosh (1981), p. 45. Reproduced by permission of Pergamon Press from *Accounting, Organizations and Society*, Vol. 6, No. 1, pp. 39–53.

system. The reservation clerk needs to know whether or not a seat is available on the flight requested; and in the latter case the system generates the next best alternative flight route. The information generated is of the 'go' or 'no-go' type. Other examples include credit card checks, on-line banking systems, and economic order quantity (EOQ) systems. These concise information systems are suited well to routine tasks.

For technical–professional technologies the hierarchic decision style seems appropriate. Hierarchic individuals prefer large amounts of data which they massage with great care and thoroughness until one best solution emerges. They like to develop long-range plans, using large data bases. They prefer long but orderly communications; and they like formal organizational arrangements featuring broad spans of control and elaborate procedures. This style is an excellent match for the demands of technical groups in technical––professional technologies with its high task variety, well-understood conversion process, and feedback style of planning. Since the technical groups also have considerable power to mobilize resources and define the situations of production, a congruous management information system would be an elaborate one which incorporates a large data base, provides relatively unambiguous information, and contains facilities for managers to interact extensively with the data base while massaging the information until the one best solution emerges.

The high task variety characterizing the technical–professional technology places greater demands on the information system. So many types of problems can arise that it is not possible for the information system to be concise. Technical–professional technologies are characterized by large bodies of established knowledge. Consequently, an elaborate information system, one with a broad base and which draws upon established knowledge, is called for. Quantities of data contained in elaborate reports and in storage are appropriate in these circumstances. Consider the case of a North American automobile giant. A vast vehicle-order information system was designed to co-ordinate the complex operation of automobile orders, scheduling, production, inspection, delivery, financing, and billing.

This information system began with a customer order at a dealer. From there the order was relayed to a district office and then to a central location where it was exploded into sub-assembly and parts requirements. Accumulated orders then became the basis for inventory ordering and shipment, sub- and final assembly production scheduling, yard storage and final shipment. The system also created vehicle expediting reports, dealer invoices, wholesale financing papers, customs documents, vehicle inspection reports, and a host of other reports and documents concerned with marketing and production of automobiles. It suited the complex engineering, production, and marketing technology of the automobile industry.

Another example of a successful elaborate information system is the NAARS (National Automated Accounting Research System), which is an information retrieval system developed by a private firm in conjunction with the American Institute of Certified Public Accountants. Subscribers to the system, mainly professional accountants from public accounting firms, use computer terminals to interact with the massive central data base which is composed of public financial accounting reports (including financial statements, notes to the statements, and auditors' reports) from thousands of companies. By identifying specific subject-matter—say, reporting practices for price level changes—the user is informed of the number of company reports pertaining to it. These financial reports are then flashed on the screen at the user's command. Specific company reports can also be printed for additional examination. This system provides precise information of an extremely large volume. It is ideally suited to the technical–professional technology of financial accounting.

Turning to Row 3 in Table 11.1, craft technologies feature little variety and unanalyzable search. Power and discretion is decentralized to the supervisory groups and line production units. The flexible decision style, using minimal data but seeing it having different meaning at different times, reacting intuitively to events rather than operating to a plan, and preferring loose and fluid organizational arrangements and short to-the-point communications, seems well suited to craft technologies. In this setting management information systems should feature minimal data bases, short summary reports, and multiple-focus information. They may play only a minor role, acting as a trigger to managers who make decisions, in the main, by intuition and by drawing on their store of background experience. So information systems should be limited to cursory information, such as the number of units sold or produced. There are few rational procedures, manuals, or other data available to be used in conjunction with designing and developing such an information system. An example of a craft organization would be a specialized psychiatric care unit, where the degree of success rests largely with the skills of individual psychiatrists. The process of therapeutic change is not well understood. Formal information about, say, costs and benefits, cannot be directly related to this process and will tend to be used in a cursory fashion.

Research technologies seem inherently ambiguous due to the high variety and lack of analyzable search procedures. Organizational arrangements are highly organic. Power and discretion are shared by the technical and supervision groups who are highly interdependent. Co-ordination of tasks is accomplished by feedback and negotiated changes in task arrangements. The integrative decision style appears ideal for research environments. Integrative individuals have an affinity for large amounts of data from which they cascade several viable solutions and plans. They prefer non-hierarchical organizations featuring a great deal of both vertical and lateral communications. Diffuse information systems featuring large data bases, simulations, and multiple-focus information seem best suited to this context.

The diffuse information system, then, is suited to the high uncertainty associated with research-type technologies. Large amounts of information of various types have to be accessible or gathered. A great deal of effort is devoted to analyzing the problem and to finding and using available information in the best way. The participants need considerable experience, both concerning where to seek and how to use the relevant information to solve the problem at hand.

An example of a diffuse information system for a research task is corporate modeling for strategic planning. Strategic planning is a research-type technology. It is an unstructured, irregular process which tends to be creative as well as analytical (Anthony, 1965). Econometric models can be extremely valuable in the strategic planning process. For instance, a model of the econometric income statement of a large industrial firm was developed and linked to an econometric model of the national economy (Macintosh *et al.*, 1973). Strategic planners can then use this dual-model information system to assess future outcomes of the firm's present and future profits. It can also be used to isolate key environmental variables which affect the firm's fortunes, to formulate alternative ways of competing, to develop overall corporate objectives, and to allocate resources to profitable product-market segments—all important aspects of strategic planning. Corporate models of this nature have also been used to generate the effect of ill-defined but critical events on corporate income (Gershefski, 1978). These types of information systems contain large amounts of information. They are massaged extensively by experienced strategic planners to develop alternative answers to strategic problems.

PRACTICAL CONSIDERATIONS

Figuring out the best design for an accounting and information system is a challenging task. The above ideas, however, can be a valuable form of evaluating systems, both those in use and those on the drawing board. These ideas have been supported by systematic research (Macintosh and Daft, 1978a, 1978b; Daft and Macintosh, 1981); and they have been translated into practical design considerations by Daft and Macintosh (1978), and Daft (1983), who suggest that accounting information system design can be aided by consideration of the following guidelines.

Designers should focus initially on the technology of the responsibility center. Technology is a relatively enduring characteristic of a responsibility center. It represents the pattern of problems and activities with which managers deal. Systems that are tailored to a single person or a single problem may have a short useful life. Managers shift around from position to position and problems come and go; departmental technology usually outlasts both. It is easy to get a mismatch between the information system style and technology. The initial design consideration, then, should be an analysis of the technology of the responsibility center. Understanding this aspect can solve genuine accounting and information system problems. Consider a few real-life examples.

The site for the first example is a large institutional food preparation company. Investigation indicated, astoundingly, that nearly 75 percent of the food prepared for institutional consumption ended up in the garbage. As a result an information system designer, after several years of exhaustive research, developed an elaborate linear programming model for institutional food preparation. The information system could provide daily menus with substantial savings in food costs and significant improvements in nutrition. The firm installed the system at considerable expense and made it accessible to potential users throughout the organization. After eighteen months the system was still unused.

Analyzing this information system failure with the above ideas indicates that an elaborate information system was designed for a craft technology. Many aspects of food preparation—local tastes, aesthetics, favorite recipes, special talents of cooks—are not sufficiently well understood to be incorporated in the linear programming system. Yet the cooks have experience with these intangible factors. They know on the basis of training and experience what to prepare in their institution. So the cooks, rightly so, will ignore the linear programming model. Experience is a better source of information than a formalized information system for this type of task. The company finally dropped the linear programming model and went to a cursory information system which made menus, recipes, and food preparation ideas for the cooks to interpret and use as they wished. The cursory information system, although less precise than the one replaced, was highly successful.

A more dramatic example comes from Robert McNamara's experience in the office of the Secretary of Defense. The US automobile industry is noted for development of sophisticated elaborate accounting and information systems to make decisions and control the awesome logistics of engineering, producing, and marketing automobiles on a global scale. These systems proved highly successful in this technical–professional context. When McNamara become Secretary of Defense he is credited with implementing a similar system in the Defense Department. This system was used in part to manage the war in the Vietnam jungle. Jungle warfare was not well understood. New problems arose every day. Factual and technical information did not exist. A sophisticated, elaborate information system was ill-suited to the technology of jungle warfare. The Defense Department's use of an elaborate information system for what was essentially a research task was met by compliant underlings who supplied the system with fictitious information. The resulting inconsistency between reported and actual performance in Vietnam, experts such as Halberstam (1972) argue, contributed to President Johnson's decision not to run for re-election.

Technology, then, places important constraints on the accounting and information system, and once the general work unit requirements are identified designers know they are on the right track. When the system fits the underlying technology it also will serve the managers well.

Once the technology of the responsibility center has been analyzed, designers can turn to consideration of the personal decision style of the manager. This can be accomplished in several ways given, of course, that the manager consents to participate. Alternatives include: the IST developed by Driver and Mock (1975), the short questionnaire used by Daft and Macintosh (1981), the Myers–Briggs personal style inventory, as described in Chapter 5, or the Witkin embedded figures test (Witkin *et al.*, 1967). Although the relationship of cognitive and decision style types to information system needs have not as yet been identified and spelled out in much detail, these instruments, regardless of which is used, would provide clues for the designer about the appropriate characteristics for the accounting and information system. When the results surface they can be compared to the requirements of the technology. If the needs converge, and this should be the most likely outcome, designers can proceed with confidence. If the needs are not congruent the designer can discuss the difference with the manager and jointly they can converge on a solution for the system.

The idea of using psychological tests to develop information-related behavioral profiles of managers is neither as far-fetched nor as difficult as might be thought at first glance. Barriff and Lusk (1978) provide a detailed description of such an approach in a public sector organization. The authors administered a series of psychological instruments, including a cognitive style test, to the seventeen individuals—primarily administrators and field supervisors—identified as constituting the organization's decision network. The organization was in the midst of designing and implementing a new evaluation and control system since the previous one failed to provide management with appropriate information for evaluating and controlling its service. The user behavior profiles guided the design of the new system which proved to be substantially different from the old one. The experiment proved a great success. Both administrators and supervisors used the new system willingly and with an unusual spirit of co-operation; and the individuals in the decision network were highly satisfied with it. The authors warn, however, that user information behavioral profiles must be evaluated within the context of each particular organization. The results of this exploratory study are highly encouraging.

Designers should also be cautioned about transferring an accounting and information system from one organization to another. This is a common mistake. In fact, many designers are hired on the basis of the system they implemented in their previous organization. They import the entire system, including manuals, flow charts, forms, documentation, and protocols, into the new organization. Managers tend to trust systems that worked well in the past. What they often fail to realize is that the system worked well because it matched the underlying technology of their former organization. The system, of course, will not work well unless the technology is the same. Along similar lines, designers forget or ignore the fact that there is a wide range of technologies in any organization.

Finally, researchers have spent considerable time developing accurate measurements of technology and decision style. For example, the instrument for measuring the concept of technology used in this chapter was assessed rigorously by Withey *et al.* (1983) who put together a new technology scale consisting of an amalgam of several previous scales. But for the designer, refined measures are not necessary for most accounting and information systems applications. Designers should simply try to avoid the big, costly systems errors. Providing an elaborate system for craft activities, or imposing a diffuse system for a flexible decision style manager, is likely to turn out to be a costly error. By the same token designers should not expect technical–professional tasks to struggle along without adequate information backups and providing an elaborate system with a large data base to decisive-style managers in routine technologies will be equally disastrous.

A technology decision-style focus is a promising development for problems of accounting and information systems design. But this approach requires both managers and designers adopt a new way of thinking about information needs, and to look beyond the special requests of particular managers to see the nature of the work unit technologies and the personal decision styles of the managers. This should arm them with powerful new tools to help solve problems of accounting and information system design.

CONCLUSION

Decision style and technology combine into a much richer representation of the organization setting of a management information system than is possible if only one of these dimensions were used. Each of the four decision styles can be fitted to one of the four cells of technology with a remarkably accurate matching. This organizational context gives the clues for the appropriate design characteristics of the best management information system. The central idea is that management information systems should be designed to be congruent with the organizational contexts which they serve.

Like any model, however, this view has its limitations. In the first place many organizational work units embrace more than one technology. A production line manager, for example, may have several technologies within his organizational boundary. They might include: programmable work such as inventory control, technical–professional work like industrial engineering, craft tasks such as machine maintenance and molders, and even research technologies for designing new processes. The systems designer should recognize these differences and treat the separate tasks accordingly.

A second limitation of the model is that in some cases technologies span several departments and organizational locations. Students go to the maths department, then to economics, on to philosophy, to the library, and even to the gymnasium as they are 'processed' through a university. Similarly, a new product passes to and from R&D, engineering, production, marketing, and accounting during its evolution from idea to development, prototype manufacturing, and eventually pilot testing by customers. The organizational boundaries of a technology are not always limited to one department.

Another limitation rests with the assumption that personal decision style is a relatively enduring cognitive trait of an individual. It may be that design styles are merely behaviors undertaken within certain contexts. At present this issue is under debate, and is in need of empirical investigation. If it turns out that decision styles are generated by certain contexts, the general thesis might be modified to posit that, to be effective, information systems and decision styles should be congruent with the nature of the technology.

Another potential problem is that a purely technological and decision style view of information system design would attribute, in most cases, a much greater store of influence to technology than is likely the case in reality. After all, other important variables are also at work. Factors such as interdependencies, managerial climate, degree of decentralization, and even size have been shown to have some influence on organizational systems. There are lots of possibilities.

It also should be noted that theories positing a rational alignment of environment and management structures have been modified recently to include dimensions of power. As Burns and Stalker (1961) noted, some firms were impeded by the career ambitions and political maneuverings of key management personnel in making the correct mechanistic or organic alignment of their management systems to their environment. More recently, organizational theorists have returned to examine Burns and Stalker's views of the effect of political maneuverings and ambitions on organizational structure. The assumption that organizations automatically strive for a rational fit between environment and task requirements and their administrative structures has come into question. As a result, this view has been broadened to one which argues that organizational design is as much a political process as it is a rational one. These two views, however, are not incompatible. This point has been stressed by Pfeffer (1978), one of the proponents of the influence of the political process, who wrote:

> There are it appears, two perspectives for analysing social structure. One asks for the appropriateness of a given structure for the coordination of interdependence to achieve some task; the other asks why and how structure is a result of organizational influence processes and the consequences of a given structure for the distribution of control and power within organizations. It is likely that these are complementary rather than competing perspectives (Pfeffer, 1978, p. 26).

The view of organizations seeking a technical–rational alignment of management structures with organizational context must be tempered by considerations of the internal power distribution and political tensions within the organization. Accounting and information systems, however, may be less vulnerable to these political impediments than other management systems.

Further, the personal decision style of the manager, however, may not always match the technology of the responsibility center. When it does not, the designer must trade off design configurations and warn the manager of the mismatch. Still, if you think about it, technology should influence information system characteristics; after all, information systems help people do their work. Technology, in the sense used here, is one way of describing different types of work. It provides a simple but rich way to analyze the organizational context of information systems.

Notes

1. Parts of this chapter are adapted from the article by Norman B. Macintosh, 'A contextual model of information systems', *Accounting, Organizations and Society*, Vol. 6, No. 1, pp. 39–53, and are reproduced by permission of Pergamon Press. Other parts of it are adapted from the article by Daft, R. L., and N. B. Macintosh, 'A new approach to design and use of management information', *California Management Review*, Fall 1978, pp. 82–92; Copyright © 1978 by the Regents of the University of California. Permission granted by the Regents.
2. Driver and Mock used a business game simulation with MBA students as subjects to test their decision style model. The results of the test and the consistency of their interpretations were later critiqued by Tiessen and Baker (1977). McGhee *et al.* (1978) and Savich (1977) were unable to support their findings in other experiments which measured the variables in an indirect and different way. In an empirical study of over 250 managers in twenty-four organizations Macintosh and Daft (1978a), however, found some support for the Driver and Mock decision style theory. Consequently, the results with regard to the effect of decision style differences on the use of formal information systems are mixed. These studies raise the question of whether decision styles are a result of more or less stable personal traits or are the result of the task environment. This issue, then, remains one which still requires empirical confirmation.
3. Here Perrow (1970) used the term bureaucratic structure for the more or less stable patterns of behavior based upon a structure of roles and specialized tasks. He emphasized that he does not use it in the more common, pejorative sense of '. . . rigid rules and regulations, a hierarchy of offices, narrow specialization of personnel, an abundance of offices and units which can hamstring those who want to get things done, impersonality and resistance to change' (p. 50).
4. Duncan (1972), for example, based his study of organizational environments and perceived uncertainty on Perrow's technology concept. Hage and Aiken (1969), using Perrow's definition of technology, found considerable support for Perrow's ideas in their study of the relation of social structure of organizations to routine work. Grimes *et al.* (1972) found that certain managerial styles and management techniques may be more useful for a given technological setting than others. Lynch (1974) established a link between Perrow's technology model and its empirical domain in her study of library departmentalization. Overton *et al.* (1977) also operationalized Perrow's concept of technology so as to differentiate among different nursing subunits. Randolph and Finch (1977) found a relationship between Perrow's technology and the direction and frequency dimensions of task communications. Glisson (1978) related Perrow's technological routinization to

structural variables. Van de Ven and Delbecq (1974) found that it was associated with communication and co-ordination patterns.

References

Anthony, R. N., *Planning and Control Systems: A Framework for Analysis*, Graduate School of Business Administration, Harvard University, Boston, Mass., 1965.

Barriff, M. L., and E. J. Lusk, 'Designing information systems for organizational control: the use of psychological tests', *Information and Management*, Vol. 1, 1978, pp. 113–121.

Burns, T., and G. M. Stalker, *The Management of Innovation*, Tavistock Publications, London, 1961.

Daft, R. L., *Organizational Theory and Design*, West Publishing Company, St Paul, Minn., 1983.

Daft, R. L., and N. B. Macintosh, 'A new approach to design and use of management information', *California Management Review*, Fall 1978, pp. 82–92.

Daft, R. L., and N. B. Macintosh, 'A tentative exploration into the amount and equivocality of information processing in organizational work units', *Administrative Science Quarterly*, June 1981, pp. 207–224.

Driver, M. J., and T. J. Mock, 'Human information processing decision style theory and accounting information systems', *The Accounting Review*, July 1975, pp. 490–508.

Duncan, R. B., 'Characteristics of organizational environments and perceived environmental uncertainty', *Administrative Science Quarterly*, September 1972, pp. 313–327.

Gershefski, G. W., 'The development of the Sun Oil corporate financial model', in Thomas, W. E. (ed.), *Readings in Cost Accounting, Budgeting, and Control*, South Western Publishing Co., Cincinnati, Ohio, 1978.

Glisson, C. A., 'Dependence of technological routinization on structural variables in human service organizations', *Administrative Science Quarterly*, September 1978, pp. 383–395.

Grimes, A. J., S. M. Klein, and F. A. Shull, 'Matrix model: a selective empirical test', *Academy of Management Journal*, Vol. 16, 1972, pp. 1028–1039.

Hage, G., and M. Aiken, 'Routine technology, social structure, and organizational goals', *Administrative Science Quarterly*, March 1969, pp. 366–379.

Halberstam, D., *The Best and the Brightest*, Random House, New York, 1972.

Lawler, G. G. III, and J. G. Rhode, *Information and Control in Organizations*, Goodyear Publishing Company, Inc., Pacific Palisades, Calif., 1976.

Livingstone, J. L., *Managerial Accounting: The Behavioral Foundations*, Grid, Inc., Columbus, Ohio, 1975.

Lynch, B. P., 'An empirical assessment of Perrow's technology construct', *Administrative Science Quarterly*, September 1974, pp. 338–351.

Macintosh, N. B., 'A contextual model of information systems', *Accounting, Organizations and Society*, Vol. 6, No. 1, 1981, pp. 39–53.

Macintosh, N. B., and R. L. Daft, 'A technology–decision style model of information systems'. Paper presented at the 1978 Annual Meeting of the American Accounting Association, Denver, Colorado, August 1978(a).

Macintosh, N. B., and R. L. Daft, 'User department technology and information design', *Information and Management*, Vol. 1, No. 3, 1978(b), pp. 123–131.

Macintosh, N. B., H. Tsurumi, and Y. Tsurumi, 'Econometrics for strategic planning', *Journal of Business Policy*, Spring 1973, pp. 49–61.

Mason, R. O., and I. I. Mitroff, 'A program for research on management information systems', *Management Science*, January 1973, pp. 475–487.

238

McGhee, W., M. D. Shields, and J. G. Birnberg, 'The effects of personality on a subject's information processing', *The Accounting Review*, July 1978, pp. 681–697.

Overton, P., R. Schneck, and C. B. Hazlett, 'An empirical study of the technology of nursing subunits', *Administrative Science Quarterly*, June 1977, pp. 203–219.

Perrow, C., 'A framework for the comparative analysis of organizations', *American Sociological Review*, April 1967, pp. 194–208.

Perrow, C., *Organizational Analysis: A Sociological Review*, Wadsworth Publishing Inc., Belmont, California, 1970.

Pfeffer, J., *Organizational Design*, AMM Publishing Corporation, Arlington Heights, Ill., 1978.

Randolph, W. A., and F. E. Finch, 'The relationship between organizational technology and the direction and frequency of dimensions of task communications', *Human Relations*, 1977, pp. 1131–1145.

Savich, R. S., 'The use of accounting information in decision making'. *The Accounting Review*, July 1977, pp. 642–652.

Simon, H., *The New Science of Management Decision*, revised edn; Prentice-Hall, Inc., Englewood Cliffs, New Jersey, 1977.

Tiessen, P., and D. M. Baker, 'Human information processing, decision style theory and accounting information systems: a comment', *The Accounting Review*, October 1977, pp. 984–987.

Van de Ven, A. H., and A. L. Delbecq, 'A task contingency model of work-unit structure', *Administrative Science Quarterly*, June 1974, pp. 183–197.

Witkin, H. A., D. R. Goodenough, and S. A. Karp, 'Stability of cognitive style from childhood to young adulthood', *Journal of Personality and Social Psychology*, November 1967, pp. 291–300.

Withey, M., R. L. Daft, and W. H. Cooper, 'Measures of Perrow's work unit technology: an empirical assessment and a new scale', *Academy of Management Journal*, Vol. 26, No. 1, pp. 45–63.

CHAPTER 12

A Technology Model of Management Control Systems

The concept of management control systems (MCS), a special kind of accounting and information systems, has been with us for a long time. It emerged in the early part of this century with General Motors Corporation in particular playing a leading role in the development of this idea. At the time General Motors faced a series of terrible crises which kept it on the brink of bankruptcy. This predicament was precipitated, in the main, by the failure of its management systems to cope with rapid growth, large size, and a volatile environment. In response to this situation Alfred Sloan, as president, formulated a philosophy of management which he dubbed 'decentralization with co-ordinated control'. This concept proved central to GM's survival and ultimate position as the largest industrial enterprise in history.

The basic idea underlying decentralization with co-ordinated control involved the realignment of duties and responsibilities amongst the various managers in the firm by separating the executive function from the administrative function. Administrative offices were charged with the responsibility for operations of car divisions including the design, production, and marketing functions. The executive office concerned itself with formulation of long-term corporate strategy, developing critical competitive policies, and measuring and monitoring the efforts of the administrative offices. Key committees, including members from both offices, provided the necessary vertical and horizontal co-ordination and integration.

The lever to success, however, for this new management blueprint, proved to be the concept that: 'if we had the means to review and judge the effectiveness of operations we could safely leave the prosecution of those operations to the men in charge of them' (Sloan, 1963, p. 140). The means proved to be financial controls. They made the final but critical link in the principle of decentralization with co-ordinated control.

These devices became known later as management controls. This distinguished them from operational controls which employed established techniques for controlling resources and activities such as cash, credit, inventory, production, orders, sales, and shipping. Management control focused on the performance of entire responsibility centers under the jurisdiction of a manager. As Sloan's principle of management became adopted by a majority of the large industrial enterprises in North America, MCS emerged as a separate speciality area of management accounting. It is MCS that are the focus of this chapter.

MCS in all organizations tend to have a great deal in common. They are built on financial information. They feature the operating budget as a key report. They also include statistical reports containing information about resource consumption, activity levels, and output creation. They often embody qualitative and quantitative long-term plans; and in some systems they include formal policies, procedures, and practices.

Yet for all this commonality, MCS also differ in obvious ways. Some are specific and contain large quantities of detailed data; others are restricted to small amounts of general information. Some feature frequent reporting; others report only once or twice a year. Some include difficult performance targets; while others have targets that are easy to achieve. MCS have as much variety as they have commonality; and, as will be demonstrated later in this chapter, this variety can be traced to differences in organizational technology.

Further, organizations subject their managers to multiple management control mechanisms. A typical MCS configuration includes: an annual qualitative strategic plan for their area of responsibility, a monthly operating budget, a bi-weekly activity statistical report, several books of standard operating procedures and practices, a bi-annual personal performance review including written objectives for the coming period, and an operations audit inspection and report. Although this seems like a large amount of control, Macintosh and Daft (1982) report, in their study of MCS in nearly ninety departments in twenty companies, that this is a typical pattern. They also found that the MCS in their sample were both important and useful. The managers did not perceive them as either restrictive or repressive; rather, they saw them as necessary and valuable, and they were well satisfied with the way these controls were used in their organizations. Management controls, the key ingredient in Alfred Sloan's concept of 'decentralization with co-ordinated control', have emerged as a vital dimension of modern organizational design.

Management control systems defined

Management control, however, is a term that requires a more detailed definition than that given thus far. One way of doing this is to compare MCS with two other major systems employed by organizations for controlling the activities, resources, and processes in the pursuit of their goals. These are operational and strategic control systems. MCS are related to, but can be distinguished from, both operational and strategic planning and control systems (Anthony, 1965).

Operational control systems are used to help ensure that the specific tasks and transactions undertaken within the various responsibility centers are carried out in the most cost-effective way. They are employed within departments at the level where organizational inputs are processed and resources are consumed to produce outputs for other departments, customers, and clients. Examples include: standard cost systems for direct labor and material, inventory economic order quantity (EOQ) models, manpower utilization reports, and material usage reports.

Strategic planning and control systems are quite different from the above examples. They deal not with logistics, but with the basic character and direction of the overall organization. They are concerned with defining organizational purpose, stating global objectives, and formulating key policies for matters including products, markets, capital acquisition, diversification, and organizational design. They tend to be used only when needed, rather than being part of a regular procedure. They focus on expected results rather than actual outcomes; and they rely on imprecise, external, and value-oriented information.

MCS are qualitatively different from either operational or strategic control systems. They are used by upper management to measure, monitor, and motivate the managers of an organization's various responsibility centers. The unit of analysis of an MCS is the entire responsibility center, as opposed to the various activities or parts within these centers. The manager in charge of the responsibility center is the focal point. The purpose of management control is to ensure that the resources of the responsibility center are used effectively and efficiently in pursuit of the organizational goal.

MCS generally are built around a financial structure and involve information about revenues, costs, and resources. The information covers both planned and actual levels, such as is found in a budget. In addition to financial information, MCS often include data about order levels, number of personnel, volume of resources, as well as quantity and quality of output. MCS tend to follow a regular rhythm. Plans are presented and approved at certain dates each year. Reports are submitted, reviewed, and evaluated in a prearranged sequence according to a fixed timetable. The management control process is an integrated one, encompassing programming, budgeting, accounting, reporting, and analysis.

Two specific examples of MCS follow. They serve to demonstrate the scope and composition of these systems; and they demonstrate the extent to which MCS can differ in important characteristics.

The first example is the system employed in a nationwide banking organization. This system contains seven major components: the branch opportunity plan, the profit plan or budget, the statistical report, the policies and procedures manuals, the branch inspections, the personal review and evaluation of branch manager performance, and, by extension, the district manager himself. Each will be discussed in turn.

Each year, branch managers are required to develop a strategic opportunity plan for their branches. The plan includes an assessment of the business environment and economic outlook for the territory served by the branch. In addition, branch strengths and weaknesses are identified and related to business potential. Specific action plans are developed for exploiting business opportunities, capitalizing on strengths, and reducing weaknesses. The branch opportunity plan is submitted to the district manager who reviews it and either accepts or rejects the contents.

The branch managers also draw up a detailed branch profit plan for the coming year. The profit plan consists of details of expected branch revenues and expenses. It is reviewed by the district manager in light of the district profit plan. It is also reviewed by the corporate headquarters finance staff. Discussion and negotiation take place until a final profit plan is agreed to by all parties. Actual outcomes are compared to target levels every quarter. If outcomes deviate from the plan, branch managers are required to submit written explanations along with a revised profit plan for the rest of the year.

Each month, branches submit to their district manager and to the corporate office a detailed document known as the statistical report. The format for the report is prescribed in a procedures manual. It covers every aspect of the branch activity including: the number and dollar value of loan accounts, collections, details of branch expenses, analysis of overdue accounts, new accounts, the number of transactions processed, business development data such as calls to customers and prospective customers, the number of branch employees, overtime hours, and supper money. A shorter version, known as the 'short report', is submitted each week. It contains a few key statistics on loan and deposit levels. These reports are necessary for central bank reporting of weekly loans and deposits. The statistical reports from all branches are amalgamated into district, region, and corporate summaries which are used to compare performance across the organization. The statistical reports are submitted to computerized regression analyses which relate personnel levels to the volume of transactions. This enables early spotting of overstaffed branches.

Branch managers are guided by twelve books and over 8000 pages of formal policies, procedures, and practices. These cover nearly all aspects of running a branch including: record-keeping, administrative practices for branch operations, office procedures, detailed job descriptions for all branch positions, branch reporting and control procedures, personnel policies, and explanations of key corporate policies and objectives. The policies, procedures, and practices are expected to be followed closely: branch managers who deviate from them are vulnerable to severe reproof.

Internal auditors make unannounced visits at least once a year to each branch in their districts. During these visits the branch operations are scrutinized in great detail. No nook or cranny is overlooked. Records, paperwork, and files are inspected to see if branch operations are being carried out in accordance with policies and procedures. A detailed letter commenting on the outcome of the inspection is sent to corporate office. Branches that perform below satisfactory levels are inspected more than once a year, and district staff personnel are temporarily assigned to problem branches to improve specific aspects of their performance.

The district manager also formally reviews the performance of the branch manager every six months. The appraisal is completed on a 'formal performance report form' consisting of two pages with general headings, including: main responsibilities, demonstrated managerial skills and qualities, career interests and ambitions, development activities and needs, performance appraisal and rating, and placement recommendations. The completed form is discussed by the district manager with the branch manager and then signed by both parties.

The district managers are also an important control. They constantly monitor the performance of each branch in their district by reviewing the profit plan, the statistical reports, and the weekly summary. They also participate in decisions regarding the appointment of branch managers—in effect they carry a vast store of information about each branch and branch manager. The district manager, in fact, is a key link in the control chain.

The total amount of control employed is impressive. Explicit plans are required. Economic performance is monitored closely, as are activity levels. Formal manuals prescribe precisely how duties and functions are to be carried out, and on-the-site inspections and personal performance reviews keep district managers in close touch with almost every detail of branch operations.

At first glance this management control system may appear excessive. Yet the various control devices complement each other. Each serves a well-defined purpose. The branch opportunity plan and the operating budget meet the planning needs. The statistical report and the weekly summary are the primary tools for measuring and monitoring performance. The policies, procedures, and practices, and the periodic inspection, prescribe the appropriate specific behavior required to run a branch. The personal evaluation review, which incorporates all the information from these sundry sources, contributes to decisions on salary raises and promotion. Collectively, these controls comprise an integrated management control system. It is of more than passing interest to note that the branch managers felt that this system provides them with a good deal of freedom and challenge; and they are well satisfied with the way it works in their organization generally.

The second MCS example provides a sharp contrast with the one used by the bank. It was designed for the engineering department of a food-processing firm. This department is responsible for improving the existing manufacturing equipment and for developing new production processes. The operating budget, which is issued monthly, consists of ten line items of salary, materials, and travel expenses. Most of the items are long-term fixed commitments. The budget, then, helps the manager plan for the department. Budget performance, however, does not receive a great deal of emphasis. The budget is little used for measuring performance.

In addition to the operating budget, a statistical report is issued monthly, consisting of about 100 line items regarding current spending levels on projects in process. Each year the department head is subjected to a personal performance evaluation and review. This review covers six major topics. Its main function is to make salary and promotion decisions.

These controls seem minimal. The budget and statistical reports contain only a few lines. There are no books of standard procedures and practices. The controls are used mainly to facilitate planning and co-ordination. They are not of much use for monitoring and measuring performance. These controls differ markedly from the first example; yet they are appropriate to the organization in question, and the department manager is content with the way the controls were designed and used.

Key characteristics of management control systems

These two examples provide a striking contrast in MCS design. Both are used to control the managers of the respective responsibility centers; both seem well suited to the needs of their respective organizations; and in both cases the managers are satisfied with them and believe they work well. Yet the two are quite different in several important characteristics, which will be identified next.

The degree of detail of information used in the controls differs widely in the two cases. In the first example the controls monitor and guide nearly every aspect of the branch operations. The control information is detailed and specific. In the second example only small quantities of general information are reported. At one end of a continuum controls are very detailed and specific. This is analogous to what is known in organizational behavior as a close style of supervision. At the other end of the continuum the control reports feature small amounts of general information. This is analogous to a general style of supervision. This suggests that MCS can vary substantially in terms of detail, and can still be appropriate.

MCS also vary in how often they report. Some report frequently, almost continuously. In the bank, for example, some sort of a report comes out weekly. In the engineering department it is monthly. In one of the research sites from our sample, reports are issued only once a year. In another, information on key activities levels at all locations across the country is collected daily and tabulated in a report for the president. The frequency of reporting, then, can vary considerably.

MCS also differ in respect to the level of difficulty of the yardsticks incorporated in the reports. Some systems use standards which are easy to reach; others set difficult but achievable targets; while still others strike very difficult, even impossible, yardsticks. The level of difficulty of the controls for the bank branches is moderate, whereas for the engineering department targets are relatively easy to achieve. Although the level of difficulty is thought to have a strong effect on the behavior of the managers, the precise nature of the impact has not yet been uncovered.

Another characteristic of control systems is the pattern of participation in setting standards. In some systems standard setting is dominated by top management. In others the responsibility center manager has a great deal of influence. In still others the employees in the responsibility center have the largest influence. In some instances the influence is shared widely by all three levels. In the case of the bank, top management is dominant in setting targets. Branch managers and employees have little say. By contrast, in the engineering department, the manager and employees have more influence than does upper management. Many authorities believe that the pattern of participation in standard-setting is crucial to the motivation and desired behavior of the managers. However, although a large number of studies on this assumption have been conducted, the results, as yet, are still inconclusive.

MCS also vary in the amount of motivational force they exert. Sometimes the impact is very strong. The controls have a great deal of influence on the day-to-day activities in the department, and managers tend to respond with quick action if actual performance deviates from planned levels. In other cases the system has little or no impact on either the managers or the daily activities in the department. For both the bank branches and the engineering departments in our study, the MCS contain a good deal of motivational force, the systems are taken seriously, and the managers respond quickly when actual levels differ from planned ones.

The original purpose of management control was to enable the executive office to measure and monitor performance of the administrative offices. A felicitous side result, however, was that the controls also proved to be important in motivating the managers of the administrative offices.

MCS also play an important role in helping managers perform the basic administrative functions of planning, coordinating, measuring, and rewarding. For some systems the key function of MCS is planning, for others it is measurement of performance, and for still others it may be co-ordination or rewards. But for most control systems it is all of these. In the case of the bank the monitoring and measuring function is dominant; but planning and rewards are also important. Co-ordination is not an important function. In the engineering department planning and co-ordination are the prime functions served by the system. The controls are not important for measuring performance or decisions on rewards.

These six characteristics of management controls can be used to compare and contrast the two examples described earlier. In the first example the control system was specific and detailed. Reporting was frequent. Top management dominated the standard-setting process and standards were difficult but achievable. The system was used primarily for measurement and monitoring, but the planning and reward functions also loomed large. The control system appeared close, even restrictive, yet branch managers reported that they were well satisfied with the way it worked and the way it was used.

To recapitulate, MCS can be defined in terms of both their structure (the various reports, instruments, and instructions) and their process (how they are used and what they accomplish). The two examples cited showed that they have several common characteristics. They also demonstrate that these characteristics can vary from organization to organization and from department to department within an organization. Next we focus on these variations and outline a model of MCS which links differences in the structure and process of MCS to differences in departmental technology.

A TECHNOLOGY MODEL OF MANAGEMENT CONTROL

During its formative years, management control systems theory concerned itself with the development of general principles and ideal types of MCS. It was thought that once these principles were developed they could be applied universally. This line of reasoning, however, is giving way slowly to a different idea. The new approach argues that impersonal forces of environment, markets, and technology have a good deal of influence on the structure of any MCS. These forces also influences the process of how the systems are used, along with important personal forces. Consequently, the search for the ideal configuration with universal applicability has lost support.

Many studies followed this lead. Several of them are covered in earlier chapters. They established that organizational context, environment, strategy, and technology are key factors, not only in shaping organizational structure, but also may have a great deal more influence in the design and use of MCS than was previously thought. The logic can be summed up as follows. If environment, technology, and goals shape the type of organizational structure, it seems reasonable that they also would influence MCS. Management accounting and information system managers, then, should attempt to design control systems that are congruent with these factors. Once articulated, of course, this may seem almost self-evident. Yet this first step is always a most difficult one to take.

This general premise, however, as was shown in Chapter 8, poses a major problem. There are a large number of contextual variables that might influence MCS; so it might be concluded that we have gone from one extreme of seeking universally applicable rules to the other extreme of recognizing that each organization has a particular context and must be studied as a unique case. If this is so, we are not much further ahead.

One way through this problem lies in finding frameworks which adopt a position somewhere between the approaches of universal principles and unique context. Such frameworks would recognize patterned variations in organization contexts and trace these to systematic differences in management control. This would establish a middle ground between the two extremes. These frameworks would need to be capable of absorbing the inherent variety of any context, and yet be simple enough to permit useful analysis of the ubiquitous environment of any organization. The technology model of management control, which is outlined next, is of this order.

As in the previous chapter, Macintosh and Daft (1982) selected technology as the key variable to develop a model of the kind proposed, because it is one aspect of organizational context that has been used widely as a key determinant in shaping organizational arrangements. Again, the specific definition of technology selected is based on Perrow's (1967) use of the term—a combination of task variety and task knowledge. When these two dimensions are combined, they form the basis for four major categories of technology.

Routine technologies have little task variety and have a store of well-understood task-conversion procedures. The work is typically routine. Technical–professional technologies tend to be fairly complex because substantial variety exists in the tasks performed. But the various problems can usually be handled by referring to a store of established knowledge and decision-making techniques. Craft technologies entail a fairly predictable stream of activities, but the conversion process is not well understood. No store of rational knowledge and techniques exists to apply to the conversion process. Tasks require extensive training and experience on the job before they are mastered. For craft-type tasks a decision-maker responds more on the basis of wisdom, intuition, and experience than by reference to an established body of rules and procedures. Finally, research technologies feature high task variety and poorly understood task knowledge. Here uncertainty stems from two sources—the wide variety of inputs and the inability to predict the best way to reach the desired output. A great deal of effort is devoted to analysis. Typically, it is difficult to identify a single correct solution because several acceptable options can be found, and a great deal of energy is devoted to finding the most satisfactory one.

The technology framework is also a simple but effective way of analyzing the management control needs of any particular organizational unit. Macintosh and Daft used it to derive four distinct styles of management control, each of which would seem to be ideally suited to one of the four technologies. Each of these styles of management control and the results of their research testing the theory is discussed in turn.

In their research, Macintosh and Daft gathered data, in questionnaire interviews with nearly ninety managers of various responsibility centers in twenty large organizations. The data collected included characteristics of three major organizational controls—the annual operating budget, the sundry statistical reports which outsiders receive about departmental activities and outputs, and the set of formal standard operating procedures and rules (SOPs) which guide the managers in running their organizational component. The results of this investigation are summarized in Figure 12.1.

Close management controls for programmable technology

Routine technologies contain well-understood, low variety tasks. Work is repetitive and uncertainty is low. Efficiency and orderliness are, thus, the order of the day for reaping the greatest possible gains from the stated goal. Management controls in this situation require several distinctive features.

248

In comparison with the total sample, controls are more detailed, and reporting is more frequent. Upper management have a greater influence in setting target levels than do employees in the department; yet target levels are, on the whole, fairly easy to achieve. The controls are important for the measuring and monitoring of performance, as well as for helping to make pay and promotion decisions; but they are less important for planning and co-ordination.

The pattern of motivation exerted by controls varies. The operating budget has less influence on departmental activities than it does in other technologies, while the SOPs have more, and the emphasis on meeting the targets of the statistical reports increases modestly. In routine technologies the budget tends to make departmental activities more visible to upper management. Finally, department managers are more satisfied with the controls than on average across the sample.

This profile suggests a close and supportive management control style—one

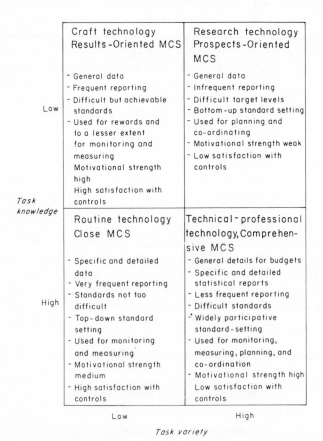

Figure 12.1 A technology model of management control systems

which seems well suited to routine technologies. The rationale for this fit is as follows. The best way to perform the routine and repetitive tasks can be readily determined and committed to policies and procedures as a permanent guide for job behavior. Thus, the amount and influence of various controls increases. The need for steady, reliable, and orderly output accounts in part for the frequent reporting, as well as for the increase in upper management influence in target setting. This, along with the fact that the repetitive tasks are well understood, leads to performance expectations that are well established and widely agreed upon. Consequently, target levels are of medium difficulty and employees in the department have little influence in setting them. The measuring and monitoring of performance is critical to ensure maximum results from routine work. For the same reason the coupling of rewards to the controls increases. Since much of the work can be programmed in advance, the role of controls in planning and co-ordination is less important.

It might be expected that the motivational force of the management controls would be strongest in routine technologies. This prediction, however, is only modestly supported. The SOPs had more influence on departmental activities while the emphasis on meeting target levels in the statistical reports increased modestly. The budget, although having less influence than average on day-to-day departmental operations, did increase upper management visibility of departmental activities; and satisfaction of department managers with the controls was high.

The controls, however, were not being used in a coercive manner to increase the pressure on the department for more output. Although they featured detailed and frequent reporting, considerable behavioral control, predominantly upper management influence in target setting, and a close correlation to decisions on measurement of performance and rewards, the potential danger of creating a coercive system was defused because the target levels that were set were reasonably easy to meet.

In sum, the need to guarantee reliable, orderly, and efficient output in routine technologies is well served by detailed controls, SOP guidance, frequent reporting, and upper management influence in target setting. Repetitive, well-understood tasks lead to reasonable expectations of performance that are widely accepted because the targets represent only moderate difficulty. Since much of the work can be programmed in advance, the planning and co-ordination aspects of the controls take on less importance; and since controls tend to work best in routine situations, satisfaction with them is higher than it is in more complex technologies. A close and supportive style of management control is well suited to programmable technologies.

Prospects-oriented management control for research technologies

Research technologies feature a great deal of uncertainty which stems from two sources. First, stores of knowledge do not exist to guide task performance, and second, the tasks undertaken by the department tend to vary a great deal. Most discretionary cost centers would fall into this category. Purpose, mission, and objectives are difficult to articulate in any concrete way. Neither the length of time required to complete a research project nor its eventual form can be confidently predicted. Not surprisingly, then, the pattern of management control which emerged for research technologies is strikingly different than that for programmable ones.

Controls are less detailed and reporting is less frequent than across the sample. Both upper management and department managers have less influence in target-setting than do the employees. Yet target levels are more difficult to achieve. The controls are used more for planning and co-ordination than they are for the measuring of performance and allocation of rewards. Less emphasis is placed on meeting target levels than in routine technologies, but the influence of the budget increases slightly. SOP controls, ill-suited to the prevailing uncertainty and ambiguity of research technologies, are much less dominant. Department managers are less satisfied with statistical reports and SOPs.

With research technologies, then, general rather than specific reporting is appropriate, because task knowledge is poorly understood. Greater detail would be of little help to upper management for monitoring performance and progress. Frequent reporting would be inappropriate for the lengthy task conversion cycle, and since the benefits of efforts expended, and the time it takes for results to be apparent, cannot be anticipated, the controls would be less valuable both for the measuring of performance and for rewarding effort. Estimating future prospects and integrating efforts with other departments, however, are important functions of control in this context. Consequently, controls would be used more for planning and co-ordination.

Since employees in the department are more knowledgeable than upper management or even department managers about the requirements of specific projects, they have more influence in the target-setting process than is otherwise normal. Surprisingly, however, their target levels are often very ambitious. It may be that they tend to be overly optimistic and underestimate the difficulties of achieving the goals they set themselves. Or perhaps they are less cautious than they otherwise might be since the controls are not important indicators of measurement of performance. However, since research tasks are frequently prone to time and spending estimate overruns, controls can bring these estimation errors to light. Controls, although they have a part to play, are less useful here than they are in other technologies. Consequently, satisfaction with them is low.

Paradoxically, in research establishments the budget has more influence on departmental activities than it does in other technologies. This may be attributed to its propensity to reduce role ambiguity and to its ability to provide some direction to what would otherwise be a highly unstructured situation.

In sum, controls for research technologies feature little detail and infrequent reporting. Employees have a good deal of influence in target setting, yet target levels are difficult. The controls are used mostly for planning and co-ordination, little emphasis is placed on meeting target levels and SOP controls are not much in evidence. Department managers are not much concerned with controls. This prospect-oriented style of management control, although less important generally than those used for routine technologies, seems best suited to the prevailing uncertainty of research technologies.

Comprehensive management control for technical–professional technologies

Technical–professional technologies feature high task variety and a well-developed store of task knowledge. Tasks tend to be more difficult, complex, and time-consuming than for routine technologies. A management accountant, for example, might be called upon to design a cost accounting system for a new refinery. A great deal of technical knowledge is available to him through advanced accounting books and well-documented case examples. Generally accepted ways of accumulating and allocating costs have already been developed. Most accountants tend to design similar systems. Even so, such projects take months to complete; and a good deal of professional training and experience is required. It is not surprising, then, that management controls for technical–professional technologies are intricate. The general pattern is as follows.

Control reports are highly detailed, for two reasons: first, the well-understood tasks can be broken down into parts, providing detailed information; second, the increased variety in the stream of tasks calls for more variety in the control information. Both factors necessitate detailed controls. The statistical reports are issued more frequently than across the sample, while budget reports are issued less frequently. Since the statistical reports help to monitor the complexity caused by the increased variety, they are needed more frequently. The budget, however, is more general in nature. In consequence, frequent budget reporting would be less useful than for repetitive tasks.

Department managers and employees in technical/professional work have more influence than usual in setting budget targets, although management influence, always strong, remains the same. Thus, participation in target-setting is widespread. This is probably because the available task knowledge is distributed among the three levels and the participation of each is helpful, if not vital. Although participation is widespread, target levels incorporated into the controls are more difficult to achieve than is usual. The reason for this may be that it is easy, before the fact, to underestimate the magnitude of the complex tasks ahead.

Regarding the various functions of the controls, the budget is used more for the measuring and monitoring of performance because, as task knowledge increases, it is better suited to this purpose. Under these conditions budget performance is a good surrogate for actual performance. The statistical reports are used little for the measurement of complex work; they are better suited to repetitive tasks. It may also be that, for high variety tasks, attempts to provide comprehensive statistical information result in overloading the information system. Thus, managers would look to more aggregated information, such as contained in a budget, in order to measure and monitor departmental performance. For example taxation filing firms, such as H&R Block, are well suited to process straightforward individual tax returns where clients are mainly salaried employees. Statistical reports on how many returns were processed would be valuable for the monitoring and measuring of performance. By contrast, such statistics would be much less useful for the complicated and intricate corporate income tax returns done by professional accounting firms.

The importance of the functions of planning and co-ordination, both for the budget and the statistical reports, increased in technical–professional technologies. An explanation for this is that the increased variety leads to more complexity; however, since tasks are well understood, planning and co-ordination should greatly ease the managing of such complexity. Consequently, the information contained in control reports would be extremely helpful. The statistical reports, however, were used less for decisions on rewards. This, too, may be related to the high task variety. Connecting rewards to performance is less likely to be useful when task variety is high than when it is repetitive. Also, since little emphasis was placed on meeting targets in the statistical reports, reliance on them, and on the SOPs, declined accordingly.

Developing appropriate management controls for technical–professional task departments seems to be more problematic than for other technologies. The wide variety in the stream of complex tasks makes for difficult administration. Yet, despite this variety, tasks are well understood. Attempts, therefore, would be made to develop comprehensive and elaborate controls. In these circumstances the satisfaction of the departmental managers with the controls would decline.

Results-oriented management controls for craft technologies

Craft technologies, such as money market managers, investment funds, fashion boutiques, advertising agencies, professional athletic teams, and political parties seeking election, might be considered the most difficult to 'match' with an appropriate MCS because efficiency is difficult to measure: the optimum relationship between inputs and outputs is not known. Neither detailed breakdowns of work patterns nor close monitoring will ensure efficiency or effectiveness. Nevertheless, since the desired results can be determined in advance the appropriate management controls are simple, involving instrumental tests which focus on results. For the investment fund the appropriate test is the annual percentage increase in the fund's value. This can be compared readily with other funds. For the boutique mark-ups, profits, and cash balances are suitable controls. For the advertising agency gross billings to clients is the appropriate test. For professional sports the team's won and lost record, and gate receipts, are sufficient. For the political party, it is the number of seats won in the election. These are instrumental tests in the sense that either the predetermined goals are reached or they are not. They focus on simple measures of results.

The survey data support the idea of results-oriented management control for craft technologies. Control reports are general, rather than detailed. The frequency of budget reporting increases, while it decreases for the statistical reports. Target levels are fairly easy to achieve and department managers have great influence in setting them. The budget is not very useful for the measuring and monitoring of performance, nor is it of much help in making departmental activities visible to upper management. On the other hand, statistical reports are valuable for the reward function, are useful in clarifying target levels, and are important in helping people to do things correctly.

In sum, the management controls in craft technologies are general, involve infrequent reporting and, although they are not heavy-handed, they have more motivational impact. Uncomplicated, instrumental tests are featured. Results-oriented controls are well suited to craft technologies.

IMPLICATIONS FOR MANAGEMENT CONTROL SYSTEM DESIGN

This study has important lessons for accounting and information systems managers involved in designing and administering management control systems for their organizations. For example, it is easy to get a mismatch between the technology of the responsibility center and the control system. In the example given earlier, the new controller of a nationwide advertising firm spent two years developing and implementing a computer-based expense budget system that tracked both target and actual expenses for each client for about twenty-five expense categories. The new system excited the managers and they genuinely tried to use it to advantage. The author, along with several cheering executives, managers, and employees, witnessed the arrival of the new computer as it was craned up the side of the office building and carefully brought in through an enlarged window. Every month, account executives received reports in great detail about billings and expenses. A year after the system was installed the controller learned that the account executives no longer bothered even to look at the reports.

Analysis of the problem indicated that a comprehensive information system had been designed for a craft technology. Many aspects of advertising campaigns—consumer tastes, winning clients, creating new advertising themes—are not well understood. Account personnel have experience with these intangible factors. They know on the basis of training and intuition how to win clients and create campaigns. They will tend to ignore budget targets, especially expense targets. Different personnel have different expenditure styles. The firm later dropped the comprehensive budget in favor of a general information system that reported actual costs and gross billings for each account. Gross billings were critical to agency success, and personnel were allowed to spend money in their own way to increase billings. The results-oriented control system, although less precise than the one it replaced, was successful.

A second example involves the R&D department of a multinational aluminum company. The department was the subject of a budget system that provided an intensive line-by-line analysis of actual spending compared to budgeted amounts for energy research project. Over a period of years, as the detail and intensity of the control system increased, the satisfaction and productivity within R&D actually decreased. Every month, the R&D vice president spent several days explaining and bickering with the budget officer over differences between actual and budget. Finally, the R&D vice-president resigned.

A technology-based analysis indicates that a close MCS was used, whereas a prospects-oriented one was called for. Research is not a well-understood process. Precise, detailed reports, along with close scrutiny and analysis of each line item, are quite inappropriate for the ambiguity of the R&D activities. Minor deviations from the budget are the rule rather than the exception. A prospects-oriented MCS, which focuses on plans and future accomplishment and features infrequent and general reporting, would be more suitable. This would shift the concern of the R&D department to future problems and to keeping the research output consistent with the overall company strategic plan, and away from minor past deviations from budget.

SUMMARY

This chapter began by arguing that elements in the contextual environment of an organization influence the design of its management control systems. Technology was selected as a key contextual variable and was used to derive a model of management control. Two dimensions of technology, task variety and task knowledge available, were employed to derive four distinct technologies—routine, technical–professional, research, and craft. Appropriate characteristics of management control then were outlined for each of the four technologies. Collectively, these characteristics merged into four general styles of MCS—close, comprehensive, prospects-oriented, and results-oriented. It was proposed that each style was suited to one of the four technologies.

The underlying idea of the model can be summarized as follows: organizations seek organizational structures that are congruent with their environments and technologies—it follows that they would also seek a congruence between these factors and their MCS. The model can be used by accounting and information systems designers to help avoid designing inappropriate systems for management control.

This chapter summarized the results of a survey for each of the four technologies. The survey supports the idea that different styles of management control are uniquely suited to each technology. It must be remembered that the support for some of these relationships was only modest, while for others it was more pronounced. Technology, therefore, can be compared to the skeleton, the general shape of which is similar, but individual members of each species will differ in height, weight, and color. In a like manner, technology determines the general shape of the appropriate controls, although each individual MCS may differ somewhat in terms of specific characteristics. Nevertheless, it seems that departmental technology is a powerful and simple way to analyze the MCS needs of any responsibility center.

References

Anthony, R. N., *Planning and Control Systems: A Framework for Analysis*, Graduate School of Business Administration, Harvard University, Boston, Mass., 1965.

Macintosh, N. B., and R. L. Daft, 'A departmental technology model of management control systems'. Paper presented at the Annual American Accounting Association Meeting, San Diego, California, August 1982.

Perrow, C., 'A framework for the comparative analysis of organizations', *American Sociological Review*, April 1967, pp. 194–208.

Sloan, A. D. Jr, *My Years with General Motors*, Doubleday and Company, Inc., New York, 1963.

Note

The research reprinted in this chapter was sponsored by the National Association of Accountants (U.S.A.) and the Society of Management Accountants (Canada).

CHAPTER 13

The Shape of the Future

Accounting and information managers would be wise to prepare for the future rather than be taken by surprise as events unfold. It is appropriate, therefore, to include in this book some speculations about the shape of that future. These are, it must be stressed, only guesses and I do not expect that every expert will agree with them. I hope, however, they will provoke others to pause and formulate some visions of their own. Who knows, perhaps together we might come close to anticipating a few important trends. There is, nevertheless, one aspect of the future that nearly all will agree on—accounting and information systems will play a dominant role in organizations of the future. The reasons for this will become apparent as this chapter unfolds.

This chapter reviews the new information technology, including its astonishing developments. It then outlines a few of the dominant future organizational prototypes made possible by the new information technology and argues that an information system strategy is critical to organizational survival. It also speculates on the impact of the new information technology on work in organizations and employment in general. And it concludes that our emerging understanding of the social software of accounting and information systems is the crucial link in harnessing the new information technology.

THE NEW INFORMATION TECHNOLOGY

The new information technology is so powerful that many scholars argue that it has propelled us out of the industrial age and into the information era. Already the majority of the workforce is involved primarily in gathering, processing and distributing information. Just as industry and manufacturing supplanted agriculture fifty years ago, information processing work has overtaken industry and manufacturing as the mainstay of the economy.

Electronics and communications are the twin engines of this transformation. They will be the focal point of the information era just as steel, with its ability to assume almost any shape and perform a vast variety of roles, was the heart of the industrial revolution (Gregory and Etori, 1981). They will replace steel as the symbol and the essence of economic prowess. They will shift the center of economic might from the Atlantic coasts of Western

Europe and the Eastern USA to the Pacific rim of California and Japan. They will transfigure not only organizations, but society.

The computer

The central character in this metamorphsis is the computer, yet most managers still have only a blurred and imprecise notion of how a computer works or of what it is capable of accomplishing. This is not only unfortunate, for it makes our job more difficult, but it is also unnecessary. A computer is based on one simple stroke of genius—it uses pulses of electricity to pass along binary information through a series of electrical gates arranged according to the rules of true–false Boolean logic. This enables it to solve highly complex problems at incredible speeds. The computer is made up of three components—the central processing unit, peripheral input–output devices, and teleprocessing equipment. Each of these will be reviewed briefly.

The central processing unit

The heart of the computer is the central processing unit, or CPU, as it is commonly called. The CPU contains a primary storage area, an arithmetic–logic element, and a control unit. The primary storage area is made up of locations called 'bits' which contain either a positive or negative electrical impulse corresponding to the zero or one binary digit. Several bits are arranged into 'bytes' each of which have a unique address making them identifiable and accessible for storage. The number of bytes determines the size of programs and the amount of data available for processing at any one time.

The arithmetic–logic unit performs subtraction, addition, multiplication, division, and other logical operations according to the instructions it receives and sends the results to prime storage. The control unit contains the instructions which operate the computer. It tells the CPU to find the data in different storage locations, channel them through the circuitry of the logical unit that will add them together and send the results to another storage location.

All of this, of course, is common knowledge. What is not so widely known, however, is the extent to which miraculous developments have taken place recently in CPUs, peripherals, and teleprocessing.

The miracle of the chip

The major miracle of the new information technology is the chip, a tiny piece of silicon invented at the Bell Laboratories. Silicon, made from purified rock or sand, has properties somewhere between an insulator and a conductor of electricity and so acts as a semiconductor. It is given a known electrical charge, melted down, sliced into thin wafers, polished, etched under intense heat with the desired series of gates or circuitry and, finally, cut into individual solid-circuit chips called transistors. Integrated circuits are formed by etching a large number of transistors and the connections amongst them on a single piece of silicon. Remarkably, an entire computer can be contained in a chip the size of a fingernail.

This is a long way from the first computer which used electromechanical relays or switches to open and close the circuitry gates physically. It weighed fifty tons, cost over a million 1951 dollars, and measured processing times in seconds. In comparison, the modern microcomputer has the entire CPU etched on a chip the size of a postage stamp which costs less than ten dollars to manufacture and measures processing time in nano-seconds or one thousandth of a millionth of a second. Superchips containing 264,000 bytes of addressable main storage are already on the market and million byte chips are on the drawing board. The miracle of the chip has led to remarkable happenings in all aspects of computer operations, including storage, peripherals, teleprocessing, integrated data base management, and software. We will review these developments quickly and then speculate about their combined impact on organizations.

Data storage

Limited storage in the past was a major impediment to making full use of the computer's capability. This bottleneck has now been all but removed by several new techniques. Primary storage is linked to auxiliary storage devices so that blocks of data and instructions can be shunted around according to the job requirements of any given moment. These auxiliary devices include magnetic tape, disks, drums, and cassettes, all of which have vast storage capacities. Magnetic strips, for example, although cumbersome to access, can store nearly 500 billion bytes; and 'buffer' storage and 'cache' memory techniques are used to collect frequently used data and instructions and make them instantly available to the arithmetic–logic unit. As a result of these advances, the problem of computer storage has been overcome. Storage, even today, is virtually unlimited.

Peripherals

Peripherals are devices used to input data into the CPU, instruct it as to which tasks to perform and receive the output when the computation is complete. Punched cards for input and high speed printers which, until recently, were the major peripheral devices now are as outdated as the steam locomotive. They soon will be supplemented by a host of new techniques, led by the cathode ray tube (CRT) terminal.

A couple of illustrations of the new peripheral technology may be helpful. One is the electronic printing and copying station called an intelligent printer. It combines lasers, chips, xerography, software, memory and imaging resolution to produce virtually any image directly from a digital source such as a

CPU. The desired output format, including graphs and charts, is designed on the spot with the aid of a 'user-friendly' programmable touch control panel. Output can be offset, printed in color and collated. The intelligent printer is capable of communicating with satellite computers, word processors and terminals.

A more exotic example is the optical point of sale scanner. This peripheral uses laser technology to read point of sale information at the cash register. Products, carrying universal product codes, are passed over the scanner by the sales clerk and automatically all the data required for accounting and inventory management purposes is collected and fed into computer storage. At the same time the scanner is used to collect information about family purchases for market research purposes, as well as to assess the success of various promotional efforts such as coupons, samples, advertising and displays.

Already screens, keyboards, central panels, spinning tape readers, intelligent printers and point of sale scanners have relegated punched cards and printers to the computer archives. These new peripherals, which can be seen and touched, will replace the CPU as key symbols of the information age.

Teleprocessing

Teleprocessing, the fastest growing segment of the new information technology, entails moving data over both short and great distances between peripherals and CPUs. As with storage and peripherals, remarkable accomplishments have taken place in this segment of the technology. For example, several devices have now replaced the CRT terminal, with its maximum speed well below that of the telecommunication line, the traditional workhorse for moving data. Multiplexers, concentrators, simplex channels, duplex channels and broad based transmission lines capable of computer to computer teleprocessing are but a few such new devices.

There are also many other ingenious devices available for teleprocessing. Modems, hooked up at each end of a transmission line, convert digital data into analogue form suitable for transmission by line. Datapacks are available to split data into batches and then delay transmission during peak load periods or divert it to less busy circuitous routes. Front end processors for interfacing computers with remote data entry points are capable of handling masses of data arriving simultaneously from a host of sources. They organize, control, and buffer the stream of incoming data as well as perform some routine stand alone processing chores thus taking some of the load off the CPU.

These developments in line transmission are remarkable, yet they pall in the face of achievements in satellite teleprocessing. Consider the example of a Canadian daily newspaper, the *Globe and Mail*, which is distributed throughout the nation by satellite. Each page of the newspaper is scanned by a microwave radio signal of 400 watts at a frequency of 6 billion vibrations per minute. It is then beamed across North America and the Pacific Ocean to a solar-powered satellite hovering about 36,000 kilometers above the equator. The satellite picks up the microwave message and relays it back to earth at the rate of one page per second. The beam has travelled more than 77,000 kilometers in a fraction of a second, travelling 21,000 times as fast as telecommunication lines and with unimaginable accuracy. At each location, the beam is received by another dish, fed into an argon laser and beamed across a photographic film which produces a newspaper page size negative. Printing plates are made from the negative and the newspaper 'goes to print' simultaneously across the country. This teleprocessing miracle has enabled the newspaper to achieve its century and a half old aim of producing a national edition. With little or no additional trouble it could produce a world edition. Notably, the technology has also permitted a reduction in the price a customer pays for the newspaper.

The possibilities for satellite teleprocessing are staggering. The commercial market will likely exceed $100 billion dollars by 1990. Firms in this new industry, such as Satellite Business Systems—a joint venture of IBM, Comsat, and General and Aetna Life and Casualty—are equipping themselves with satellites, high speed modems, digital earth stations and communications copiers in order to provide digital, voice and video data transmission services to private and public sector organizations of all sizes.

In fact, the teleprocessing sector of the new information technology is so important that in the early 1970s the French government launched a far-reaching program, known as Telematique, with the aim of developing a national integrated telecommunications system utilizing sophisticated digital technology including a new telephone network (Stratte-McClure, 1980). The system is to be the fundamental component of a comprehensive information-based society. Its aim is to incorporate telephones, television, computer terminals, and other media into a harmonious high-speed, advanced transmission and switching network. This integrated services network will meet all communication needs on a single line. The telephone will become a multi-functional tool for data voice and video communication. The network plan includes an overwhelming array of compatible peripheral equipment such as: intelligent terminals, fiber optic cables, electronic time division multiplexing, data packets, springless alphanumeric keyboards, telewriters, high density integrated circuitry, computer driven switching centers, coaxial cables, communication satellites and microwave links. This network will provide the citizenry with access to a vast number of data bases, information banks, as well as video and TV programs.

The French Telematique program is an heroically ambitious initiative, requiring a dedicated central government, experience and faith in long-range national planning and a cadre of highly trained technical elites to get the venture under way and to keep up its momentum. It is clearly a technical–social experiment on a scale never before attempted in the history of civilization. It is not surprising, therefore, that implementation is lagging seriously behind the planned timetable. But even if it fails to gain customer support for many years, or is set aside until one after another of the inevitable but unpredictable technical hurdles are surmounted, or even if it grinds temporarily to a halt, it does not matter. The impressive point of the experiment is that it has been undertaken. It is unlikely that the French will succeed in having their nation hooked up in one compatible network until at least the next century, but when they do it will be expanded to include the other European Economic Community countries. After that, we will be looking at global networks.

Teleprocessing, then, will lead to larger and larger networks. Slowly but surely, for better or for worse, organizations, countries, trading blocs, and eventually the entire world will be hooked up in a nest of networks. The teleprocessing technology will be in place within the decade. As always, however, it is expected that the social resistance to change will prove to be the major hurdle to overcome.

Integrated data processing networks

Teleprocessing developments have made possible integrated distributive processing configurations within organizations. The basic idea is that two or more processing centers within a single organization are linked although each has its own program execution and data storage facilities (Hussain and Hussain, 1981). The various organizational centers, of course, can be linked in a wide variety of configurations by selecting the appropriate mix of architecture, controls, peripherals, teleprocessing, software and, of course, CPU capacity. The final network permits any user, no matter how small or how occasional, to be added at minimal cost. The ultimate goal is to create a fully integrated interactive network which can meet fully any user's requirements on the spot.

The impact of fully integrated–interactive networks on organizations is not easy to predict. Yet it seems obvious that if information at any location is available at any other location there are bound to be profound and far reaching implications. Work roles, interaction patterns, lateral relations, interdependencies, power and authority hierarchies and decision making patterns will be permanently altered. The precise nature of these changes will reveal themselves over time. In the future, however, accounting and information managers will find that these considerations will be seen to override technical ones.

Integrated data base management

The chip, peripheral developments and advances in teleprocessing have combined to make possible the creation of very large data bases that can be accessed by a vast network of common users. This has not always been the case. Until very recently organizations developed computer applications one at a time. Each application, although sharing the CPU with other applications, had its own data files and programs. But as the numbers spread, difficulties were encountered in supplying information that cut across departmental boundaries and redundancies occurred across the various data bases (Nolan, 1973). In response to these problems the notion of an integrated corporate data base with pooled data available for common use as a shared resource emerged. Integrated data base management is the system required to collect, keep track of, and organize data into a common data base that can be accessed efficiently and effectively by a large number of users (Hussain and Hussain, 1981).

The 'data element' is the basic building block of data base management and is used to identify any piece of data, such as an employee, a pay rate, or a sales invoice. Data elements can be in the form of raw data or they may be derived from other data elements. They have a unique, unambiguous, and easy to recall name. They serve a variety of purposes, including the creation of a logical file, linking with other files, authorization for access, and checking transactions for completeness. Data elements are listed on input–output tables, which identify all shared data elements in reports and aid the logical addition or deletion of material. They are shared throughout the organization and are contained in data element dictionaries. Data elements are joined into logical and physical records enabling the computer to integrate and organize information into a data hierarchy by character, data element, record, file and data base data by addresses and fields. Data are located by an address which identifies the location of the data on the physical file. The physical organization depends upon many factors, including frequency of use and retrieval time requirements.

Data collection media and coding schemes are another key part of integrated data base design. Universal coding schemes such as media (from cards and tapes to badge readers and point of sale scanners) and coding schemes are critical to an effective and efficient data base.

Procedures for the utilization and control of the common data base must be designed carefully if it is to be used effectively and efficiently. A key element of this is the 'data directory' which is a list of all information about data elements and data dictionaries. Its purpose is to facilitate quick reference to pertinent information. Off-the-shelf programs for directories are now available from software and equipment suppliers, although some companies prefer to develop their own. Short, unique, and easy to process identifiers or names, called 'labels', are often substituted for the data element. Dictionaries and directories also provide organizational information about data elements. Indexes, designators, keywords and classwords are all included in the directory which must document all information related to processing in order to provide the standards governing the creation and use of data.

The data directory system has several auxiliary purposes. It generates a matrix of data elements and users to help streamline the data base by identifying the relative importance of data elements, including those not used. It identifies which departments create and maintain each data element. It also generates a transaction matrix which identifies those transactions that would be affected by deleting or redefining a data element. And it helps the computer check security codes for access to specific data elements and files, control access, bill users, identify storage locations by name and test new programs for compatibility with general code files. Obviously, the data directory system is a critical part of any data base management system and requires considerable organization and control.

An essential tool for this purpose is a data base management system (DBMS). This includes software for greater integration of data, on-line access, manipulation of complex file structures, as well as supplementary software for data base reorganization, data privacy, breakdown recovery, and independent applications. The DBMS provides a single door for access to the data base and services programs while they are in execution. It also intercepts requests to access and manipulate data and provides semantic and proper authorization security. Importantly, it also keeps track of all events and changes affecting the data base (Everest, 1976).

These developments have given rise to new administrative needs. In response to this, many organizations have created a new position, called data base administrator (DBA). The DBA is responsible for managing all aspects of the data base, including the basic architecture, accuracy, and quality of data, performance audits, continuity precautions, access and security, as well as the maintenance and upkeep of active data, storage of old data and elimination of useless data. Software programs, called data base managers, are being developed to aid the DBA and his or her staff in the technical parts of the job and data base Committees, composed of technical people and users, are set up to guide the DBA. Obviously, however, access to and responsibility for the entire data of an information makes the DBA an essential and sensitive post.

Although integrated data base management is a critical link in the chain of new information technology, it is still in an early stage of development and is often ignored and certainly overshadowed by the more glamorous developments such as super-chips, virtual storage, satellite transmission, intelligent printers, and societal networks. Universal standards have still to emerge and agreement on data base models has not as yet taken place. Data base machines have only reached the drawing board stage, while much research is needed urgently for graphic interfaces, query languages and data base definitions. It seems fair to conclude that while we have identified the major issues and problems of integrated data bases the ensuing technology is only beginning to emerge. Thus, the development of data base management will be the major task for the next decade in the evolution of harnessing the new information technology.

Software

The computer, of course, can do nothing until a set of programs outlining instructions and rules tells it what to do. These programs, called software, represent the intangible but essential intellectual process of the computer. Software contrasts with the hard and tangible computer hardware (transistors, circuitry, metal and plastic terminals and printers) which can be touched and seen. Software is the language of computers.

Like natural languages, software comes in a wide variety. It ranges from low level binary language to very high level natural voice recognition. Software is required for every operation the computer performs. Machine languages incorporated into compilers instruct the CPU. Interpreters and compilers convert application program language into machine language. Operating systems software tells the machine how to coordinate the CPU, schedule jobs, organize queues, allocate storage and keep track of job status. Processing programs are needed for fundamental chores such as sorting, merging, transferring data between storage media, filing, program debugging, and testing.

Most of the operating system software is provided by the computer hardware suppliers. Software known as 'canned' programs, to signify convenience as in canned foods, are available from a variety of firms for almost any purpose. Software packages have the advantage of spreading developmental costs over many users and eliminating debugging time. They come in a wide variety, ranging from payroll to sophisticated statistical packages for high powered social science research; and organizations, of course, develop their own software for their special needs.

Recently, a variety of interactive software has been developed, including menu selection, blanks, parametric requests, and query languages. Menu selection software, for example, offers the user a series of lists of choices until the wanted information is extracted. Interactive software is now used commonly in libraries for tracking down authors and subjects. Menus have the advantage that the user needs knowledge neither of the data base nor of computers to use the system. A similar technique involves software which presents a checklist of questions to the user who supplies the necessary input. Parametric request programs interrogate the user until the specific information required is identified and delivered. In the past few years several query languages have been developed that are close to the English language. Some can be learned in less than two hours and permit individuals to have a spoken exchange with the computer to extract information. Interactive programs also include simulation programs where the user is asked to supply the necessary input data and assumptions.

Software is unquestionably a key aspect of harnessing the computer's possibilities. In fact, it represents a large new industry, accounting for a surprising 70–80 percent of the total cost of large systems computer installations and more than half of the cost of micro systems. During the 1970s the

US Department of Defense alone spent over $30 billion on software; and it is anticipated that during the next decade a continuing shortage of skilled programmers will cause the software segment to lag behind other advances of the new information technology, thus delaying its onslaught.

Outlook for new developments

It is remarkable to recall that most of the developments touched on above have occurred only within the last decade or two. It is all the more remarkable to realize that even more incredible developments are in the offing that will push the technology beyond anything even imaginable ten years ago. Each segment is brimming with exciting new ideas and breakthroughs.

CPU memory, for example, will feature immense storage and incredible internal speeds. Bubble memory chips, tiny cylindrical domains of reverse magnetism in certain magnetic materials formed by applying a biasing magnetic field normal to its surface, will permit almost infinite memory capacity. Circuitry integration will evolve from large to massive scale with information manipulation interconnections and concentration of circuitry which includes up to 250,000 gates for integration of control logic. Parallel developments are also taking place in the field of structured molecules. DNA engineering and molecular rectifiers built from molecules with anode- and cathode-type binding energies, point towards the crystal lattice computer of the future modeled on systems from the life sciences, rather than from the material sciences (Hammer, 1977).

Peripheral equipment will feature video and optical capabilities, including optical readers with special fonts, digital (flat) screens with high resolution, and even voice-to-print or CRT transmission. Teleprocessing will take the form of digital electronics, with optical communication incorporating lasers or light-emitting diodes, glass fibers and cryptographic controls. Data base management systems will witness the introduction of information nodes, specialized information storage computers, and interconnected functional modules rolled into data base machines featuring relational and flexible, rather than hierarchical and rigid, structures. Software will feature very high level languages, including voice recognition, built-in modular pockets based on firm initial specifications, and combined hardware/software input devices. It is now anticipated that the photon will replace the electron as the work-horse of electronics, giving rise to integrated optical circuits incorporating lasers, amplifiers and detectors on a single chip. And it even looks as if 'intelligent' computers (called 5th generation computers) will soon emerge on the scene.

Even without these remarkable advances the new technology has begun to reshape our organizations by creating new ways of getting work done. Two such developments include the 'electronic office' and 'integrated distributed processing'.

The electronic office

One outcome of the onslaught of the new information technology is the concept of the 'electronic office', also known as the office of the future, the wired office, the automated office, and the integrated electronic office. Information related work, which now engages the majority of the workforce, involves gathering, storing, manipulating and communicating information and, of course, most of it takes place in the office. It is no surprise, therefore, that the new information technology is slowly but surely profoundly altering the nature and organization of office work (Giuliano, 1982). In its basic form the electronic office means replacing the typewriter, teletype, and copying machine with computers, related peripherals, and teleprocessing equipment. Each of these devices could, of course, be introduced singly, rather than as part of a wholesale switch to an electronic office. Either way, they are restructuring office work in organizations.

The electronic office includes a variety of devices, including electronic mail, teleconferencing, electronic funds transfer, and 'war rooms'. Electronic mail consists of sending messages from one CRT terminal to another. While electronic mail usually consists of a two-party exchange of information, tele-conferencing involves simultaneous communication amongst a number of persons in different locations who talk to each other with their CRTs and so save on travel time and expense. However, the meeting also has access to stored information and presentations previously made on overhead projectors or flip charts are made on the CRT screen. The computer can also make records of proceedings and take minutes. Electronic funds transfer involves using CRT terminals, instead of cheques or charge cards, to make payments at the point of sale. War rooms involve multimedia communications centers where top management congregate and use one line retrieval systems, simulation models, closed-circuit television, and videotapes to make decisions, monitor progress and formulate policy.

The heart of the automated office remains the word-processor which functions as a sophisticated typewriter with a CRT screen instead of paper. Centering, left and right justification, spacing, and corrections are done on the screen and, when completed, the text is printed on a high speed printer. The word-processor, however, can be much more than a super typewriter. It can store dictionaries, mailing lists, standard paragraphs for responding to common queries, statistics, quotations and even information from trade journals. Input, in addition to the typewriter terminal, can be achieved with optical character recognition, facsimile, and even voice recognition equipment. Output, selected with a font, can be chosen from a wide variety of size and type. Applications, then, range from a single letter to the storing of several hundred standard paragraphs to produce thousands of 'individualized' letters about a variety of topics, including specific products or product groups. Word-processors, linked up to computerized electronic printing and copying systems, add many of the facilities of a commercial print shop to the typewriter keyboard.

Electronic offices can be purchased on a turnkey basis. Data Corporation, for example, has an off-the-shelf configuration which can include over 200 computers linked by coaxial cables, interfacing devices, and lines to work stations, local and global magnetic disc storage units, printers, word-processors and color graphics. The potential market possibilities are so tantalizing that in 1980 Volkswagenwerke, the giant German automaker, acquired a variety of companies in Europe and the US, including computer firms, office equipment, word-processing, typewriter, copiers, and computer-terminal manufacturers, as well as a dealer and marketing network, and put them all together to form a large, fully integrated office automation and electronic office of the future firm as a hedge on its investment in the troubled world-wide automobile and truck industry. The array of new products for the office is impressive; and there is little doubt that the information technology has a massive market potential in this area.

The personal computer

Another remarkable aspect of the new technology is the advent of the personal or desk top computer which has all the features of a large computer yet can weigh less than 20 pounds and will fit under an airline seat. It can store and process large quantities of data and programs using auxiliary storage and memory configurations, including read-only memory (ROM) and random access memory (RAM), floppy and hard discs, disk drives, and adapter cards. It can also include a small high-speed printer, a modem for telephone linking with other computers and data bases across the country and a joystick for video games. As well, a wide range of excellent software packages are available for the personal computer including: accounting and banking, financial forecasting models, sophisticated multidimensional spread sheets, financial ratio analysis, statistical analysis, and graphics. It can also be used for teaching children skills in reading, writing, and mathematics, not to mention video games. In fact, computing power is now available to almost anyone who wants it.

The personal computer is particularly appealing to a new group of young professionals and managers. Frustration with the data processing arrangements in their organizations, along with the desire to have an independent source of computing power, have created a large new market. The personal computer thus represents a powerful weapon for the new generation of young ambitious managers. This group will make up a new elite corps who have sophisticated analytical capability at their fingertips, putting their computer illiterate rivals at a serious disadvantage. Already many such managers are bringing personal computers into work in the morning and taking them home at night. The portable computer has replaced the bulging briefcase as the status symbol of the important executive.

Computerization of products and production

The influence of the computer on organizations is not limited to information and communications. It also extends to products and production processes. While early applications of computers into products were mainly for military usage in missile and weaponry control, and in the exploration of space, the race to computerize commercial products is under way in earnest.

Let me put the point into the context of some concrete examples. Pocket cameras automatically read the intensity of light and adjust shutter speed and focus as the picture is taken. Hearing aids with a microphone and amplifier fit into the stem of a pair of glasses and automatically adjust the loudness of the signal. Digital watches not only keep time but also act as a stopwatch, calendar, alarm, and radio. Pocket-sized pagers, with chip memories and light-emitting diode displays and printers, provide two-way verbal and written communication. Digital audio disk players for highly superior sound reproduction print sound on a mirror-like disk in microscopic pits which are read by a laser beam and reconverted into music by a large scale integrated or LSI chip. Microwave ovens use miniature television screens to give instructions, recipes, and lists of ingredients, respond to vocal instructions, and verbally announce when cooking is complete. Of course, microprocessors in large numbers have been an integral part of airplanes for some time and, more recently, of automobiles and trucks. These are only a few examples and any reasonable extrapolation of this trend makes it obvious that in the near future the microprocessor and its related technology will be as ubiquitous in our products as are wheels and gears today.

The use of the new information technology in the production process is even more widespread. Automobile assembly, precision metal cutting, engineering designs, medical diagnosis and medication prescriptions, commodities exchanges, and tax return preparation are but a few examples of the computer's key role in the production process. The F-15 fighter airplane is a specific example of a computer dominated production process. Nearly all parts are made by computer controlled machine tools, assembly is computer planned, and soon will be a fully automated process, featuring robot manned work stations.

There are countless examples. Freight train yards are operated by computers and automated equipment. Totally mechanized warehouses are controlled by information networks incorporating a 'boss-computer', a series of terminals, an on-line data base, peripheral control units, robots, and an automated reporting system, including audit trials and transaction logs. Mechanized car and truck painting stations utilize numerically controlled painting machines, supervisory computers and body recognition systems. Investment dealers and stockbrokers are hooked up in real-time information networks which include all the data necessary for trading on stocks, bonds, and currencies. Commodity exchanges use similar networks to link producers and purchasers. In many industries, such as banking and airlines, where the production process is mainly information processing, the computer is indispensable.

This trend will continue for some time, as computerized robots begin to replace workers for tough, dirty, boring and repetitive jobs. Robotics features combinations of electromechanical servomechanisms, microprocessors, photo and digital data transmission, and optical probing and control. Robots have been used for some time now for spot welding, materials handling, assembly work, and painting; and they are now being developed to 'see' with a tiny television camera, 'feel' with tactile sensors and 'think', using advanced data processing capabilities. Already a few Japanese television assembly plants using robotics have reduced the number of production workers by 80 percent, while at the same time increasing output by 50 percent.

Summary

It is apparent, then, that the invasion of the new information technology into our organizations is well under way. The computer, in one way or another, will touch nearly every aspect of organizational life. Already it is an integral part of our products and services. It plays a large role in nearly all phases of our production process. It has taken over office work. It will be used to build information webs that will link all managers into one distributed network and so completely change our traditional authority and power hierarchies.

If this proposition seems far fetched, one need only imagine the consequences if all the computers in the world were shut off for a few weeks. The resulting clamor would be heard far and wide. Airlines, banks, stock markets, defense systems, refineries, research institutes, television stations, and telephone systems, to mention only a few, would shut down overnight. Shortly thereafter trains, automobile factories, steel plants, chemical works and grocery chains would grind to a halt. Our industrial and commercial enterprises would be in disarray; and most public sector institutions would come to a standstill. Computers are already the central nervous system of our organizations. Without them, accounting and information systems, the lifeblood of organizations, could not deliver their essential data and information. The importance of information systems can only grow in the future.

FUTURE ORGANIZATIONS

One outcome of the new information technology will be the emergence of new species of organizations. The dominant organization during the industrial era was the classical, large industrial enterprise. These firms specialized in one industry and integrated their operations vertically only from a need to protect their sources of supply and their markets. They generally concentrated on one industry (steel, automobilws, oil, meat packing, aluminum, retailing, textiles, farm equipment, furniture, etc.) and most of their activities were domestic. A repertoire of appropriate accounting and information systems techniques was developed which enabled their administrators to make decisions and control operations including: operating budgets, cost allocation schemes, transfer pricing systems, cash flow analysis, market forecasting and production scheduling, inventory ordering models, and capital budgeting systems. These tools served their organizations well.

Today, however, the large single-industry enterprise is no longer dominant. Already it has given way to the diversified global industrial giant which operates in nearly every corner of the earth. Take for example the giant energy corporations. At any given moment they are negotiating with government officials in Indonesia for offshore exploration rights; searching for new fields of hydrocarbon in the Arctic Circle; distributing heating oil in Scotland; providing asphalt to Brazil; carrying crude oil to Japan; refining chemicals in Saudi Arabia; pumping gasoline into automobiles in France; researching energy cells in Switzerland; and negotiating for new capital in New York. These are massive firms with vast arrays of markets, immense resources, complex technologies and armies of highly trained technical and professional people. They employ hundreds of thousands of people, compete in thousands of markets, and operate in a couple of hundred countries around the globe. Royal Dutch Shell, Mitsubishi, Lever Brothers, Volkswagen and IBM are typical.

The outstanding feature of these organizations is their complexity. The complexity, of course, is caused by constantly changing technologies, shifting markets and ever increasing size. But it is impossible for a handful of executives at the top to understand the various technologies or comprehend the types of problems faced by the various parts of the organization. In order to cope, these goliaths must employ armies of highly trained professionals who are experts in one technical area such as chemistry, geophysics, marketing, or accounting. Consequently, the process of managing features multilateral brokerage and the widespread inclusion of specialists in the decision making process. This widespread use of collective leadership is also fueled by the social democracy movement that is making headway in most Western industrialized nations, some of which even have laws requiring worker participation at the board level.

The demands for accounting and information systems in these firms are almost insatiable. Currency conversions, foreign exchange fluctuations, complex consolidations and differing accounting practices around the globe are enough in themselves to explain the crushing demands, not to mention the requirements of unions, sundry government bureaus and agencies and joint venture partners, for information systems resources. In the future, information will loom larger and larger as the key ingredient to organizational effectiveness. Information about sources of supply, markets, products, competition and government actions and inclinations for a hundred nation states will be required, in addition to the vital traditional accounting and information systems.

Another prototype organization of the future is the firm that competes in a few, or even one, product or service and also operates globally. Cola companies, fast food chains, wine merchants, marine insurance brokers, lock manufacturers, and sportswear outfits, are a few well known examples. These firms operate around the world and feature sharply defined competitive strategies, centralized decision making, and close monitoring of the activities of the far flung operating units. For these firms, effective and efficient accounting and information systems are essential. This type of organization is superbly placed to harness the new information system technology to advantage. Only those that do so will prosper. The effective design and utilization of accounting and information systems has also been found to be the most critical factor for international marketing effectiveness in small firms (Kirpalani and Macintosh, 1980).

At the same time, large and complex bureaucracies have arisen in the public sector. Large private organizations and massive public bureaucracies, it seems, go hand in hand. What is fascinating about these organizations, of course, is that most of their activities consist almost entirely of processing information. Regulatory agencies, foreign service offices, revenue collecting departments, social welfare agencies and census bureaus are a few examples of almost pure information processing organizations. Their accounting and information system needs, especially financial controls and assessment systems, differ dramatically from those of their private sector counterparts. These needs unfortunately are being met at present with a repertoire of woefully inadequate information tools. New techniques and tools are urgently needed; yet will be painfully slow in coming.

The giant Japanese general trading companies, known as 'Shogoshosha', are typical of yet another organization of the future. These firms do not make or market their own products; rather they deal in thousands of products acting on behalf of other firms in distributing goods and services domestically in Japan as well as acting as exporters for domestic firms and importers for foreign firms. Their critical skill is the management of a global market intelligence network which identifies markets, products and technologies needed by Japanese and foreign firms. So it is not surprising that they have always adopted the latest in communication technology.

Mitsui, one of the largest Shogoshosha, is a typical example. As far back as 1876 it had already developed its own private code for telegrams inside Japan; and when international telegram services became available in 1881 it began to use its own private English code for offshore communications (Tsurumi, 1980). Today Mitsui operates major intelligence centers (in Tokyo, New York, London, Sydney and Bahrain) which are connected up with 180 subcenters in Japan and in countries overseas. In addition to conventional means such as telephones and telex, the centers utilize a network of highly sophisticated computers linked by privately leased satellite channels. This remarkable network operates 24 hours a day, seven days a week, as tens of thousands of Mitsui 'brokers' spotted around the world use it to seek out, cultivate and make complex deals for clients in every nook and cranny of the globe. Mitsui and the other Shogoshoshas, and this is the striking point, deal purely in information; their business is to manage a complex information network.

Perhaps the most intriguing organizational prototype to emerge in recent years is the large joint venture involving a curious assortment of partners, intangible purposes, illusive goals, multiple and conflicting objectives, imperfectly instrumental technologies and multinational spheres of operations. Consider the bizarre case of the Marine Resources (MR) company, the largest American joint fishing venture.

The American government, after the Soviet invasion of Afghanistan, denied the Soviets fishing rights in American waters. Under an act of Congress, however, the United States grants its fish to foreign countries in exchange for assistance in modernizing its out-of-date fishing industry. So MR, owned jointly by a private American fish company and the Soviet fisheries ministry, was formed to circumvent the ban on fishing rights. MR contracted with 30 American fishing boats to catch and deliver fish to 16 Soviet giant processing ships which are leased by MR. The company sells the processed frozen fish and fish meal to the Far East. The fish, mainly pollack, are not popular in America so domestic stocks of wanted fish are not depleted. The long-term agreement transformed what was formerly a cyclical and volatile business into a steady operation, thus making it viable for American fishermen to modernize their fishing fleets. The result is a thriving international business which helps the American fishing industry, provides fish for the Russians, and acts as a prototype for agreements with other nations.

The information requirements of MR, however, go well beyond the capabilities of traditional accounting and information systems, even though the organization is relatively small. These difficulties are magnified many times in the case of similar but larger organizations, including the federal governments of any advanced industrial nation, the United Nations, the European Economic Community, the North American Treaty Organization and the World Bank. For all of these, political and social ends outweigh economic goals and their informational needs are also more closely connected to political and social ends than to economic ones. Such demands go far beyond the traditional strengths of accounting and computerized management information systems (MIS) in the areas of profit measurement, production control and transportation models. Yet the number of these large scale geopolitical organizations continues to grow.

These new organizational prototypes, then, pose unique problems and offer new opportunities for accounting and information systems. It seems likely that the traditional scope of these systems will have to be expanded drastically to incorporate political and social, in addition to economic information. Yet the present state of knowledge in these areas remains primitive. Obviously, a new set of generally accepted accounting and information systems principles is urgently required to guide these organizations towards their goals. A great deal of research and creative thinking will be required to close the gap.

The demand for new and better accounting and information systems to serve the organizational prototypes of the future will continue to grow for a long time. Although this poses problems it also presents a great opportunity since the way in which organizations develop and utilize accounting and information systems will emerge as the most critical aspect of any organization's competitive strategy, whether it be in the global market place or in the area of public funds and resources.

Traditional means of delivering this information will no longer be adequate. Fortunately the new information technology, which was reviewed earlier in this chapter, is rapidly reaching maturity. Whether its availability is spurring organizations to widen their scope or whether the ever expanding need for information is spurring the development of sophisticated technological information systems is a moot issue, with observers arguing on both sides. What is likely is that a symbiotic relationship exists, by which information technology fuels growth and complexity, which in turn requires new and better information systems. Either way, accounting and information systems will be in greater demand and will prove pivotal to the success of these global giants.

INFORMATION RESOURCE STRATEGY

By and large, the emergence of new types of organization as well as the potential for harnessing of the new information system technology has been ignored by diffident top management groups who neither understand the new technology nor appreciate the vital need for competence in accounting and information systems. It is not surprising, then, that system resource plans tend to be formulated in a haphazard fashion by the technical people and by the hardware vendors. It is because of this that one of the most important challenges that will face accounting and information systems managers in the next few years is to have accounting and information considerations not only included in, but seen as the paramount aspect of, the organization's corporate strategy.

The concept of corporate strategy, of course,.gained widespread acceptance in the mid-1970s. It defines how an organization will compete over time, sets out its overall goals and lays down measures of performance. It prepares conditional plans for allocating scarce resources to changing opportunities, and plans for the administrative structures, systems and arrangements to be used for implementing the competitive strategy and reaching the organization's objectives (Macintosh *et al.*, 1973). Formulation of corporate strategy involves identifying opportunities and risks, analyzing corporate competences and weaknesses, and directing competences toward opportunity. Corporate strategies tend to focus on identification of market segments and appropriate products, plans for production technology and engineering, projections of funding needs and financial structures and anticipation of how the firm will meet scientific and research requirements. A corporate strategic plan, then, is a set of policies and objectives which incorporate the plans and prospects of the key organizational components——marketing, manufacturing, finance, engineering and R&D—into a master plan for guiding the various managers throughout the organization.

Yet the plans for the accounting and information system components are, almost without exception, left out of the corporate strategic plan. This is, if we pause and think about it, senseless. Information is the key competitive factor of success. Organizations compete not only in products and services but in accounting and information systems excellence. The management of information will soon be the critical competitive aspect of most organizations. An information system strategy should be an integral aspect of any corporate strategic plan. Information is obviously the main business of managers.

The idea of an information system resource strategy may be novel for many accounting and information systems managers. One of the pioneers of the concept defines an information systems strategy as,

> a component of the overall strategic thinking in an organization, by which top management determine their longer term needs for investment in computing and communications, the management of the data resource and the development of organizational structure and management style, in line with the mission of the enterprise and in light of available resources recognizing the strategic issues and opportunities facing the enterprise. (Tricker, 1982, p. 112–113.)

This is a rich and far-sighted definition. It suggests that the information system component of corporate strategy goes well beyond simply planning for computing power to many other critical questions. Where should the ownership and control of information be located? Who should have access to which dimensions of information? What sort of organizational arrangements are required for the accounting and information systems people in the organization? What configuration of CPUs, peripherals, and teleprocessing would best serve the organization? And what are the policies and plans for the people side, or social software, of these systems?

To speculate in too much detail about the answers to these questions would not be fruitful at this juncture. They must be thought out in the context of each individual organization, the stage of its development in the accounting and information systems area and the information needs of the rest of the organization. Rather we will sketch out the two generally accepted alternatives—the decentralized and the centralized models—and make an earnest proposal for a third type of arrangement.

The decentralized model is the most common approach taken by organizations to date. Under this model each major organizational component is responsible for the design and development of its own informational requirements. They decide what configuration of computing power, peripherals, and teleprocessing suits them best. The information system resource people report directly to, and work for, the local line managers. The local organizational component has ownership of the information and data bases. They decide who, including top management at headquarters, may or may not have access to the information, and they employ their own style of social software for designing and implementing these systems.

The decentralized model has several advantages. As they know best the local needs, conditions and prospects for environmental changes, the local units are best situated to make these decisions. If they waited for a grand, global strategy, systems developments would not only be delayed, they would run the risk of being inappropriate. When it is done locally, it produces results quickly (Lincoln, 1977).

More and more, however, the major limitations of the decentralized model are being recognized. The individual systems that spring up throughout the organization prove to be incompatible with each other and so make communication between information files impossible. Long-run total system maintenance costs also tend to increase dramatically as new systems are developed and grafted on to the old ones. Perhaps most importantly, the local units may hoard, suppress, and withhold critical strategic information from upper management.

The centralized model, by contrast, features tight control by headquarters of systems development. A central steering group ratifies all decisions regarding acquisition of computer hardware, peripherals and teleprocessing. Personnel involved in accounting and information systems at the local level report directly to a vice-president located at headquarters. All information, including that used only at the local level, is available to top management, who share ownership with the local units. Both have access to the information data bases, some of which are located at headquarters. In this way central policies and guidelines shape the implementation and subsequent management of the accounting and information systems.

A key advantage of the centralized approach is that systems throughout the organization interlock in a compatible way. Communication amongst the various units is possible, when required, and priorities can be established from a corporate, rather than technical perspective (Lincoln, 1977). A centralized approach also means that ownership of data is controlled from the center. A key requirement for this approach to be successful is for accounting and information systems people at the top to have a good grasp of the informational requirements throughout the organization. This will be more the case in the single industry firm than in a widely diversified one.

The success of the centralized approach is typified in the example, cited in Chapter 7, of a consumer finance corporation which operated over a thousand branches across the nation. Each branch, hooked up by terminals to a large CPU in a mid-western city, enters daily all its loan, collection, and expense transactions. All the files are kept centrally and performance reports are available throughout the organization each day, about all branches, regions and districts. There are several reasons for the success of this approach. First, branch operations are relatively routine and homogeneous across all branches; so a uniform central system suits all units. Second, and perhaps more importantly, central and tight control of cash is absolutely essential since a finance company must be a very sharp operator on the short-term money market, as it earns a profit by maximizing the margin on interest rates on loans outstanding and rates on capital borrowed in the market. In most large complex organizations, however, central knowledge of the sundry management systems and the total information flowing within the organization is not possible.

What is more likely to happen in the future is that organizations will take a position somewhere between these extremes. They will centralize some accounting and information systems (say cash, foreign currency, and inventory) and decentralize others (such as market research, production scheduling, and payroll) depending on the needs of the overall organization and the requirements of the various far flung units. Central management will take responsibility and initiative for the overall planning and guidance of systems development throughout the organization. They will also design, implement, and run those systems which affect most of the organization. The various units, however, also will initiate information system projects for their own local needs. These will be approved by central management after checking them for consistency and duplication with the local systems of other units. In short, accounting and information systems development will be achieved by co-ordination and collaboration.

Either way, the information resource strategy for the organization will become an integral part, if not the cornerstone, of overall corporate strategy. Already there are overwhelming reasons for including information resource plans in corporate strategic plans. The size of the accounting and information systems budget alone is enough to justify its inclusion. In many organizations, budgets for this are as large as those of any other corporate operation; and they continue to grow even when business activity falls off. It is not uncommon for the large multinational firm to have an information resource budget in the hundreds of millions of dollars and to employ thousands of people. But perhaps the most compelling reason lies in the fact that the information and communication function is rapidly becoming critical to organizational survival. Organizations are discovering that information management is the key ingredient for success. Those who fail to develop a coherent and insightful master plan for the information system resource will place themselves in great jeopardy.

CONCLUSIONS

The new technology is both remarkable and awesome. However, opinion divides sharply on its likely impact. Some authorities see it as a timely blessing for mankind. While other informed experts predict that it will only add to our already long list of complex problems.

The critiques make several telling arguments. The new information technology, they predict, will put nearly half of all clerical, secretarial and industrial employees out of work within the next decade. The brunt of this redundancy will be borne by women simply because they dominate the low-skill segment of the white collar work population. An important side effect, however, is that most of the gains women have made in the past decade to win a place in the workforce also will be wiped out. In addition, alienation and conflict in the workplace will increase as management utilizes the new technology to monitor almost every movement employees make. Many of our daily business transactions will also be de-humanized, as customers interact only with machines as, for example, in the case of instant cash banking.

Perhaps the most profound negative consequence predicted by the critiques, however, is that the new technology will lead to a havenot class of low-skilled, computer-illiterate, information-poor people. This class will come to be dominated by individuals from the new computer-literate, information-rich class who hold the necessary skills to exploit the new technology. The result will be a new class struggle between the 'information-rich' and the 'information-poor'.

By contrast, advocates of the new information technology contend that what is more likely to happen is that the new technology, because of its inherent job-creation propensity for wide-scale commercial application of micro-computers and electronics technology, will create more jobs than are lost. Historically, they argue, every major new technology from the wheel to the automobile has dramatically increased the total number of jobs. They compare the critics to the Luddites, a band of workmen who, in an effort to save jobs, rioted and wrecked new textile machines in England during the first part of the nineteenth century.

The new information technology will require large numbers of engineers, technologists and managers to design, build and market the computers and related products and services. The by-products of the new technology will lead to new industries just as tractors and combines were spin-offs of the internal combustion engine and mass production automobile assembly lines. Large increases in staff will be required to process and use the huge output of information from the computer. So instead of mass unemployment, they contend, we will be witness to more jobs and greater prosperity.

The advocates also assert that jobs will be enhanced, not degraded. Computers and robots will replace people only in back-breaking and in dreary routine jobs. At the same time, other jobs will become more creative as employees gain access to large amounts of information and learn how to utilize powerful computer decision aids.

Although the outcome of the debate remains for the future to decide, a few of the crucial elements are easily identified. To begin with, mechanization throughout history has proven to relieve many humans from heavy mean labor. It has, for example, through a host of labor saving devices from sewing machines to automatic washers and dryers, paved the way for many women to escape the confines of tedious drudgery at home (Ginzberg, 1982). In a similar way, the new information technology will relieve white collar workers from routine menial office work and open up a host of new opportunities in the computer and related fields. As these jobs are taken predominantly by women this presents an opportunity for them to move out of the 'white collar ghetto' into more interesting and higher paid jobs. There is, however, one important wrinkle in this line of reasoning. The new opportunities naturally will be taken up by people with the requisite training; and although there appears to be no natural advantage to either sex to acquire these skills, it remains to be seen whether or not white collar women workers will seize this opportunity (Ginzberg, 1982).

It also seems inevitable that the new technology will lead to important shifts in employment. It will undoubtedly make some jobs obsolete while at the same time creating new ones. There will, however, be a new twist to the historical pattern. Many of the jobs will be lost in the developed countries while the new jobs will move to low-wage third world nations. So the net effect will be double edged. The developing nations will experience a marked improvement in their economies; while at the same time the developed nations will go through a long period of large-scale unemployment for their low-skilled workers. As always happens during the aftermath of a new major technological development there will be winners and losers. Still, the net effect for society is likely to be a marked improvement.

The point of departure for this book, however, was the idea that our technical knowledge about accounting and information systems has outstripped our understanding and appreciation of the social software. Yet it is the social software which ultimately means the difference between their success or failure. Just as physics lacks a grand unifying theory of both the universe and the subatomic world, we still lack a coherent all-embracing theory of the social software of accounting and information systems.

The emerging social software

Nevertheless, we are slowly but surely developing a number of valuable insights and theories which make up the cornerstone of a solid foundation of behavioral accounting and information systems. Prior to these developments, notions of the behavioral aspects of such systems were limited to a few ideas from information economics which assumes that systems users assess the utility of any information system by determining its marginal or incremental cost by direct calculation or through estimates obtained using probability theory. More information is gathered as long as its marginal value exceeds its marginal cost. Highly sophisticated quantitative methodologies are harnessed to sharpen this incremental analysis of information.

We soon discovered, however, that individuals, groups and organizations do not seem to behave in accordance with 'economic-man' assumptions. At first we thought that people could be coaxed in this direction through a concentration on human relations. We knew that in some circumstances these systems were used in a fashion which led to negative attitudes, hostile relationships, job dissatisfaction, and poor job performance. We thought that if democratic processes were employed in setting the targets for financial controls and if the leadership stressed consideration of the workforce, positive attitudes, friendly relationships, job satisfaction, and optimum job performance would follow. Careful research, however, indicated that the human-relations model was naive. Nevertheless, we are more appreciative of the potential utility of engineering good human relations into our accounting and information systems.

The focus of investigation soon shifted to a concern for tailoring accounting and information systems to the personality of the user. Psychologists had discovered that different individuals process information in quite different ways. Experiments confirmed that cognitive style influenced preferences for information format, decision making and, at times, performance. Simple cognitive style concepts, such as analytic versus heuristic, gave way to richer theories of decision style, such as the Jungian personality typology as the basis of matching accounting and information systems with individual traits. This approach shows great promise for practitioners, although a good deal of research and theory building is still required.

Accounting and information systems which focus on the individual user in isolation from the organizational context tends to be limited. So other researchers, following clues unearthed by the human-relations investigations, began to study the relationship of important impersonal forces on the shape and use of accounting and information systems. Taking their cues from organizational theory they postulated that patterned variations in macro forces, such as environment, technology, interdependencies and organizational design, define the structure and process of financial controls and other information systems. Although the precise nature of the contingencies and the causal train amongst the forces is difficult to unravel, these investigations have shed a great deal of light on the fundamental reasons for the major differences encountered in these systems and have pointed to valuable directions for designers.

The organizational theory approach proved to be a more complete and richer approach to accounting and information systems theory building than were previous trails. It was only natural that the next step involved conceptual schemes which merged personal traits and impersonal forces. While it is true that only individuals use accounting and information systems, they use them in the context of the macro impersonal forces facing the organization. It may be inspirational to recall that at one time man thought the earth to be the middle point of the universe. From this perspective, with man at the center, the sun and planets were seen to be revolving around the earth. This theory, however, made the paths of the planets complicated, even perplexing. It was only, as Bronowski (1978) reminds us, when Copernicus, taking a fresh approach, thought of putting the sun at the center of the solar system that the true nature of the universe fell into a single simple mathematical description. It is not surprising, therefore, that at the outset, behavioral accounting put the manager at the center of its theory building. Accordingly, the managers' cognitive pattern, his leadership style and his participative behavior were thought to be the key factors in effective accounting and information systems design. These aspects, however, now play a much smaller role in the scheme of things when environment and technology are placed at the center. Surely, they are key factors for comprehensive theories of accounting and information systems and organizational design.

The social software of accounting and information systems, then, has come a long way since Argyris observed their ramifications, both negative and positive, on the workplace. We have proceeded well beyond a simple economic-man perspective; and while we are still in the early evolution of this important aspect of organizational life, we are nevertheless at a critical juncture. Within the next decade we will witness the merging of the new information technology with the body of knowledge on social software. The process will be enhanced as organizations learn how to go about formulating an information system strategy. This will give rise to a remarkable alteration, not only of our organizations, but of society at large. The precise nature of the changes remains to be seen; but they will depend to a large extent on the outcome of the clashes of different perspectives of organizations and society. We turn now to identification of a couple of these key issues and to a few speculations about their resolution.

References

Bronowski, J., *The Common Sense of Science*, Harvard University Press, Cambridge, Mass., 1978.

Everest, G. C., 'Data base systems tutorial', *Readings in Management Information Systems*, McGraw-Hill Book Co., New York, 1976.

Ginzberg, E., 'The mechanization of work', *Scientific American*, September 1982, pp. 67–75.

Giuliano, V. E., 'The mechanization of office work', *Scientific American*, September 1982, pp. 149–164.

Gregory, C. A., and A. Etori, 'Japanese technology today: the electronic revolution continues', *Scientific American*, October 1981, pp. J5–J46.

Hammer, C., 'A forecast of the future of computation', *Information and Management*, November 1977, pp. 3–9.

Hussain, D., and K. M. Hussain, *Information Processing Systems for Management*, Richard D. Irwin, Inc., Homewood, Ill., 1981.

Kirpalani, V. H., and N. B. Macintosh, 'International marketing effectiveness of technology oriented small firms', *The Journal of International Business*, Winter 1980, pp. 81–90.

Lincoln, T., 'A practical strategy for MIS', in Tricker, R. I., and R. Boland (eds), *Management Information and Control Systems*, John Wiley & Sons, London, 1982.

Macintosh, N. B., H. Tsurumi, and Y. Tsurumi, 'Econometrics for strategic planning', *Journal of Business Policy*, Winter 1973, pp. 49–66.

Nolan, R. L., 'Computer data bases: the future is now', *Harvard Business Review*, September–October 1973, pp. 98–114.

Stratte-McClure, J., 'French telecommunications: digital technology and the Telematique program', *Scientific American*, September 1980, pp. 25–43.

Tricker, R. I., *Effective Information Management*, Beaumont Executive Press, Oxford, 1982.

Tsurumi, Y. (with R. Tsurumi), *Shogoshosha: Engines of Export Based Growth*, The Institute for Research on Public Policy, Montreal, 1980.

CHAPTER 14

Epilogue

We are told that as the industrial revolution fades the new information technology will reshape society and organizations in new forms (Abelson and Hammond, 1977). The underlying reason for this belief is that energy and information are the basic currencies of all organic and social systems; any new technology that alters the terms on which these are available to a system works the most profound changes in that system (Simon, 1977). I would like to close this book by hazarding a few guesses about the potential impact of the information revolution on two of our major institutions. I do not expect everyone to agree with these speculations; in fact, I expect many will disagree and some will even be outraged. Nevertheless, the new information technology is such a powerful and important force in society that we should at least attempt to formulate some of the choices for its long-term impact.

INDUSTRIAL DEMOCRACY AND THE NEW INFORMATION TECHNOLOGY

One aspect of the dawning information era, an aspect which may catch most accounting and information executives by surprise, is that the new information technology will prove to be the battlefield where the forces of traditional management meet those of industrial democracy. For some time now researchers such as Mumford and Ward (1968) and Bjorn-Andersen and Hedberg (1977) have seen the fading of the industrial revolution as the dawning of a new era for the industrial democracy movement.

Industrial democracy views organizational designs as containing important social arrangements and attributes. Its proponents argue that the traditional technical–economic perspective, summarized in Table 14.1, contains a host of assumptions which have had a profound effect on the quality of working life. The traditional view features centralized power and authority in the hands of a small group of elite managers who make all the key decisions and get the lion's share of the organization's status and rewards. At the lower levels, by contrast, jobs are narrow, routine and dull; attitudes are negative; workmanship is shoddy; and absenteeism, turnover, and alcoholism are widespread.

Table 14.1 Traditional and industrial democracy perspectives of organizations

Social system attributes	Traditional technical–economic perspective	Industrial democracy perspective
1. Rules for decision-making	Made by the dominant coalition of top management	Widespread participation in a democratic fashion
2. Work roles for most employees	Narrow, routine, and dull jobs	Widened task handling to form self-contained and interesting jobs
3. Attitudes to work	Degradation of lower-level work	Positive and humanistic concern for work
4. Organizational structure	Outside control of inter-dependent work units	Autonomous, self-contained work units
5. Power	Centralized in the hands of the dominant coalition top management	Widespread, and shared by workers and management alike, who elect a democratic parliament to decide policies and procedures
6. Reward structure	Dominant coalition and managers get the best of the rewards	Organizational rewards shared equally by workers and managers

The remedy, it is argued, lies in industrial democracy, a humanistic concern for work and relationships at work. This view, also summarized in Table 14.1, features a parliamentary style of management whereby the leaders are elected by the employees, with widespread distribution of power and rewards. This ensures that upper management have a genuine concern for the creation of widened and interesting jobs and autonomous, self-contained work groups. The ultimate goal of industrial democracy, of course, is to alter work organizations in both capitalist and socialist economies until they became truly democratic social institutions. Basic humanistic values are to be pursued along with technical–economic ones.

The new information technology, and it is important to seize this point, threatens the goals of industrial democracy because it is used, both wittingly and unwittingly, to reinforce the traditional organizational design (Hedberg, 1975, 1980). The argument goes as follows.

The new information technology is capital-intensive. Accounting and information systems, once designed, are consequently locked into place for long periods of time, in order to recoup the large initial capital outlay. Any systems designed around the traditional organization will serve to reinforce and perpetuate its priorities. Careful research has shown that systems designers, and indeed the wider profession of accounting and information systems, are concerned mainly with tailoring the new information technology towards economic goals of efficiency and towards the existing social arrangements of the current organizational design.

Information and power, of course, go hand in hand; and it is predicted frequently that in the information era, information, not capital and labor, will be the critical scarce resource. It follows that if new computer-based accounting and information systems consolidate upper management's hold on information access and flows, then the technical–economic rationale for organizational design will prevail over that of industrial democracy. Importantly, this would be accomplished with the aid of a new breed of elite computer-literate administrators, imbued with the traditional view. Thus, computerized information systems designed according to the assumptions of the traditional organizational social system loom as the major impediment to the goals of industrial democracy.

Yet this threat can be turned into an opportunity for industrial democracy. The key lies in having employees participate in the design of new information systems. It is not enough, as was learned at the Volvo car plant in Halmar, Sweden, to have excellent physical working conditions, enriched jobs, and work rotation. Social–technical organizational design must also include employee involvement in the accounting and information systems that permit work groups to plan and co-ordinate their own work. These systems must be capable of supporting expanded jobs and autonomous work units. Only then will employees experience true self-determination in the workplace.

It is crucial, the argument concludes, that democratic processes penetrate the design stage of new computer-based accounting and information systems. Where employees are unfamiliar with the new technology they will have to be supported by their own technically literate union representatives. Otherwise they will be readily hoodwinked by the organization's computing and accounting experts. Without some experienced representatives it would be almost impossible for them to confront traditional management head-on. Technical and philosophical support must be provided to the work groups during the design phase.

From the industrial democracy viewpoint, then, systems design in organizations must no longer remain unaffected by changing values and power balances in the larger society. The new information technology could be the main engine for the transformation of our traditional technical–economic-oriented work organizations into more democratic and humanistic institutions. For this to happen, employees must participate as equal partners with managers, not only in the design phase of specific computer-based accounting and information systems, but also in the formulation of corporate-wide strategic plans.

It may come as a surprise to accounting and information systems designers to learn that their systems are pivotal to the goals of the industrial democracy movement. Yet after all, information is power, and the tensions between those who seek industrial democracy and those who hold to the traditional views of organizational design will center on the way in which information (and thus power and control) will be owned, shared, and distributed. Accounting and information systems designers generally are unversed in such matters. They are well advised to do their homework, for they will be in the middle of the fray.

IMPLICATIONS FOR SOCIETY

We now shift our discussion to a more general level in order to hazard a few guesses about the implications of the new information technology for one of the major institutions in society—the manufacturing of material goods. These speculations borrow the analytical techniques of sociology, the main focus of which is the study of societal institutions, including their idea systems, and the conditions and causes of their transformation (Giddens, 1982). Sociological methodology involves the recognition of important forces in society, the identification of how these forces affect the emergence of institutionalized behavior, and how that behavior persists in recognizable form across generations.

A few illustrations will serve to demonstrate the power of this type of analysis. A simple example is how the advent of mass-production technology made cheap private transportation widely available and this, in turn, led to the development of suburbia along with its related lifestyle, as well as to the decline of the central core areas of many large cities. Similarly, the arrival of the new information technology, particularly the cheap mass-produced personal computer, will make information, both private and public, readily available at a low cost to everyone around the globe. This development is likely to have an even more profound impact on lifestyles than did cheap private transportation. More will be said about this later.

A more complex illustration of sociological analysis is the idea that industrialization, urbanization, and population explosion lead to 'developed' societies. Development, a liberalizing and progressive force, leads to the decline of traditional values and the emergence of the nation state and its related institutions of citizenry, nationalism, giant private corporations and their countervailing large public bureaucracies. Underdevelopment, by comparison, spawns conservative and regressive institutions.

An even more complex illustration is given by Heilbroner (1980) in his brilliant exposition of Marx's analysis of the most powerful social invention of mankind—capitalism. According to Marx, our struggle with our material circumstances, principally our constant need to produce material goods, gives rise to our social consciousness and the necessary legal and political superstructure to support and sustain these requirements. From this perspective it is not, as previous philosophers argued, our consciousness that determines our being; rather it is our economic existence which produces the ideas that shape our historical evolution and the conditions of our social, political, and intellectual life processes. In short, our material setting contains and breeds the ideas we hold about how society should work.

It follows, the argument continues, that the essence of social existence is preserved in disguise within its existing institutions. The principal institution, of course, is the mode of production for our material requirements. The mode of production, capitalist or socialist, contains two internal sets of institutionalized ideas—the forces of production and the social relations of production. The forces of production are the means we use for the reproduction of material goods and properties—that is to say our tools, machines, techniques, skills, and people. The social relations of production are the social arrangements which dictate what, how, and by whom goods are produced, as well as the arrangements for distributing them. Important institutionalized ideas, then, are embedded in the forces of production.

Under a capitalist mode of production one social class, the superior one, owns the forces of production and directs them towards markets which return the most profit. This powerful profit drive forces routine on to labor and regularizes it, thus reducing it to a homogeneous commodity that then can be bought at the cheapest price possible. This, in turn, gives rise to an inferior class made up of indistinguishable laborers. The profits of production which materialize from the market exchanges for labor and production accrue to the superior class. As a result they get the major share of the material goods produced by the forces of production. So access to, and ownership of, a disproportionate amount of wealth becomes the prerogative of the superior class.

The result of these unequal relations between the two classes is a state of extreme tension. This systematic inequality gives rise to the class struggle whereby the superior class defends and tries to preserve these social arrangements, while the inferior class attacks them and struggles to change them. Embedded in the capitalist system, then, is a fundamental contradiction involving the interaction between the forces and relations of production. Paradoxically, the two classes must co-operate to sustain the flow of material reproduction. The unity of opposites within the system must be sustained to assure the continuity of the capitalist mode of production. Capitalist society, therefore, and this is Marx's great insight, can reproduce itself only under conditions of tension that constantly threaten to disrupt and destroy its socioeconomic structure. Capitalism exists because of the class struggle within itself.

This internal conflict, Marx argued, would lead inevitably to a socialistic mode of production with its related supporting institutions. These include three central ideas. First, all property, including the forces of production, should be owned by the state; second, all citizens should contribute to the forces of production, according to their abilities; and third, the output should be shared equally by all citizens in accordance with their needs. The ultimate goal is a classless and unalienated society.

The wisdom of Marx's sociological analysis remains, of course, for history to decide. Certainly, capitalism has evolved in a form that could not possibly be imagined a century ago. The emergence of massive public bureaucracies has taken most of the rough edges off its most pernicious inclinations; and presently there are few, if any, signs of an impending revolt by the inferior class in any of the advanced capitalist nations.

At the same time it should be recognized that socialist nations also have racked up impressive records in the production of goods. The USSR, for example, rising from the ashes of massive devastation during World War II, built the second-largest industrial production machine in the world, the largest oil and coal sector in the world, the largest military build-up of any nation in history, and an impressive social welfare system. Yet socialism has not escaped class distinctions, alienation of part of the labor force, and disproportionate distribution of the material output of its productive forces to elitist bureaucratic, military, and cultural groups. Paradoxically, many socialist nations are experimenting with private enterprise for particularly troublesome sectors of their economies.

What the future holds for capitalism and socialism is a matter of much academic debate, and well beyond the scope of this book. What is relevant is the enormous power of sociological analysis to provide insights into the nature of our institutions and their transformations. It is on this note, then, that we shall turn to speculations about the likely consequences of the new information technology on the conditions of emergence of our major institutions.

For one thing, I do not think that the new information technology poses a direct threat either to the capitalist or the socialist modes of production. Even today we are witness under both systems to material abundance well beyond the wildest dreams of either Adam Smith or Karl Marx. The socialist system will harness the new information technology to fill the missing link that until recently has plagued their efforts to provide sufficient material needs—accurate, timely, and detailed information about the consumer needs of the citizenry. The capitalist system will exploit the new information technology to produce and market a constant stream of ever-better consumer products and services around the globe, thus fueling its needs for continued growth. The new information technology can only enhance the already awesome capability of both systems to produce material goods.

The electronic revolution does, however, pose a far greater threat to both systems than the possibility that capitalism might give way to socialism, and vice-versa. The materialistic base of society, which has been the fundamental force shaping the two competing social systems, will give way to a new power base—that of knowledge and intellectual power (Simon, 1977). This new base will give rise to progressive forces, which like its predecessors, eventually will cause the decline of our traditional social institutions, including capitalism, socialism, citizenry, and nationalism. The amassing of material goods will no longer be our prime concern. We will see ourselves as citizens of the world; and the nation state will decline in importance as new supranational institutions emerge to provide the legal, political, and social bonds that legitimate and enforce the knowledge and intellectual power base.

For some of us, particularly those of us that work in institutions of higher learning, this is already a fact. Our major institution is neither the university nor the state that employs us; rather it is the college of scholars and researchers spotted around the globe who work in our own narrow area of specialization. For us the important social arrangements are contained in our particular academic societies, scholarly journals, annual conferences, research-granting agencies, and the professional literature. The same holds true for doctors, psychiatrists, lawyers, accountants, and sundry other highly trained professional experts.

Similarly, we are transcending local boundaries in our non-working life. It is awesome to realize that in the summer of 1982 over four billion people around the globe simultaneously watched, with commentary in the language of their choice, the finals of the World Cup football match. The new information technology will give rise to new dominant social institutions for both our work and our leisure.

It seems inevitable, then, that the production of material goods as the base of our social arrangements will be replaced by a knowledge and intellectual power base. Industrial expansion, with its dependence on energy and materials, will be curtailed as we realize the enormity of the destruction that is taking place in our physical environment—air, water, and soil. The information sector will overtake manufacturing, capitalism and socialism will be transformed, and nationalism will fade.

Best of all, we will come to realize, through new global information networks, that there is a rich and rewarding life that goes well beyond materialism. Even today, to our children around the globe, whether they live in Russia, France, Japan, Cuba, or the United States, global bickering about which social system should most successfully produce material goods seems very strange. They understand that societies around the world have created a material abundance far beyond their needs at the enormous price of acid lakes, polluted air, plundered forests, toxic wildlife, and arid deserts. They know our values are turned upside-down; and they realize the insanity of a world where both capitalism and socialism have geared up to defend their materialistic way of life by deploying weapon systems capable of destroying the entire planet many times over. The new information technology is the social institution which will, if we come to our senses, propel mankind beyond the mere amassing of goods and forward in the evolutionary chain to a new and better but totally different world. Accounting and information system designers, then, will have to expand their way of thinking about formal information flows beyond merely providing data on the economics of the enterprise to incorporate the political and social rules and ramifications of these systems on society at large (Tinker, 1980; Tinker et al., 1982).

The most important information systems in the new era will not be the traditional hard-copy reports about financial and economic facts based on generally accepted accounting rules and guided by the principles of good systems design. Rather, they will be real-time systems delivered around the world by satellite teleprocessing capable of providing information of all kinds—world money supply, global grain requirements for next week, scientific data bases, technical and professional knowledge, up-to-the-minute reports on the ton-loads of nitric acid and sulfuric acid emissions pouring into the atmosphere around the globe, education systems of all kinds ranging from mathematics to foreign languages, and a host of other systems beyond our imagination. These information systems will pave the way for the enhancement of the mind and spirit.

Wouldn't it be a tremendous challenge and great fun to design an information system which reported daily on the level of global food consumption, inventories, deliveries in transit, and crop and livestock under cultivation? One thing seems certain: the next couple of decades is going to be an exciting period for accounting and information systems managers around the globe.

References

Abelson, P. H., and A. L. Hammond, *Electronics*, March 1977, p. 1085.

Bjorn-Andersen, N., and B. L. T. Hedberg, 'Designing information systems in an organizational perspective', *TIMS Studies in the Management Sciences*, North-Holland Publishing Company, Amsterdam, Vol. 5, 1977, pp. 125–142.

Giddens, A., *Sociology: A Brief But Critical Introduction*, Harcourt Brace Jovanovich, Inc., New York, 1982.

Hedberg, B., 'Computer systems to support industrial democracy', in Mumford, E. and H. Sackman, (eds) *Human Choice and Computers*, North-Holland Publishing Company, Amsterdam, 1975.

Hedberg, B., 'Using computerized information systems to design better organizations and jobs', in Bjorn-Andersen, N. (ed.), *The Human Side of Information Processing*, North-Holland Publishing Company, Amsterdam, 1980.

Heilbroner, R. L., *Marxism: For and Against*, W. W. Norton & Co., New York, 1980.

Mumford, E., and T. B. Ward, *Computers: Planning for People*, Batsford, London, 1968.

Simon, H. A., 'What computers mean for man and society', *Science*, March 1977, p. 1186.

Tinker, A. M., 'Towards a political economy of accounting: An empirical illustration of the Cambridge controversies', *Accounting, Organizations and Society*, Vol. 5, No. 1, 1980, pp. 147–160.

Tinker, A. M., B. D. Merino, and M. D. Neimark, 'The normative origins of positive theories: Ideology and accounting thought', *Accounting, Organizations and Society*, Vol. 7, No. 2, 1982, pp. 167–200.

Index